Making Room for Mystery

"Christianity without real mystery and anomalous events is not only blind to the facts but just not that interesting—unlike Holley's book, which is more than interesting. Thought-provoking and open-minded—yet at the same time critical—this is a truly welcome addition to the literature on religious and metanormal experiences. Do yourself a favor: Buy it and then read it attentively."

—**Dale C. Allison Jr.**, author of *Encountering Mystery: Religious Experience in a Secular Age*

"David Holley's *Making Room for Mystery* is truly a remarkable book. By far the most comprehensive and illuminating book on paranormal experiences I have read. The twenty chapters cover everything from dreams and visions to ghosts, near death experiences, intercessory prayer, and much more. Theologically and spiritually astute and approachable, *Making Room for Mystery* will enlighten and encourage laypersons and scholars alike. Joining personal accounts, scientific research, and theological reflection, this text provides hope and inspiration without magic and hyperbole. It presents a vision of reality in which paranormal experiences are part of the fabric of life and not supernatural intrusions. I highly recommend it for the seeker, skeptic, and spiritual adventurer."

—**Bruce Epperly**, author of *Angels, Mysteries, and Miracles*

"God moves in paranormal ways, Holley suggests, in this spectacular book about some of the world's stranger things, from clairvoyance and telekinesis to prophetic dreams and ghostly visitations. The work's inviting tone makes room for genuine dialogue, as do the many intriguing case studies. Believers and skeptics alike will find much to appreciate here."

—**Ryan J. Stark**, Professor of Humanities, Corban University

"Standing on the shoulders of William James, David Holley provides us with a significant advancement in the study of the paranormal and the extraordinary. Readable and riveting, *Making Room for Mystery* provides the reader with a typology of the paranormal. This book is highly recommended as a text for a course in comparative religion or for a course in paranormal and primary religious experience. It is also recommended for the book club seeking to engage in lively discussion."

—**Allan W. Eickelmann**, Teaching Professor, The University of Southern Mississippi

"Dr. Holley makes a clear and carefully reasoned case to take mystery seriously. It is not that we should always expect extraordinary and unusual events to occur nor think we can perform them, but—and this is his real point—if we don't think mystery is in the world, we will miss seeing it, and, consequently, miss seeing the hand of God working with nature and free individuals to heal and redeem creation."

—**Dennis L. Sansom**, Professor Emeritus of Philosophy, Samford University

"Barring anti-vaxxers and conspiracy theorists, most of us believe in science most of the time. We may not think science has the explanation for absolutely everything, but we assume that the events of our lives take place only in ways consistent with the laws of science. However, there are many reports, some of them apparently credible, of happenings that seem to violate these limitations. David Holley urges persuasively that we ought not automatically disbelieve such reports, but rather 'make room for mystery' in the world and in our lives."

—**William Hasker**, Emeritus Professor of Philosophy, Huntington University

"Despite public interest in the paranormal, many reflective people today are distrustful or uneasy about paranormal activity due to scientific skepticism. In this nuanced, well-researched book, which is the best of its kind and suitable for a wide audience, David Holley reveals in his usual engaging style reasons that Christians and other religious believers might embrace mysterious dimensions of conscious experience in ways that deepen their faith without denying science its proper role of explanation."

—**Todd R. Long**, Professor, Philosophy Department, California Polytechnic State University

"For all its admirable accomplishment, modern science too often serves up drearily prosaic descriptions and points us toward flattened horizons. Without gainsaying science's explanatory uses, *Making Room for Mystery* reminds us of the shadowy fathoms and sky-piercing peaks of human experience that science, for now and perhaps always, cannot elucidate. Although there are superstitions to reject and riddles to unravel, Holley invites curiosity, wonder, and reverence at real mystery without which real wisdom falters."

—**Douglas Henry**, Dean of the Honors College, Baylor University

Making Room for Mystery

Anomalous Events, Extraordinary Experiences, and Christian Faith

David M. Holley

CASCADE *Books* • Eugene, Oregon

MAKING ROOM FOR MYSTERY
Anomalous Events, Extraordinary Experiences, and Christian Faith

Copyright © 2025 David M. Holley. All rights reserved. Except for brief quotations in critical publications or reviews, no part of this book may be reproduced in any manner without prior written permission from the publisher. Write: Permissions, Wipf and Stock Publishers, 199 W. 8th Ave., Suite 3, Eugene, OR 97401.

Cascade Books
An Imprint of Wipf and Stock Publishers
199 W. 8th Ave., Suite 3
Eugene, OR 97401

www.wipfandstock.com

PAPERBACK ISBN: 979-8-3852-3894-1
HARDCOVER ISBN: 979-8-3852-3895-8
EBOOK ISBN: 979-8-3852-3896-5

Cataloguing-in-Publication data:

Names: Holley, David M., 1948– [author].

Title: Making room for mystery : anomalous events, extraordinary experiences, and Christian faith / by David M. Holley.

Description: Eugene, OR: Cascade Books, 2025 | Includes bibliographical references and index.

Identifiers: ISBN 979-8-3852-3894-1 (paperback) | ISBN 979-8-3852-3895-8 (hardcover) | ISBN 979-8-3852-3896-5 (ebook)

Subjects: LCSH: Curiosities and wonders. | Parapsychology. | Extrasensory perception. | Psychokinesis. | Ghosts. | Experience (Religion). | Miracles. | Near-death experiences. | Spiritual healing. | Theology.

Classification: BL53 H65 2025 (paperback) | BL53 (ebook)

VERSION NUMBER 07/24/25

Scripture quotations are from the New Revised Standard Version Bible, copyright © 1989 National Council of Churches of Christ in the United States of America. Used by permission. All rights reserved worldwide.

To Joyce

who welcomes the extraordinary
and delights in the ordinary

Contents

Introduction: Strange Phenomena | ix

1. Christian Skepticism | 1
2. Science, Religion, and Mystery | 12
3. The Miraculous and the Paranormal | 22
4. Believing Weird Things | 32
5. Anomalous Phenomena | 43
6. Crisis Revelations | 54
7. Dream Messages | 65
8. Revelatory Visions | 76
9. Glimpses of the Future | 87
10. Mind Over Matter | 99
11. Tales of Extraordinary Powers | 110
12. Remarkable Rescues and Mysterious Helpers | 121
13. Petitionary Prayer | 131
14. Extraordinary Healing | 144
15. Hauntings, Organ Transplants, and Past Lives | 156
16. Mediums | 169
17. Near-Death Experiences | 179
18. Visits from Dead People | 192
19. Deathbed Phenomena | 205
20. God Moves in Paranormal Ways | 214

Bibliography | 225
Name Index | 233
Subject Index | 235

Introduction

Strange Phenomena

MAGIC ACTS ARE FASCINATING because they show us what we know does not happen. You can't really make an object disappear in one place and reappear in another. You can't saw a woman in half and then have her reemerge, whole and unharmed. We realize that we are watching an illusion. But when the illusion is skillfully performed, we seem to see what we think is not possible.

There is a type of story that evokes a response resembling our reaction to magic performances. It's a tale that describes something that strikes us as too strange to fit into our standard explanatory frameworks. The account suggests the operation of powers or forces that differ from those we are used to dealing with. Sometimes we simply dismiss such reports with the thought that such things cannot happen. But sometimes our incredulity is tempered by the fact that the report comes from a source we trust. In such cases we may find ourselves wondering whether the world could be more mysterious than the predictable order we have taken for granted.

I begin with an example of the kind of story I am talking about. Morton Kelsey, a professor at Notre Dame for many years, says that when he was a young boy his mother told him about an experience she had as a teenager. She awakened suddenly in the middle of the night and seemed to see a young man she had been dating, standing at the foot of her bed. When the appearance vanished, she looked at the clock and saw that the time was 2 a.m. The next day she learned that this young man had become despondent over a medical diagnosis and had fatally shot himself at 2 a.m.

Kelsey says that this story made a significant impression on him. He adds that he later heard similar stories and ultimately became convinced that experiences like this one could be taken seriously.[1]

This story resembles a great many other accounts of experiences that have been labeled "crisis apparitions." Emily Williams Kelly, a research professor at the University of Virginia, includes in this category "experiences in which a person sees an actual apparition, hears a voice, has a dream or intuition, or feels the presence of another person, and the experience coincides with the time that the other person, at a distance, is undergoing some sort of crisis, usually death."[2] She notes that there are numerous well documented reports from the nineteenth century of this kind of phenomenon and that many people in our own era continue to describe the same type of experience.

It is easy to see why people might find accounts of this kind astonishing. What is described is not merely out of the ordinary. Given standard assumptions, it shouldn't happen at all. The person who has the experience appears to get a kind of message related to what is happening at a distance, but doesn't acquire this information through any recognizable physical means. To accept such accounts as true, we would have to think that there is a way for people to receive information about what is happening elsewhere that comes through some source other than sense perception.

The standard crisis-apparition story involves awareness of a danger, typically to someone with whom there is an emotional connection, that can't be explained in terms of our usual assumptions about how we know things. But there are also stories in which the person who has an extraordinary awareness is the one in crisis. Consider an example: A nurse had spent many months caring for a quadriplegic man. The patient had some complications that led to a transfer from the facility where the nurse worked to a larger teaching hospital. The nurse kept up with how the man was doing by staying in contact with his sister. One night the nurse dreamed about being in the unit where he had been moved: "I was talking to him and telling him to keep fighting and not give up hope."[3] His sister called soon afterward to say that her brother was better. The sister also said that he told her that his former nurse "was with him in the middle of the night and was telling him to get

1. Kelsey, *Christian & Supernatural*, 26.
2. Kelly, "Mediums, Apparitions, and Deathbed Experiences," 76.
3. Kelly, "Mediums, Apparitions, and Deathbed Experiences," 84.

better and to keep fighting." He described the nurse as standing at the end of his bed. On reflection, the nurse wrote "The dream had been so real, and I felt like I saw him clearly in the dream.... I felt really strange but recognized that I went—somehow—to him."[4]

No doubt there are alternatives to the nurse's interpretation of what happened. The sense of reality the nurse felt could be dismissed as subjective. We might also wonder whether the words the man heard were words that the nurse had used previously, which he recalled and incorporated into his own dream or vision. But as with standard crisis-apparition stories, there are numerous accounts of people in need receiving what looks like a communication from someone concerned for their wellbeing that doesn't come through normal physical channels. Sometimes the message received by the person in crisis comes as thoughts that seem to emerge from nowhere. Sometimes it takes the form of a vision or a dream. Even if there are plausible ordinary explanations of what some of these stories describe, there is a kind of cumulative force that comes from hearing repeatedly of the same kind of thing happening. Acquaintance with such stories can lead us to wonder whether there is more going on than our ordinary modes of explanation are able to deal with.

Both the standard crisis-apparition story and stories about someone in crisis receiving an apparently telepathic message suggest a kind of connection between minds that seems extraordinary to us. We typically think of what is going on in our minds as inaccessible to other people. But the stories suggest that under certain conditions our minds may be linked in ways that conflict with this assumption. Furthermore, the story of the nurse suggests the remarkable idea that there can be mental influence that affects the physical condition of someone at a distant location.

Some people think that all such stories must be flawed. They suggest that there is misremembering or confusion or deliberate deception. Or they posit that striking correlations between the experience and real-world events are exaggerated or coincidental. There are many reports for which this kind of response is adequate. However, when skeptics offer reasons for doubt, they sometimes leave the impression that no matter what the evidence, they would not entertain the possibility of an event that challenges their fundamental assumptions about what can happen. Because they are confident that such things can't occur, they are

---

4. Kelly, "Mediums, Apparitions, and Deathbed Experiences," 84.

also confident that there is an ordinary way to explain any reports that conflict with this expectation.

On the other hand, there are people who are willing to consider the possibility that events we find strange and hard to explain might really happen. Sometimes this willingness is a product of having a strange experience of their own. Sometimes it is connected with hearing about such things from trusted friends or relatives. New Testament scholar Dale Allison says that his openness to possibilities that many people dismiss is connected with stories he has heard from family members. These stories

> include a teenager interacting with an apparition identified only later from a picture album; a boy recurrently dreaming about a girl who turns out to live across the street after he moves to a new city; a man hearing the voice of his dead father asking him to call a woman he does not know in order to wish her a happy birthday, after which, upon doing so, he learns it is in fact her birthday; a high school student dreaming about entering her church's sanctuary by the side entrance on Sunday morning, seeing all the lights go out, and hearing a friend say, "We lost the electricity," after which, a few weeks later, she walks into the church . . . observes all the lights are off, and hears her friend say, "We lost the electricity because of the storm . . ."[5]

The family stories also include a father receiving a call from his son asking to be picked up at the train station at a particular time. In the days before cell phones, this was a call that the son could not have placed because he was on the train at the time the call was received. The son had expected to surprise the family, but is met at the train station by his brother who had been sent to pick him up.[6]

How We Think About Reality

I don't believe every story I hear. Neither do you. We all have what we might think of as maps of reality that we use to distinguish between what can happen and what cannot happen. We don't invent these maps on our own. They come to us in the ways that we acquire many cultural assumptions that shape how we think, and what we do or don't do. Among the assumptions that educated people in Western cultures tend to acquire is

---

5. Allison, *Encountering Mystery*, 169–70.
6. Allison, *Encountering Mystery*, 170.

the idea that there is a scientific explanation for whatever happens. Not everyone in our culture fully agrees with this claim. Some people, after all, have religious beliefs that posit things happening that cannot be explained in scientific terms. For example, some believe that there are instances in which God miraculously overrides the natural course of events or instances in which they experience the presence of God. However, events caused by a power beyond nature or encounters with a reality beyond nature would be beyond the scope of scientific explanation.

Nevertheless, even people who believe things that don't fit with the idea that science can explain whatever happens may feel a kind of pressure to adjust their thinking in areas where it might conflict with this assumption. In our culture scientific ways of understanding things are often contrasted with religious superstition. Typically, this contrast is connected with the idea that scientific views have superseded religious accounts. Educated people don't generally want to put themselves in the position of defending a religious account that might be replaced as science advances, and they certainly don't want to come across as superstitious. So, they often adjust their beliefs in ways that bring them closer to the views of their scientifically minded fellow citizens. They might still believe that God could act to bring about something that would be unexplainable in scientific terms, but they would be reluctant to say in a particular case that something scientifically inexplicable actually occurred. They may accept the possibility of experiential contact with God, but treat most claims about such contact with a skepticism that resembles that of their secular peers.

In a culture where science has a great deal of prestige, calling a way of thinking unscientific often means not just that it is different from scientific thinking, but that it is less rational. However, judging that some account is or is not scientific sometimes depends on assumptions about nature that have been adopted on nonscientific grounds. At the beginnings of modern science in the seventeenth century, scientists and philosophers posited that there could be no such thing as action at a distance. They developed a conception of nature in which the only causal powers were those that could be accounted for in terms of interactions between material things. The assumption that nature was fully explainable in mechanistic terms was explicitly formulated by some Christian scientists and philosophers as a way of ruling out the idea that nature could produce miraculous events. They reasoned that if nature couldn't produce miracles, then miraculous events described in biblical texts would have to be ascribed to God's power.[7]

Ultimately, this strategy for defending their religious faith was unsuccessful. As people who had learned to think of the world in mechanistic terms considered scriptural accounts of extraordinary events, which they were confident nature could not produce, they increasingly found it more plausible to doubt whether the events actually occurred than to accept that they had occurred and were produced by a power beyond nature. But the main point here is that science was conceived in a way that involved thinking of natural phenomena as explainable in terms of causal interactions involving adjacent physical entities. Given this assumption, there was no need to even consider evidence of telepathic connections between minds or direct influences of minds on physical phenomena.

It is ironic that the idea of action at a distance crept back into scientific accounts of quantum phenomena in the twentieth century. At the subatomic level, physicists have accepted what they call *entanglement*. At the quantum level, it is no longer possible to think of subatomic entities as isolated from each other. Experiments have confirmed that what happens at one location correlates with what is observed at a distant location in ways that our ordinary ideas of physical causality cannot explain. Many scientists accept this claim in relation to the subatomic realm, but maintain that such connections don't apply to the world of larger objects. However, we might suspect that confidence in this view is fueled by a commitment to the mechanistic vision that came to be identified historically with legitimate scientific explanation. For someone who is less committed to that vision, mysterious phenomena like those I have mentioned earlier in this chapter could suggest that conscious minds are connected with other things in ways that seem reminiscent of the entangled reality of quantum physics.[8]

People in our age tend to assume that the only alternative to conceiving what happens in the world as explainable in terms of the physical forces recognized in contemporary science is to posit supernatural causes. But assuming this dichotomy distracts us from consideration of a third possibility. There are describable events like some of those I have mentioned that we can be fairly confident cannot be explained in terms of the accounts of nature recognized in contemporary science,

---

7. Griffin, *Parapsychology, Philosophy, and Spirituality*, 16–25.
8. Radin, *Entangled Minds*, 231–32.

but don't look like supernatural interventions either. If we think we have good reason to accept that anomalous phenomena of this kind actually occur, perhaps we should wonder whether the natural order is stranger than dominant scientific paradigms lead us to expect. Perhaps nature is strange enough that under the right circumstances it could produce the kinds of extraordinary events that were ruled out when the foundations of modern science were being constructed.

I think that there are reasons for believing that nature is more mysterious than standard scientific pictures suggest. In subsequent chapters I will be discussing some of these reasons. But my primary concern in this book is to consider what it would mean for Christians to think about their faith in the light of a conception of reality that allows for the kind of phenomena Kelsey and Allison describe. Educated Christians in our era have often attempted to reconcile their faith with science by reducing their sense of mystery. This kind of adjustment can be thought of as an adaptation to maps of reality we thought we had to accept. Rather than adjusting to these maps, I will be exploring an alternative way of reconciling faith with science, a way that leaves more room for mystery.

CHAPTER 1

Christian Skepticism

ANTHROPOLOGIST JACOB LOEWEN DESCRIBES a time when he was doing Bible translation while living with members of a Choco Christian church in Panama. Aureliano, a leader of the local church, had invited Loewen and his colleague David Wirsche to be his guests. During their visit Aureliano's wife Neta became seriously ill with what Loewen recognized as pneumonia. Loewen immediately sent a messenger by canoe to a town about half a day away to buy medicine, but the medicine was not available, and it was evident that the pneumonia was becoming more virulent each day.

Loewen reports that during this time he was reading the New Testament book of James. In the fifth chapter he read an instruction about calling the elders together, anointing a sick person with oil, and offering prayer. The text promised, "The prayer of faith will save the sick" (5:15). Loewen says that the biblical text put him into an inner struggle. He explains:

> Since germs for me belonged to the category of the material, they could be "killed" by specific other materials, but I didn't have a category for the Spirit of God in the germ-killing function. I suddenly realized that I didn't have the faith to truly believe that God would heal.[1]

1. Wilson, "Seeing They See Not," 202–4.

In his own Christian culture, Loewen had been taught that in praying for healing, he should always add the phrase "if it is God's will." For Christians like him, the biblical promise in James didn't generate an unequivocal expectation that healing would occur, even if the text might be understood that way. But, says Loewen, "I also knew that these Indian Christians were literalists. If they would see this biblical injunction, they would do just what it said."[2] In spite of his struggle, Loewen wrote out a translation of the passage and gave it to the husband of the ill woman. Aureliano asked Loewen why he hadn't said anything about this biblical passage earlier when he saw that his wife was dying. Loewen replied that he was afraid the prayer wouldn't work, an answer that made no sense to Aureliano. "Why might it not work?" he asked.

The leading members of the church, along with Loewen and Wirsche, gathered and followed the procedure described in James. The sick woman showed some improvement, but she suffered a relapse the next morning. The local leaders met later without inviting Loewen and Wirsche to join them. Immediately after they anointed Neta and prayed for her, she was well enough to get up and do her housework. After observing the remarkable recovery, Loewen asked Aureliano why the church leaders had not invited David and him for the prayers. He was told, "I am sorry, but it doesn't work when you and David are in the circle. You and David don't really believe."[3]

The point of the story is not that Loewen wasn't a dedicated Christian. It is instead that he had been socialized into assumptions that are in tension with expecting extraordinary healing. The Choco Christians had no such difficulty. Their worldview made it natural for them to think that the power of the divine Spirit can overcome whatever spirits may be causing disease. Aureliano comments after the successful cure, "Yes, that Spirit of God is really powerful, when he goes after those fever spirits, they really run!"[4] In Loewen's worldview what happens in cases of illness is understood as a product of material forces operating in ways scientists describe. While he presumably accepts the possibility of God acting in the world, he is unsure how to integrate that idea with expectations based on his scientific understanding of how things work.

---

2. Wilson, "Seeing They See Not," 203.
3. Wilson, "Seeing They See Not," 204.
4. Wilson, "Seeing They See Not," 204.

Loewen's account is quoted in an article by another anthropologist, C. Roderick Wilson.[5] Wilson's article is focused on the question of how anthropologists should deal with extraordinary experiences that they encounter during their field work. He suggests that central to the issue is a difficulty in perceiving phenomena that don't fit with one's own ways of thinking. To illustrate the perceptual problem, he tells about a time when he was trying to determine how members of a group in Amazonian Ecuador understood various color terms. He showed one man a card with a bluish tinge, and the man called it "leaf-colored." Surprised, Wilson asked where he had seen a leaf this color, and the man pointed to a group of trees in the distant hills where Wilson could see that his description was accurate. In later tests some people called a card with a purplish sample "sky-colored." Later Wilson verified that they were correctly describing the sky's appearance under conditions that were common in the vicinity. He realized that his own assumptions about leaves being green and the sky being blue were a product of his scientific understanding of how colors were produced. Thinking of these objects as having a normal color had made it difficult for him to observe actual appearances. As he put it, "I could not see what was literally in front of my face."[6]

Wilson's more general point is that the assumptions that go with our cultural background can block us from being able to recognize some phenomena. If our scientific views don't allow us to make sense of particular events, we may not be able to perceive those events. Something can occur right in front of our eyes, but fail to register with us if it doesn't conform to our expectations of what can happen. Or we may observe something anomalous, but redescribe it in ways that make it cohere with our scientific assumptions.

Wilson uses Loewen's story to show that it is not just those people who reject beliefs about the supernatural whose ability to perceive extraordinary phenomena is limited by their scientific ways of thinking. Those who have theistic religious views, but who have learned to accommodate their views to the assumptions of a scientific culture, may also have difficulty taking seriously what does not fit with scientific expectations. Loewen's remarks make it clear that he has carved out a domain where a scientific understanding of how things work is definitive. He calls this domain the "category of the material." He would undoubtedly affirm

---

5. Wilson, "Seeing They See Not," 197–208.
6. Wilson, "Seeing They See Not," 199.

belief in the Spirit of God, but he is puzzled about how the Spirit of God interacts with the material realm. While he presumably believes that God could affect what happens, he doesn't really expect healings that are contrary to the natural operation of material forces. If he prays for someone to be healed, he will be careful to add the qualification about God's will, which reminds him to temper his expectations.

There is, of course, good reason to resist thinking of prayer as like a kind of magic in which following the proper procedure is all that matters. Loewen is right to think that promises like those in the passage in James should not be understood as an unqualified basis for expecting cures whenever the specified procedure is followed. No doubt Loewen's "non-literalist" reading of the text is connected with knowing from experience that the sincerest prayers do not always lead to the desired result. Nevertheless, there is still a kind of sting to Aureliano's judgment that the visiting Christians do not really believe.

What don't they believe? Perhaps the key to understanding what Aureliano means is his assessment that the prayer for healing doesn't work when Loewen and Wirsche are present. Somehow, they are blocking the kind of connection with the divine Spirit that is needed for healing power to flow. How might that be? I want to suggest a baseball analogy. There is a widely understood rule for baseball players that when your pitcher is throwing a no-hitter, you don't mention that fact because it might jinx him. This prohibition might seem like pure superstition, but it is presumably based on the realization that the pitcher's performance depends on maintaining the right frame of mind. The frame of mind in question is one in which abilities that are not under conscious control are coming together in a way that puts the player "in the zone." There is, in other words, a delicate balance that might be disturbed by refocusing awareness on the achievement.

My guess is that Aureliano and his neighbors are able to engage in a process where self-consciousness recedes and something like a communal consciousness that is receptive to powers beyond their own arises. But when the Westernized Christians try to participate, their inability to let go of distracting thoughts blocks this receptive state. It is not exactly that they don't believe that God has the power to heal. But the kind of belief they have is one in which skeptical thoughts are part of whatever belief they affirm. Like the pitcher who can't maintain the right state of mind when the focus shifts, they can't let go of their awareness of reasons for doubt about what they are doing.

The kinds of doubts that block wholehearted participation in the prayer for healing for people like Loewen are products of a tension between different ways of thinking. He has learned to think of the world as a physical system in which particular acts make sense. It makes sense, for example, to treat pneumonia with penicillin or other drugs that have been proven to be effective against it. But for someone who has come to think in this way, prayer seems to belong to a different thought world, a world in which God's power may produce results that differ from what scientific accounts would lead us to expect.

When you are thinking scientifically, you are not entertaining the idea of God bringing about some result. But the habits of thought you learn in thinking scientifically aren't easily switched off in a way that enables you to enter a different thought world. I want to illustrate the difficulty of combining these different thought worlds with another story.

A Surprising Healing

Ed Wilkinson, a member of a Christian church in the United States, had a background in neuropsychology that disposed him to take a critical attitude towards fellow Christians whose faith he thought led them to expect divine rescue from the problems of life. He tended to be skeptical about claims of miraculous cures or other kinds of supernatural interventions. His views were challenged when his eight-year-old son Brad was diagnosed with an atrial septal defect. There were two holes in the boy's heart that compromised the function of both his heart and his lungs. Brad's activities were severely limited as he awaited a scheduled surgery.

Ed tried to give his son an honest assessment of the seriousness of his condition. Apparently, Brad took the message to heart. He started giving away his toys in the expectation that he would not survive. One day Brad asked his father directly if he was going to die. Ed told him that he hoped the operation would be successful, but that it might not be. Then Brad asked whether Jesus could heal him. Ed didn't know what to say. He replied, "I'll get back to you on that." Later, after some anguished prayer and reflection, he told his son that God does heal, but that if it didn't happen in this case, there was still the hope of eternal life.

During a church service a visiting minister, who had himself been healed of a heart condition after doctors had given him hours to live, called for those who wanted prayer for healing to come forward. At the urging of his father, Brad went forward and told the minister about his condition. The minister offered a simple prayer. Tests the next week showed that Brad's condition was unchanged. The surgery scheduled for the next day was expected to last four to six hours. But after an hour, the doctors came to the waiting room and told Ed that as they were preparing to do the surgery, imaging revealed that the holes where blood had been leaking from one chamber of the heart to another were no longer there. They assured him that they had been there at the previous day's tests. There was no misdiagnosis. They said that this kind of spontaneous closure sometimes happened in infants, but wasn't expected for someone Brad's age. One of the doctors suggested that someone must have been praying.[7]

I think that the tension Ed experiences is representative of a difficulty many Christians have in integrating their faith stance with a scientific understanding about how the world operates. According to the account, Ed rejects forms of faith that seem to conflict with scientific attitudes. He thinks of hoping for miraculous cures as refusing to accept reality. Ed believes that God exists, and he is apparently willing to say that God can do things in the world that are unexpected from the scientific point of view. After giving the matter considerable thought, he tells his son that there is such a thing as divine healing. But his default assumption is pretty clearly that our expectations about what will happen should be based on what science tells us. In other words, he adopts the scientific assessment of what is likely as a kind of presumption that should be overridden only if there is compelling evidence.

In practice, this way of thinking is conducive to skepticism about claims of anything scientifically inexplicable. There is some indication in the story that Ed's experience with his son may have made him more open to the possibility of extraordinary events, but if so, the account does not tell us enough to explain how his thinking might have changed and whether he has been able to resolve the tension he experiences between his Christian beliefs and his scientific attitudes.

Skepticism About the Extraordinary

Jacob Loewen and Ed Wilkinson are examples of what I will call Christian skepticism. The term is not intended to suggest that they wouldn't

---

7. See Keener, *Miracles*, 1:431–32.

affirm standard Christian doctrines. Instead, it draws attention to a skeptical attitude about the occurrence of events that seem extraordinary from a scientific point of view. Loewen wants to distinguish between a realm in which scientific regularities account for what happens and a realm in which God operates. But his distinction undermines any expectation he might have of extraordinary healing actually happening. Wilkinson wants to reject flippant talk of divine intervention into a world that he understands to operate in accordance with natural regularities described by science. But in dealing with his son's situation, he is torn between maintaining this position and thinking that divine healing can actually occur.

The confidence that Loewen and Wilkinson have in science leads them to take a skeptical attitude about events that are unexpected from a scientific point of view. In this book I want to suggest an alternative to this kind of skepticism. I think that a skeptical attitude is appropriate for some claims to the extraordinary. But I also think that we have good reason to affirm that recognizable types of extraordinary events sometimes occur. If we do, we can treat some claims about events that are scientifically anomalous not as isolated cases but as fitting into a larger pattern of similar events. Thinking that events of these types sometimes occur does not mean that every report of such things should be accepted, but it does mean that we shouldn't start with a level of skepticism that keeps us from recognizing such things if they do occur.

Some people, of course, are not willing to take the possibility of events that don't fit with our scientific understanding of the world seriously. They think of current scientific accounts as setting limits for what can happen. I think that reports of anomalous events, along with experimental investigation of powers that might lead to such events, give us reason to suspect that reality is more mysterious than our standard ways of explaining things are able to accommodate.

It is not just uneducated or uninformed people who think that the world contains this kind of mystery. Thomas Morris was a philosophy professor at the University of Notre Dame when he edited a book containing autobiographical accounts written by noted Christian philosophers describing the relationship between their faith and their intellectual lives. Morris calls his own essay on the topic, "Suspicions of Something More."[8] He describes how throughout his life he has had numerous experiences

---

8. See Morris, "Suspicions of Something More."

that left him with the impression that "there is much, much more to reality than meets the eye."[9]

These experiences included premonitions by people he knew that were later shown to display an uncanny insight. There were also stories within his family of people with "special abilities to bring dead plants back to life" or "communicate with animals." There were accounts by his father of shooting dice one evening during his military service and "feeling his wins before they happened" as well as the story of a friend who for no apparent reason felt certain that an acquaintance was dead, well before receiving a report that confirmed it. There was also a striking personal epiphany of his own mission in life that Morris calls unexpected and powerful. He doesn't offer any of these events as proof of anything, but he found that the cumulative effect of his experiences was "a growing suspicion of something more, that something more to which religious faith was both a response and a call."[10]

So here is the point: if we don't begin with the assumption that whatever happens is explainable in scientific terms, we may discover reasons to take seriously experiences that suggest dimensions of reality that go beyond what science reveals to us. I am not talking only about experiences that might lead us to think of God. Some of the incidents Morris describes don't have any obvious religious significance. It is not clear, for example, why his father suddenly develops a remarkable ability to shoot dice on one particular evening and never after that. It is not apparent that the premonitions Morris mentions should be understood as divine revelations. But accepting events that suggest hidden depths of reality that are hard to square with standard materialistic accounts of the world opens the door to serious consideration of some religious understanding of reality.

The Place of Mind

Loewen's reference to the "category of the material" suggests a picture of the natural world in which what happens can be attributed to regularities governing the operation of physical things. He is clearly not at home with the Choco picture of spirits that cause disease and spirits that drive the disease spirits away. But how does he understand the powers of our

---

9. Morris, "Suspicions of Something More," 16.
10. Morris, "Suspicions of Something More," 18.

minds? In Western scientific culture there is a tendency to understand each human mind as a product of an individual human brain. Given this assumption, it seems plausible to think that whatever powers our minds have can be understood in terms of physical processes. If we don't believe that physical processes could produce particular powers, this way of thinking would lead us to conclude that our minds do not have such powers.

I will be suggesting throughout this book that there is good reason for thinking that events occur that reveal potentials of human consciousness that are anomalous from a scientific point of view. Accepting that there are such events is not a reason to reject science, but it is a reason for thinking that there are powers that have real effects in the world that escape our scientific net. These powers can be grouped into two main types. One type consists of capacities of the mind to receive information by means other than physical sensation. The other involves capacities of the mind to have direct causal influence on physical things beyond one's own body.

The first type of capacity is usually called *extrasensory perception*. The general idea is that we can sometimes be aware of information that we did not acquire through ordinary physical means. The phenomena known as crisis apparitions, which I described in the introduction, in which someone becomes aware of another person at a distance who is undergoing some kind of crisis experience, are an example.

There is a standard way of distinguishing between forms of extrasensory perception that represents them as different types: (1) *telepathy* (mind-to-mind influence), (2) *clairvoyance* (information about distant objects or events), and (3) *precognition* (information about future events). However, it turns out that it can be difficult to tell in specific instances which of these subcategories apply. For example, if someone becomes aware of a distant death, is it because of some telepathic connection or might it be a precognition of a later report or even a clairvoyant seeing of something at a distance?

The other type of capacity is for the mind to causally influence physical things beyond one's own body by means other than ordinary physical causation. It is usually called *psychokinesis*. Some cases of extraordinary healing might be understood to involve psychokinesis. In later chapters I will discuss the phenomenon and consider the evidence for this kind of influence. Just as there are problems in distinguishing between different types of extrasensory perception, there are instances in which it is unclear whether an event should be characterized as extrasensory perception or psychokinesis. For example, suppose I dream about the fuel pump on my car going out, and it happens the next day. Might it have been precognition or might some mental influence on my part have affected the operation of the fuel pump?

The powers of extrasensory perception and psychokinesis fall under the category of *psychic phenomena*, which are sometimes referred to by the Greek letter *psi*. Scientific researcher Dean Radin points out that there are words for such phenomena in most languages. Events of this kind, he says, "have been reported by people in all cultures, throughout history, and at all ages and educational levels."[11] However, powers of this kind don't fit with current scientific assumptions about the world. It is conceivable that they might be understood by a future science, but such a future science would have to be significantly different from the prevailing versions. It would have to embrace conceptions of reality that many scientists now regard as unscientific.

A world in which psychic powers exist is unlike what either Jacob Loewen or Ed Wilkinson is contemplating when they struggle to integrate their faith with science. Such powers are not part of their scientific pictures. Loewen is puzzled when he considers the idea of the Spirit of God producing physical effects. But in a world in which minds can influence other minds as well as physical things, influence by God's Spirit can be more easily conceived.

For the most part, the psychic powers I am referring to are not under our direct control. Our access to them involves states of consciousness that differ from the kind of reflective consciousness that is typically cultivated in Western education. We might recall here Aureliano's sense that the prayer for healing doesn't work when the outsiders are present. That is, it doesn't work when there are people present whose habitual forms of consciousness block access to these powers. Further, even when there are no such blocks, some people may be more adept than others at connecting with the unconscious sources of these powers.

Claiming that there are powers that our science doesn't account for calls for evidence, and I will be discussing some of the relevant evidence in subsequent chapters. I won't claim that the available evidence is sufficient to convince people who hold a worldview that has no room for occurrences that can't be explained in terms acceptable to contemporary

---

11. Radin, *Entangled Minds*, 6.

science. But I think that it can be convincing for people who are not closed to the possibility of dimensions of reality that are deeper than what our science discloses.

Christians who are convinced that there are remarkable powers of mind can be more receptive to extraordinary events than scientifically minded Christians like Loewen and Wilkinson were able to be. But even people who don't accept any kind of religious views may find the evidence for such powers impressive enough to rethink the assumption that extraordinary events don't occur. Reflection of this kind may not lead automatically to religious belief, but adjusting thoughts about reality to allow for the occurrence of events resembling the kinds of remarkable events described in religious texts can clear away obstacles that stand in the way of receptively hearing a narrative like the Christian story.

CHAPTER 2

Science, Religion, and Mystery

DISCUSSIONS OF WHETHER THERE is a conflict between religion and science often focus on whether accepting particular religious accounts means rejecting well-established scientific discoveries. No doubt some religious believers have conflicts of this kind. However, sophisticated believers have long recognized that this sort of problem can be resolved by adjusting religious claims in the light of new information. Augustine, for example, taught that when biblical accounts of creation are understood in ways that conflict with discoveries about the world, Christians should alter the way they have interpreted scriptural texts to remove the conflict.[1]

There is, however, a more fundamental kind of tension between religious outlooks and scientific approaches to understanding the world. At the heart of religious accounts is a sense of mystery. Experiencing the world as mysterious, as I am using the term, involves thinking that beyond or underlying the world given to us in ordinary experience is a deeper level of reality that sometimes breaks through. In most religious traditions, altered states of consciousness such as dreams, waking visions, and mystical experiences have been regarded as means of making contact with this deeper dimension. Similarly, anomalous events that go against our normal expectations of how things happen have been viewed as signs of this hidden order.

---

1. Augustine, *Literal Meaning of Genesis*, 41.

In contrast to this outlook, science attempts to explain things without any appeal to this kind of mystery. It seeks to understand the natural order as a physical system that is structured by regularities that we can verify. What happens is viewed as a causal outcome of the operation of these regularities in particular conditions. Gaining confidence in the power of science to explain the experiential world without appeals to mystery is conducive to developing a skeptical mindset about the need to posit a deeper level of reality than scientific investigation discloses.

From the point of view of the scientific quest, the places where religious traditions find indications of mystery seem dubious. Science recognizes as data for constructing accounts of the world only what can be verified through the bodily senses. Experiences in altered states of consciousness can be accepted as subjectively real, but won't be treated as conveying information about objective reality. Similarly, reports about anomalous events that don't fit with our expectations of how the world works will be regarded from a scientific point of view as either false or as explainable in terms of recognized scientific categories.

The point here is not that someone who accepts science couldn't have religious beliefs about something transcending the physical order. It is rather that for someone with a scientific mindset, it will be hard to find room for forces or causes not recognized by science that actually affect what happens. For example, saying that God brought about a particular event looks from this point of view like giving up prematurely on scientific inquiry. The response of much of contemporary theology to the prestige of science has been to adjust religious beliefs so that they don't conflict with our scientific pictures of the natural order. But the end result of this kind of adjustment has been to minimize the sense of mystery that seems fundamental to an outlook that is recognizably religious.

It is possible to show proper deference to the achievements of science but also make room for experiencing the world as mysterious. But doing so hinges on how we understand a presumption under which scientific work is conducted: the presumption that what happens can be fully explained in terms of physical interactions. This presumption is often taken as a claim that everything in the natural order is reducible to something physical. However, there is another way it can be understood. We might take it to be a strategy for simplifying the scientific task by concentrating on those aspects of reality that can be precisely measured. Viewed as a strategy, we can say that this way of thinking has turned out to be amazingly fruitful. But we can also ask whether the resultant understanding of nature is an oversimplification.

As philosopher Thomas Nagle puts it,

> The spectacular progress of the physical sciences since the seventeenth century was made possible by the exclusion of the mental from their purview.... Science will have to expand to accommodate facts of a kind fundamentally different from those that physics is designed to explain.[2]

Most scientists assume that what Nagel calls the mental can be explained as a byproduct of brain activity. Given the goal of explaining things in physical terms, what else could it be? But there are reasons to question the viability of this goal. First, no one has much of a clue about how consciousness could be produced by brain activity. Philosopher David Chalmers famously called this the "hard problem."[3] Second, some phenomena suggest that there are powers of mind that can't be given a physical explanation without fundamentally revising our assumptions about the nature of material things.

Admittedly, there are plenty of people who think that mental phenomena can be explained in terms of the physical. In other words, they think that the strategy of concentrating on the precisely measurable has resulted in a complete or nearly complete understanding of reality. However, taking this stance means minimizing the significance of phenomena that don't fit well with this assumption. Sometimes ignoring or minimizing data that conflict with well-established views can be a reasonable strategy. However, this approach can also hide from us assumptions that the data give us reason to question. As Nagel puts it, "Materialism remains a widespread view, but science does not progress by tailoring the data to fit a prevailing theory."[4]

Throughout this book I will be referring to various phenomena that seem puzzling when we think that minds can be understood in purely physical terms. But my focus will be on phenomena that people who presume that all reality is physical don't recognize as possible. A prime example is extrasensory perception. I will be referring in subsequent chapters to evidence that gives us reason to think that people sometimes become aware of information about reality beyond their own body that

---

2. Nagel, "Is Consciousness an Illusion?" para. 29.
3. Chalmers, "Problem of Consciousness," 200–219.
4. Nagel, "Is Consciousness an Illusion?" para. 29.

they couldn't have acquired through ordinary sense perception, either their own or someone else's. But someone who thinks that all reality is physical will reject claims to awareness of reality that doesn't come through a recognized channel of physical causation. Thinking that information about anything beyond the body could be acquired without sensory input would mean attributing powers to the brain that they don't attribute to physical things.

Cases that suggest extrasensory perception often seem strange to us. Notice, for example, that the incidents described by Kelsey and Allison that I mentioned in the introduction are all cases in which someone apparently knows something by some means other than ordinary causal processes. In these incidents the information comes through mysterious audible voices, apparitions, or dreams. In standard ways of thinking, these sources are manufactured by an individual's own mind. But recognizing that they can convey accurate information that is not acquired through the senses suggests that the mind has access to information by means that go beyond what we think of as ordinary.

Powers of mind to perceive things through extrasensory means seem strange enough. But another power of mind seems even stranger. In later chapters I will discuss evidence that a mind can influence what happens in ways that can't be accounted for in terms of ordinary physical causes. This power is usually referred to as psychokinesis. From the viewpoint of a standard materialist account of reality, saying that such a thing can happen sounds like claims of magical powers that science rejects. But if there is strong evidence of the phenomenon, we can't just reject it on the grounds that science doesn't know how to deal with such things.

Accepting powers of extrasensory perception and psychokinesis, makes the world seem more mysterious than we might have thought. In a world where there are such powers, we have ways of knowing that surpass our expectations. In addition, what happens in our minds has a potential for causal influence that seems amazing. These powers transform the ordinary reality we assumed into something extraordinary.

Extraordinary Events

People can make a distinction between the ordinary and the extraordinary even if they live in a culture that is prescientific. Some events are striking enough to suggest powers that go beyond standard expectations, and some experiences seem to put people in touch with a level of reality that transcends what ordinary experience gives us. However, when I talk about the distinction, I find it most helpful to think of it in relation to contemporary scientific accounts of nature. The ordinary is the world of cause and effect that we can understand in terms of the forces and entities that are recognized in our science. The extraordinary includes events that are contrary to what our scientific understanding leads us to expect or experiences that involve contact with realities that can't be accounted for in terms of recognized scientific categories.

There is room for disagreement about whether an event is extraordinary. We might think, for example, that a particular healing is unlikely, given our understanding of physiological processes, but a scientific understanding can accommodate some unlikely events. Additionally, we should acknowledge that there can be future scientific discoveries that alter our assessments about what is likely or unlikely. So, an event might seem extraordinary at one point, but not later on. Nevertheless, we can conceive of events that we can say with a high degree of confidence would not occur unless they were produced by powers or forces that our science does not recognize.

What powers are we talking about? Some people assume that only the power of God could bring about something genuinely extraordinary. Many of these believers think that supernatural interventions in which God overrides the natural course of events to bring about a desired result are frequent. They are not at all reluctant to call particular rescues from dangers or other difficulties miraculous. But this view raises a problem. The more frequent you imagine such miraculous interventions to be, the more difficult it is to explain instances in which horrible things happen but there is no divine intervention. If God is thought to act in many cases to prevent evil, then cases where evil is allowed to happen make us wonder why God does not act.

There are traditional explanations of why God does not act to prevent horrible things. In general, these answers posit that the created order is such that there are powers other than God with degrees of control over what happens. In other words, creation is understood to involve a relinquishing of control. To be effective as an answer to why God does not prevent some horrendous evil, this line of thought needs to show that God's options are much more limited than what we might imagine them to be. However, good reasons to explain why divine intervention does not occur in cases where we might have expected it are also reasons to be less confident in expecting divine intervention in situations where we might think it is needed. Furthermore, reflecting on cases where there is no divine intervention can lead to doubts about whether miraculous interventions occur at all. Even without this doubt, recognition of the extent of evil leads us to think that if interventions in which God overrides natural processes to prevent bad outcomes do occur, they are relatively rare.

But if we suppose that instances in which God overrides natural processes are rare, should we think that extraordinary events that are scientifically unexplainable are rare? Not necessarily. What if there are powers other than God that might bring about something extraordinary? If this idea sounds strange, notice that it was the way biblical people tended to think. People in biblical times were typically more receptive to the possibility of extraordinary events because they thought of the world as a mysterious place in which there were multiple powers that might produce something extraordinary. For ancient Israelites, a big part of the temptation to seek out gods other than Yahweh was the belief that these other gods had real powers to convey significant benefits. This belief was likely mixed with the thought that expertise in magical arts could produce extraordinary events. In the Exodus account when Moses uses his staff to turn water into blood by the power of Yahweh, we are told that "the magicians of Egypt did the same by their secret arts" (Exod 7:22).

The point here is that claims that Yahweh brought about extraordinary events were heard against the backdrop of a view of the world as a place where extraordinary events might be produced by powers other than Yahweh's. To be sure, the book of Exodus makes the point that Yahweh's powers surpass what the Egyptian magicians (or Egyptian gods) could do, but there is no attempt to deny that they have remarkable powers.

The powers of extrasensory perception and psychokinetic influence that I have referred to are not the same as the powers of gods or of masters of the magical arts, but if they are real, they provide a backdrop for taking claims to extraordinary events seriously. Such a backdrop is important in an age where people find it hard to believe that there are extraordinary events. When people are able to begin with the assumption that extraordinary events regularly happen, they can view scriptural accounts of such events with a less skeptical eye.

Miracle Stories in Scripture

There are people who believe miracle stories in scriptural texts because they are in the Bible. However, many people in our era tend to discount ancient testimony to anything contrary to a scientific understanding of how the world works. A common line of thought is that we can't trust reports about extraordinary things happening in the ancient past because such things do not happen in our experience. New Testament scholar Craig Keener addresses this kind of skepticism about miracle stories in an impressive two-volume work on miracles.[5] He intends his work as a defense of the credibility of New Testament narratives of extraordinary events against scholars who reflexively dismiss such stories. The bulk of his work is a compilation of contemporary accounts of miraculous events, the vast majority of which report instances of extraordinary healing. The accounts include cases from all over the world, and some of them come from people with medical expertise. So, his initial point is that stories about miraculous healings are reported not just in ancient texts but also in contemporary accounts that describe events that are recognizably similar.

But Keener wants to go farther than just saying that people report miraculous events in our own times. In his judgment many of these reports are impressive enough to support the view that God accounts for what happened as a viable option. Keener thinks of a miracle as "an extraordinary event with an unusual supernatural cause."[6] He thinks that his eyewitness accounts show why scholars should consider supernatural explanation both with regard to the modern stories and by extension with regard to the ancient stories found in biblical texts.

I think that Keener makes a strong case that testimonial evidence of extraordinary events exists in our own time and that the evidence is sometimes very impressive. However, I doubt that the kind of testimony he cites is enough to establish that these events should be explained in terms of supernatural causes. The testimony does provide evidence that events occur that conflict with what a scientific understanding of nature would lead us to expect. However, the claim that supernatural causes should be posited requires something more. If we assume that the only possibilities are God causing the event or natural regularities recognized by science causing it, as some of the scholars he addresses may assume,

---

5. See Keener, *Miracles*.
6. Keener, *Miracles*, 1:110.

then the argument may be persuasive. But what if extraordinary events like those Keener describes could be a product of powers within the natural order that science has not recognized?

In the New Testament Jesus's opponents were sometimes portrayed as recognizing that Jesus had done extraordinary things, but offering an alternative interpretation of how to understand his acts. Some attributed them not to the power of God but to the power of evil spirits (e.g., Mark 3:22). For most people today, the evil-spirit interpretation of these acts is not a viable option, but the point here is that conclusions about the causes of extraordinary events depend on what we take the viable options to be. If the options include the possibility that extraordinary healings might come about through potentials within the natural order, then people who are skeptical about God will likely find the inference to supernatural causes unnecessary. It is important to notice that thinking that the powers bringing about these events are natural possibilities would not preclude God's involvement. It is a standard Christian view that God works through the natural order to achieve particular purposes. But when we have a natural explanation, the action of God is likely to be hidden to those who don't discern what happens through the eyes of faith.

I agree with Keener that we can recognize at least some of the extraordinary events described in biblical texts as paralleling events that are reported today. But in my view, reflecting on biblical accounts in the light of evidence of extraordinary human capacities gives us reason to suspect that the powers involved, at least in most cases, are connected with human potentials that are often unrecognized. The point here is not to deny that God is the ultimate source of healing powers; rather, it is to suggest that we might think about remarkable healings not in terms of God deciding to heal or not to heal in particular cases, but in terms of whether human beings are accessing powers that the created order makes available. In other words, we might think of powers to do extraordinary things as analogous to ordinary powers to do such things as planting crops for our daily bread. We can give thanks to God for benefits that come from powers we call extraordinary, just as we can for powers that we consider ordinary.

But can such a view accommodate the fact that extraordinary events in biblical contexts are often represented as signs of what God is doing? Can they can be signs of God's involvement even if unusual human powers might be an immediate cause? Here I think we should notice that the paradigmatic New Testament portrayal of the recognition of God's involvement is to suggest that it comes about through faith. At one level, we might see a human act, but the eyes of faith may allow us to recognize the deeper truth of God working through the human act. In other words, faith in this context can be thought of as a kind of receptiveness to the deeper significance of what is going on. A sign can be an occasion for recognizing revelatory truth, even if it does not compel a recognition of that truth.

Transcendent Experiences

In most cultures before our own, dreams and visionary experiences were regarded as ways of making contact with a realm beyond the physical order. It is evident that biblical writers thought in this way.[7] By contrast, our culture is mostly suspicious of any claims about reality that can't be verified by ordinary sensory experiences. Admittedly, there is a legitimate place for critical reflection on our interpretations of experiences that seem to put us in touch with transcendent realities, but the point here is that our culture teaches us to treat experiences of realities transcending the physical order as guilty until proven innocent. And if you think you have to prove that you have actually encountered God before you accept the legitimacy of the experience, you are unlikely to get to that point.

A central reason for my interest in cases of extrasensory awareness is that verifiable instances of such a thing would show how experiential contact with transcendent realities might be possible. If the subconscious mind can sometimes give us access to truths about the world through a non-sensory process, we can conceive of such a process being a channel through which we might become aware of spiritual realities. Of course, it doesn't follow that we can regard awareness coming from subconscious sources as a hotline to heaven, and the potential for bizarre conclusions about the meanings of particular experiences is surely great. However, if we have reason to think that there are channels for knowing things about reality other than sense perception, someone who is convinced, for example, by a vivid near-death experience need not think that the mere fact that it comes through a channel other than ordinary sense experience is a compelling reason to discount it.

Throughout this book, I will be discussing various kinds of experiences that purport to reveal deeper levels of reality than what ordinary

---

7. Kelsey, *God, Dreams, and Revelation*, 31–56.

sense experience discloses. Some of these experiences are likely to seem strange to us. Many of us don't quite know what to make of it, for example, when someone reports seeing or talking with a dead person, or encountering a demonic or angelic presence. Sometimes we falsely assume that such things don't happen to normal people, that they are a sign of pathology. But there is good reason to think that a significant number of people who should not be thought of as mentally unbalanced have experiences that don't fit with our paradigm of sensing a physical object.[8] I don't pretend to have the final word about all such experiences, but I am convinced that it is too simplistic to think that we either have to understand them in literal terms or dismiss them as subjective hallucinations.

My inclination is to think that some of these strange experiences are like our dreams in that they involve some degree of human creativity and imagination. And like dreams, they are often better understood symbolically rather than literally. However, I also think that some of these experiences can be revelatory. If we grant that a crisis apparition can show truths about what is happening at a different location, it doesn't seem out of the question to think that the same unconscious channels through which this kind of apparition is perceived might also put us in touch with dimensions of reality that are ordinarily inaccessible to us.

The focus of this book is on the extraordinary, which includes events that are anomalous from the viewpoint of contemporary scientific understanding and experiences that purport to reveal realities beyond the physical realm. I'll be discussing some of the relevant evidence for striking powers of mind that seem connected to anomalous events and transcendent experiences. However, this book is not centrally about establishing that these powers are genuine. It is more about trying to think about what it means for Christian faith if we decide that there are good reasons to accept them. What would it mean in relation to such issues as religious experience, miracles, petitionary prayer, and God's action in the world? Historically, Christians have adjusted their thinking in response to discoveries about the world. So, what if we become convinced that the natural world that we inhabit is stranger and more mysterious than our culture typically represents it to be? What if we reconsider assumptions about reality that our scientific culture has taught us to take for granted?

---

8. See Murray, *Mental Health and Anomalous Experience*.

CHAPTER 3

The Miraculous and the Paranormal

WHEN THE EIGHTEENTH-CENTURY PHILOSOPHER David Hume wrote his influential argument against accepting accounts of miraculous events on the basis of testimonial reports, he knew that he was addressing Christians who were predisposed to reject claims of the miraculous from religions other than their own. Furthermore, it wasn't just miracles in non-Christian religions that they rejected. Because they thought of miracles as validating their beliefs, they were suspicious of claims to miracles by Christian groups with which they had significant theological differences. Leaders of the Protestant Reformation accepted biblical miracles, but regarded many Catholic claims of miraculous events as unbelievable.

Hume was playing on the anti-Catholic views of his British audience when he brought up a story told by a Catholic Cardinal about a man with only one leg who grew another leg after his stump was anointed with holy oil.[1] He was confident that his readers would find such a claim absurd, even though, as he pointed out, it was confirmed by the whole town. Additionally, he cites another case from France of numerous miracles near the tomb of a well-known Jansenist Catholic. Hume writes,

> Many of the miracles were immediately proved on the spot, before judges of unquestioned integrity, attested by witnesses

1. Hume, *Enquiry Concerning Human Understanding* 10.2.96.

> of credit and distinction, in a learned age, and on the most eminent theatre that is now in the world.... Where shall we find such a number of circumstances, agreeing to the corroboration of one fact?[2]

In other words, the testimonial evidence is about as good as it can be. However, Hume knows that his audience will likely reject reports of miracles that might suggest a divine endorsement of Catholic views. But how can they reject miracle stories supported by such strong testimonial evidence? Hume's answer is that in order to reject these unpalatable claims, they need to give up the idea that testimony can carry any weight when it reports events that are impossible.

The issue Hume raises should give pause to people who accept miracle stories that they take as confirmation of their own religious beliefs while rejecting those that might be used to confirm alternative beliefs. That stance might be defensible if the stories that are accepted have stronger evidential support. But an honest look at the evidence, Hume suggests, shows that some stories people in his target audience want to reject are supported by testimony that is at least as strong as the testimony supporting the accounts they accept. So, Hume proposes that if they are confident that the miracle accounts that they reject are false, they ought to decide that testimonial evidence is not a reliable basis for accepting any miracle claims. An obvious consequence of that stance is that it undermines the basis for their own claims about miracles.

Hume's suggestion for dealing with miracles in religions other than your own is not the only option. What makes miraculous events in other religions problematic is the assumption that miracles are a divine validation of the one true faith. If we think of them in that way, then miracles in multiple religions make it difficult to assert that a particular faith has a divine stamp of approval. Suppose, however, that Christians don't think of miracles as proofs that Christianity (or their version of Christianity) is correct. In that case, miracles in other religions might not be a threat. However, the viability of that option depends on how miracles are conceived.

---

2. Hume, *Enquiry Concerning Human Understanding* 10.2.96.

The Miraculous and the Extraordinary

Hume's argument for rejecting testimony to miraculous events appealed to the idea that you can reject testimony when it describes events that you take to be impossible. The claim that miracles are impossible is closely connected with the way he defines the term "miracle." He characterizes miracles as violations of laws of nature.[3] Whenever someone describes such a thing as happening, he says, we need to weigh the likelihood that it occurred against the overwhelming evidence we have of laws of nature operating as we have previously experienced them to operate. Since we recognize that testimony can be wrong for a variety of reasons, he claims that the reasonable response is to judge it mistaken when someone describes an event that would depend on a vanishingly small probability of a law of nature not working as we have consistently experienced it to work.

In considering Hume's assessment, it is important to notice that Hume defines the term "miracle" in a way that differs from how such events would have been conceived in biblical times. Biblical writers would not have described miracles as violations of laws of nature for the simple reason that they didn't have our concept of a law of nature. That concept comes from a later period. The most common biblical terms for events that we might call miracles are usually translated as "signs" or "wonders." When biblical writers use these terms, they are referring to events that would not be expected to occur except by the operation of some power beyond what they recognize as ordinary.

The source of such a power doesn't have to be God. Exodus 7–8 says that the powers of the Egyptian magicians brought about wonders. Matthew 24 suggests that false prophets can produce great signs and omens. Some of Jesus's opponents claimed that Jesus's healing ability came from demonic powers. While a sign or wonder would be impressive and maybe even awe inspiring, thinking that it comes from some extraordinary power does not imply that it involves a violation of a law of nature. It might be produced by a power within nature to bring about outcomes that don't fit with our ordinary expectations of natural phenomena.

The point here is not that we can't raise the question of whether there are violations of laws of nature. It is rather that thinking in these terms can distract us from the question of whether there could be what biblical writers called signs and wonders. There are numerous philosophical

---

3. Hume, *Enquiry Concerning Human Understanding* 10.1.90.

discussions that begin with Hume's definition of miracles and consider whether it might be reasonable in a particular case to believe that an event meeting this definition had occurred. That is, could we have good reason to accept the occurrence of an event that nature could not produce?[4]

When the discussion is framed in these terms, we are led to focus our attention on events that are so extraordinary that we have strong reason to believe that the operations of nature could not have produced these events. This focus tends to exclude from our view a larger range of events where we can't say with confidence whether what happened had natural causes but that nevertheless evoke a sense of wonder that might suggest some deeper meaning. For example, suppose there is a healing that nothing we know scientifically would lead us to expect. Even if we have no way of deciding whether it came about through the operation of natural causes, we might still think of what science tells us as only a partial truth. For example, we might find viewing the event in the light of an account of what God is doing in the world to reveal a deeper meaning.

An additional problem with framing the question of miracles in terms of laws of nature is that it is typically conducive to overconfidence in judging what nature can do. We tend assume that what our scientific understanding cannot account for is beyond nature's capacities. But those capacities may be greater than we imagine. If we were less confident that we can specify what nature can or cannot do, we might be more open to the occurrence of the kinds of extraordinary events that people regularly report. Even if we don't call such events miracles, some of them may qualify as what biblical writers would have called signs and wonders.

Judgments of Plausibility and Worldviews

People in previous historical eras thought in ways that made them more open to accounts of extraordinary events than well-educated people in our era typically are. They could be skeptical of particular tales, just as we can, but they were less likely to rule out all accounts of something extraordinary happening. In our time, however, many people find any

---

4. Defenders of the miraculous point out that even if nature could not produce this kind of event, it might have been produced by a power beyond nature, i.e., the power of God. But that claim raises the question of when positing such a power is really needed to explain what happened. Thinkers in the tradition of Hume are likely to say that in cases where we have good reason to think that some reported event could not have occurred naturally, there will be reason to doubt that the event actually occurred.

claims to what does not fit with their scientific understanding unworthy of serious consideration. There are various reasons for this kind of skepticism. One is that we have become familiar with numerous examples of fraudulent or mistaken claims about extraordinary phenomena, which has led to a generalized suspicion of this kind of story. But perhaps more fundamentally, educated people in our time have come to embrace assumptions about reality that lead to judgments that some things that are reported just can't happen.

An explicit formulation of the kind of assumptions that lead to this type of skepticism is a worldview that could be called *scientific naturalism*. *Naturalism* denies the existence of anything beyond nature. That is, it rejects anything supernatural. By itself, naturalism does not tell us specifically what cannot happen, only that nothing that happens is caused by a power beyond nature. But when naturalism is combined with the idea that nature should be understood in terms of what our best contemporary science says, the resultant worldview contains a prescription for rejecting anything that doesn't fit with the way contemporary science portrays nature. If something of this kind is alleged to occur, the scientific naturalist will rule out the anomalous event in advance.

While scientific naturalism is not a discovery of science, it can be an attractive view for people whose thinking is shaped by a scientific culture. People who reject the idea of God often think in this way. But in our social context, even people who believe in God may feel a kind of pressure to adopt a view that can be seen as a modification of scientific naturalism. It is not unusual for Christians who have learned to think scientifically to believe that what happens in the world is completely explicable in scientific terms unless God intervenes to do something miraculous. It is possible to accept this view and hold that miraculous interventions occur on a regular basis. However, Christians who have become confident of the power of scientific explanation tend to minimize the number of instances in which they are willing to claim that divine intervention has occurred. If God acts in the world to produce something scientifically unexplainable, they think that such actions will be rare. So, believers of this kind who accept the possibility of divine intervention will think like scientific naturalists about what has happened or is likely to happen most of the time.

The story of how Christians came to regard what happens in the world as explicable either by science or by miraculous interventions obviously has something to do with increasing successes of science in providing explanations. But that is not the whole story. Historically, theological reflection led to concern that Christian belief in various spirit powers and reliance on magical practices for dealing with these powers were superstitious and potentially idolatrous.[5] But as the various spirit powers and magical forces were pushed out of the picture, science increasingly came to fill the vacuum. Even if the possibility of divine intervention was retained, it was conceived of as intervention into a world in which what happens without divine intervention was viewed as explainable in terms of recognized scientific regularities.

Reflection on anomalous events gives us reason to consider an alternative view. Many of the best-evidenced cases of anomalous events do not suggest a supernatural intrusion into the natural realm. For example, when someone acquires information that our standard ways of thinking about how knowledge is acquired cannot account for, the impression we get is that some kind of human capacity of expanded awareness has been activated. While such a capacity can amaze us, instead of thinking that something supernatural has occurred, we may be inclined to speak of the paranormal.

When the term "paranormal" was coined near the beginning of the twentieth century, it was used to refer to anomalous events that didn't fit with standard understandings of physical causality.[6] Those who used this term thought that there were numerous, well-documented occurrences of this type. However, they didn't assume that these phenomena were an indication of causes from beyond the natural realm. Such unexpected events, they thought, might arise from powers that are part of the natural order, even if we lack an adequate understanding of how these powers work or how to use them reliably. In other words, the natural world may contain hidden depths that are not accounted for in available scientific representations of reality.

Reflecting on cases of events that seem anomalous from a scientific point of view suggests that unconscious processes can sometimes connect us with sources of knowledge that are beyond what we could acquire through ordinary sensation and reflection. It also suggests that at an unconscious level we know how to do things that surpass our usual conceptions of what we are capable of doing. For reasons I will be considering in

---

5. Taylor, "Disenchantment-Reenchantment," 288.
6. Kripal, *Flip*, 22–23.

other chapters, these potentials can be difficult to activate or control. But when they give rise to the unexpected, they can evoke a sense of mystery.

Christian Concerns

Some Christians may be uneasy about my suggestion that powers within the natural order can give rise to events that can't be explained by standard scientific accounts. One reason for uneasiness is the worry that thinking extraordinary events can come about because of hidden powers in nature may push God out of the picture. For example, if we can attribute an extraordinary healing to some power of telepathic or psychokinetic influence or think of some remarkable rescue as coming about because of extrasensory powers that alerted someone to a danger, then we don't have to attribute these events to God's action.

It is true that what I am suggesting would mean that there can be extraordinary events produced by psychic phenomena that are not acts of God. However, saying that not all such events signify God's action does not imply that none of them do. Christians have traditionally thought that God sometimes acts through nature, even while refraining from attributing everything nature does to God. So, if psychic potentials are part of nature, it would not be surprising if not every display of psychic power is something God does, even though God might sometimes use psychic powers to accomplish particular purposes.

Whether or not God is pushed out of the picture depends, I think, on how we conceive of God's action. Some people think that if God does something in the world, the action should be conceived of as a kind of intrusion into the natural order through which God brings about something that nature could not have produced. However, doing something that is contrary to nature is not the only way to conceive of how God might act. For example, God might for revelatory or redemptive purposes influence natural processes to make some possible outcome more likely. Our best science tells us that what happens in the physical world involves probabilities. In a given situation, some outcomes may be unlikely, but not physically impossible. If what God does leads to an outcome that is physically possible, we might not be able to detect God's action by scientific means, even if what happens would not have occurred without God's influence.[7]

---

7. Ward, *Pascal's Fire*, 230.

If we think of God as working through nature, and if nature includes psychic potentials, we can imagine God making use of these potentials. God might, for example, use paranormal processes to enable someone to access information that is not available through ordinary means. God might increase the likelihood of conditions conducive to the activation of latent psychic powers to bring about healing through touch or focused attention. In subsequent chapters I will be exploring the idea of God using psychic powers as a fruitful way of imagining how God might act in the world. But the main point here is that recognizing that what happens comes about through a natural process need not push God out of the picture.

Nevertheless, the claim that God could be acting through natural causes does not quite address what may be the underlying concern about expanding our conception of the natural to include paranormal phenomena. The worry, I suspect, is that unless there is something that goes against what nature can do, we can't be sure that some power other than nature is involved. If water can't be turned into wine by some natural process, then seeing it turned into wine would force us to acknowledge that something transcending the natural order is involved. But if natural processes might bring about this result, we don't have to attribute what happened to God.

Suppose that this line of reasoning is correct; that the only cases in which we can be absolutely sure that God has acted are cases where we are sure that something contrary to the natural order has happened. If so, it appears to me that we would not be sure very often. In the most common cases when something extraordinary occurs, we are not in a position to judge whether what happened is something that nature could not have brought about. For example, given our understanding of nature, a particular healing might seem greatly improbable, but improbable events, such as spontaneous remissions, do sometimes occur. If, however, we focus on reports where we are very confident that what is claimed to occur could not have been brought about by a natural process, another problem arises. There will almost always be room for doubt about whether the event really happened. If certainty that God brought about some event requires knowing both that an event couldn't have occurred naturally and that it did occur, then certainty is pretty hard to come by.

The point here is not that we can't believe that some spectacular event is due to God's action. It is rather that seeing God in the event depends on our receptiveness to that possibility. In the Gospels when someone recognizes the power of God in some extraordinary event, the typical characterization is that this insight was made possible by faith. Biblical texts sometimes speak of having eyes to see. What is it that triggers a faith response in this kind of case? Typically, it is the recognition that what is observed suggests the operation of a power beyond what we think of as ordinary and that the alignment of what has happened with God's purposes suggests that God is involved. One way of describing this response is to say that we recognize signs that point to God's activity. The signs of God's action may be convincing to those who are properly receptive, but being convinced does not require having a proof that cannot be doubted.

Even so, some Christians might think that there need to be some miraculous events that provide indisputable proof of the truth of Christianity and that acknowledging that there are psychic powers makes it more difficult to claim such proof. I can see why one might want such a proof, but even if psychic powers are rejected, an appeal to miraculous interventions is unlikely to yield this kind of proof. In previous ages claims about miracles were sometimes regarded as a decisive way to establish the truth of Christianity and its superiority to other religions. However, in our era this kind of argument is much less effective, since those who doubt the truth of the Christian message are likely to find its miracle stories doubtful. Many of our contemporaries are quick to take a skeptical attitude toward ancient reports of events that don't fit with a scientific understanding of nature.

It might seem counterintuitive to some, but raising the possibility of extraordinary events produced by powers in nature is a way to address the kind of skepticism that often blocks serious consideration of religious stories containing accounts of extraordinary events. If you think that nothing extraordinary actually happens, you will likely dismiss reports of extraordinary events from ancient times. But what if you have become acquainted enough with the study of paranormal phenomena to think that there are regular occurrences of events that don't fit with the standard scientific accounts of causality? Knowing about contemporary visions in which someone learns about distant events might prepare you to take biblical accounts of visions more seriously. Knowing about contemporary reports of extraordinary healing might make ancient reports seem more plausible. Admittedly, acknowledging that there may have been extraordinary events at the root of some religious stories is not the same as accepting the religious interpretation scriptural texts provide of the meaning of these events. But it opens the door to responses other than quick rejection of what is often taken to be ancient superstition.

To put the point in a different way, people in our culture have filters that keep them from recognizing the significance of events or experiences that might point toward levels of reality deeper than what science discloses. Coming to think that there are paranormal phenomena that involve powers other than those recognized by our science can be a way of loosening those filters. The point is not that accepting paranormal phenomena leads automatically to some religious view. It is rather that breaking out of the straightjacket of an understanding of the world from which mystery has largely disappeared can remove barriers to discerning signs and wonders that we have been conditioned to filter out.

CHAPTER 4

Believing Weird Things

WHEN I WAS A young boy, I remember going fairly often to the Saturday morning movies. One of the few films I remember seeing was the original version of *Invasion of the Body Snatchers*. I recall that after seeing the movie I was uneasy for several days about going to sleep, for according to the story, it was when you went to sleep that the aliens could replace you. A few years ago, I came across the novel on which the movie was based. What surprised me was how good the book was. I guess I had assumed that a fifties novel that was the source of a B movie would be of low quality, but I was wrong. The author was Jack Finney, and while he may not be a great writer, I would say that he's pretty good. He wrote several classic time-travel stories, and it was after reading one of those stories that I decided to read *Invasion of the Body Snatchers*.

Here is the first paragraph of the body-snatchers book:

> I warn you that what you're starting to read is full of loose ends and unanswered questions. It will not be neatly tied up at the end, everything resolved and satisfactorily explained. Not by me it won't, anyway. Because I can't say I really know exactly what happened, or why, or just how it began, how it ended, or if it has ended; and I've been right in the thick of it. Now if you don't like that kind of story, I'm sorry, and you'd better not read it. All I can do is tell what I know.[1]

---

1. Finney, *Invasion of the Body Snatchers*, 7.

That introduction was enough to hook me. Here is a narrator informing me that he's going to tell a story, but he doesn't really understand what happened. The account may leave the reader as puzzled and unsettled as the storyteller seems to be. That sounded like my kind of story.

The narrator is correct in saying that the book leaves some unanswered questions. For example, the story hinges on aliens replacing human beings. But the alien replacements look just like and have all the memories of the humans they replace. They also duplicate behaviors of the original person, which raises the question of how you can say that there has been a replacement at all. There are passages that give some indication of differences between the original person and the alien replacement, but none of these accounts are developed in ways that provide a clear understanding of the nature of the takeover. While it might be interesting to speculate about how to conceive the transformation, I won't pursue that question. Instead, my focus will be on a different issue that the book raises.

The main character of the story, a physician named Miles, along with a group of his friends, get fairly decisive evidence that the strange phenomenon of body replacement has been going on, but a skeptical psychiatrist friend named Mannie offers a debunking explanation that convinces this group that they must be mistaken about what they think has happened. So, they change their minds about what we readers recognize to be the truth because they have been given an alternative explanation that makes them doubt it. The issue that interests me here is when we should override convincing evidence that something has happened because it just seems too weird. Or alternatively, how open should we be to claims about the occurrence of what seems to us incredible?

Near the beginning of the novel Miles receives a visit in his office from an attractive woman named Becky whom he has not seen since they were both teenagers. Becky comes to see Miles about a strange concern. She tells him that her cousin Wilma has a delusion about Wilma's Uncle Ira. Wilma was raised by her uncle and continues to live in the same house, but she claims that the man in this house now is not Ira, but an imposter. The imposter looks just like Ira, talks like him, and acts like him, but Wilma is sure that it isn't Ira.

Miles is persuaded to come over and check things out. He goes to the house and talks to the alleged imposter, and he thinks there's no question about it: "It was . . . Ira, every hair, every line of his face, each word, movement and thought."[2] But when he tries to reassure Wilma, she remains absolutely convinced that it is not Ira. Miles raises the obvious question: "How do you know it's not Ira?" Wilma admits there are no physical differences and that the imposter could pass any memory test, but when she tries to explain how she knows, she puts it this way:

> He looks, sounds, acts, and remembers exactly like Ira. On the outside. But *inside* he's different. His responses . . . aren't *emotionally* right. . . . There's something *missing*. . . . Uncle Ira was a father to me, from infancy, and when he talked about my childhood, Miles, there was—always—a special look in his eyes that meant he was remembering the wonderful quality of those days for him. Miles, that look, 'way in the back of the eyes, is gone. . . . The facts of Uncle Ira's memories are all in his mind in every last detail, ready to recall. But the emotions are not. There *is* no emotion—none—only the pretense of it. The words, the gestures, the tones of voice, everything else—but not the feeling.[3]

It shouldn't be surprising that Miles is not convinced that Ira has been replaced. He assumes, as we would, that the problem is with Wilma. He persuades her to see a psychiatrist friend of his to sort out this delusion. Within a fairly short period, Miles also encounters other patients who have the same kind of story to tell about someone being replaced by an imposter, and he refers each of them to the local psychiatrist. I should mention that after reading this book, I learned that there actually is a psychiatric disorder like Wilma's case. It is called the Capgras delusion. The delusion involves thinking that one or more familiar persons has been replaced by imposters, who often take the form of robots or aliens. People with this delusion are apparently very resistant to changing their minds. Sometimes they will admit that their claim sounds farfetched, but nevertheless hold firmly to the idea.

In the novel, however, people whom we might be tempted to describe in such psychiatric terms have it right. We readers realize that their friends and family members actually have been replaced by alien

---

2. Finney, *Invasion of the Body Snatchers*, 15.

3. Finney, *Invasion of the Body Snatchers*, 21. This account is the first one advanced about how the alien replacement differs from the original person. Later in the story the replacements are portrayed as acting to keep their identity secret. We might speculate that there is some kind of consciousness behind the one that has been taken over, but the book doesn't pursue the matter. Perhaps we should recall that the author has warned us that everything is not going to be satisfactorily explained.

substitutes. According to the story, some large seed pods from outer space have appeared in a pasture outside of town and then spread all over town. Our central characters discover several replacement bodies in various stages of development that have grown from the seed pods, and they connect their discoveries to the stories of impostors. But then their conversations with the psychiatrist make them doubtful.

Mannie, the psychiatrist, tells them about mass hysteria and auto-suggestion. He describes a case in which person after person in a town came to believe that someone was attacking the residents with poison gas and another in which people develop a strange affliction that comes to be called dancing sickness. The human mind sometimes gets caught up in this sort of contagion, the psychiatrist says, but in cases of this kind, the delusion eventually fizzles out. Mannie proposes that Miles and his friends have leaped to connect the strange stories they have heard with some kind of explanation and adds, "we all prefer the weird and thrilling to the dull and commonplace as an answer."[4] What they have seen, he suggests, is what their overly excited minds have imaginatively created.

The psychiatrist's account leads Miles to doubt his own experience. He says, "Even though I could still see in my mind, vivid and horribly real, what I thought I'd seen in Becky's basement, I felt intellectually that Mannie was probably right."[5] This skepticism becomes stronger when the characters go back and check for the bodies they had found previously and discover that they are gone. Additionally, those who have been telling the stories about the imposters, one after another, recant their strange delusions, just as Mannie had predicted they would. The reader eventually realizes that Mannie and those who recant their stories have been replaced by the aliens and that they are motivated to keep those who haven't yet been assimilated from recognizing the truth, but Miles and his friends don't consider such a possibility. Instead, they allow themselves to be talked out of believing the weird phenomenon of body replacement.

While the psychiatrist is persuasive, Miles's friend Jack is not quite convinced by the mass-hysteria explanation. For a while he has been collecting stories of strange things that have been reported in the popular press. Some of the reports are clearly outrageous, but there are also reports of bizarre events that really happened. He notes the tendency to reject what doesn't fit into our common body of knowledge. The policy,

---

4. Finney, *Invasion of the Body Snatchers*, 75.
5. Finney, *Invasion of the Body Snatchers*, 75.

says Jack, is "you must never admit for a moment anything we don't understand may nevertheless have occurred."⁶ While Jack admits that people can have a receptiveness to accounts of strange occurrences that arises from our fascination with the extraordinary, he thinks that there is also an opposing motive: "We hate facing new facts of evidence, because we might have to revise our conceptions of what's possible, and that's always uncomfortable."⁷

I think that Jack is correct in his claim that we have opposing motivations when it comes to accounts of extraordinary occurrences. On the one hand, we are drawn to attention-grabbing stories, and when someone can tell a compelling narrative about a haunted house or visions that come true or doppelgängers or people with remarkable powers, it stimulates our imaginations, and vivid imagination sometimes turns into belief. On the other hand, we may find it disturbing to contemplate breaches of a familiar order we have learned to rely on by something that seems mysterious and possibly threatening, and just as important, we are reluctant to adopt beliefs that our peers might judge foolish. So, even though we can be more credulous than we ought to be, we can also be too ready to discount evidence that challenges established ways of thinking. No doubt we should have a bias against accepting claims about the extraordinary, but the bias shouldn't be so strong that it blocks all evidence that what seems incredible may have actually happened.

Science and the Unexpected

Strange things do happen. Everybody admits as much, but people take different attitudes toward reports of events that don't fit with standard expectations of what can happen. Some people seem eager to believe accounts of fantastic or bizarre events that many of us think are unworthy of serious consideration. We sometimes call such people superstitious or gullible. It is as if they lack a kind of critical judgment about what is credible. At the other end of the spectrum, there are people who react to stories about strange events with reflexive suspicion, and scorn for those who believe such things. They have unalterable ideas about what is implausible, and they are quick to dismiss reports that don't fit with their expectations of what can and cannot happen. In practice, their

---

6. Finney, *Invasion of the Body Snatchers*, 83.
7. Finney, *Invasion of the Body Snatchers*, 83.

skeptical attitude signals a kind of dogmatism that is closed to considering unwelcome evidence. The ideal attitude is surely somewhere in between these extremes.

It is reasonable to respond to accounts of unprecedented or unlikely events with some degree of skepticism. The story of alien body-snatching is fictional. But if we imagine receiving reports of such a thing in real life, most of us would regard the claims to be farfetched. Like people in the story, we might be receptive to alternative ways to explain experiences that seem to confirm the reports. But even if body-snatching seems strange and hard to believe, it is not obviously in conflict with a scientific understanding of how nature works. We can imagine increasing our biological knowledge to develop a scientific account of how this kind of thing could occur. Given enough evidence, we could treat it as an example of a phenomenon with which we were previously unfamiliar but that now fits with our beliefs about the world.

By contrast, imagine an extraordinary event that you don't think could be explained scientifically. Suppose that it is not just strange or unprecedented but conflicts with accepted scientific accounts of how the world works. The judgment that it can't be explained scientifically provides some reason for doubting that the event actually happened. However, we should be careful not to confuse the question of what can be explained by our current science with what science might eventually explain. One often-repeated story from the eighteenth century tells how people from the countryside would report seeing rocks falling from the sky. Scientists of the time found these tales ridiculous, writing them off as superstitious. Only later did scientific understanding advance enough to include the concept of a meteor.[8]

The point here is that our sense of what is potentially explainable scientifically is tied to assumptions that are taken for granted in current scientific thinking. If empirical reports don't fit with those assumptions, the events reported are likely to seem implausible. Some degree of skepticism about what our scientific theories cannot accommodate is warranted, but our skepticism can also block us from considering relevant data that might contribute to the advancement of scientific understanding.

Nevertheless, even if we can imagine science advancing to the point where it can accommodate phenomena that we can't currently explain, it is difficult to imagine how some events that have been reported to occur

---

8. Polanyi, *Personal Knowledge*, 138.

could ever be explained scientifically. You might be able to imagine a future science in which alien body-snatching is recognized, but be unable to consider the idea that there could be a scientific explanation of someone acquiring knowledge of distant events by telepathic means. The difficulty in this kind of case is a matter of recognizing that the revisions of our understanding of nature that would be needed to account for some phenomena are so drastic that they would undermine ways of thinking about the world that many regard as essential to being scientific.

Evidence and Skepticism

In the early twentieth-century essay "The Will to Believe" the American philosopher William James quotes a leading biologist of his time as saying that even if telepathy is real, "scientists ought to band together to keep it suppressed and concealed" because it would mean the undoing of what scientists rely on to carry out their pursuits.[9] In other words, they ought to suppress the truth in order to save science. James himself was convinced of the reality of telepathic phenomena, partly as a result of his extensive firsthand investigations of Leonora Piper, the remarkable trance medium. But he describes trying to persuade some of his scientifically minded colleagues at Harvard to come and investigate her for themselves and receiving refusals because they were closed to the possibility of something that did not fit with their understanding of the natural world. From their point of view, it was just too weird to be taken seriously.

Like the scientists James describes, some of the most prominent contemporary skeptics about psychic phenomena in our time seem to think that they can know in advance of any consideration of evidence that such phenomena don't occur. As a result, they are sometimes content to reject particular evidential claims whenever they can imagine any reason for doubt about the evidence. It is undeniably true that many claims of extraordinary events can be dismissed as suspect for a variety of reasons, including fraud, gullibility, lack of attentiveness, etc. It is also true that a significant amount of reluctance to accept what goes beyond established explanatory paradigms is warranted. Nevertheless, we sometimes get evidence that is hard to dismiss without dogmatically insisting that what is not explainable in terms of our current paradigms didn't happen.

9. James, "Will to Believe," 722.

Some thinkers operate as if we don't have to be skeptical about our debunking explanations. However, as the American philosopher C. J. Ducasse points out, the danger is not just on one side. He says,

> Although the evidence offered by addicts of the marvelous for the reality of the phenomena they accept must be critically examined, it is equally necessary on the other side to scrutinize just as closely and critically the skeptics' allegations of fraud, or of malobservation, or of misinterpretation of what was observed, or of hypnotically induced hallucinations. For there is likely to be just as much wishful thinking, prejudice, emotion, snap judgment, naivete, and intellectual dishonesty on the side of orthodoxy, of skepticism, and of conservativism, as on the side of hunger for and belief in the marvelous. The emotional motivation for irresponsible disbelief is, in fact, probably even stronger—especially in scientifically educated persons, whose pride of knowledge is at stake.[10]

Ducasse's point is that we should be wary *both* of motivations toward excessive belief in the extraordinary *and* toward excessive skepticism; either motivation can interfere with our efforts to gain truth.

But is there actually strong evidence for the reality of psychic phenomena? I won't attempt to give a full response to that question in this book. Doing so would call for a book-length discussion of its own. Fortunately, I think that good discussions of that issue are already available. Much of what I say will presume that claims about psychic phenomena are worth taking seriously. But for my purposes, it is sufficient to report that some able thinkers who have studied the matter have judged that there is powerful evidence for the reality of such phenomena. In our time these thinkers include both accomplished scientists and highly respected philosophers. I will be referring to some of these thinkers in subsequent chapters, as well as referencing them in some of the footnotes. But I will mention here a few examples of accomplished scholars who comment on why not everyone is convinced by evidence they find overwhelming.

One distinguished British philosopher from an earlier era, C. D. Broad, comments specifically on the evidence for extrasensory awareness by some trance mediums. In certain cases, he says that the knowledge displayed is "too extensive and detailed to be reasonably ascribed to chance-coincidence, and it is quite inexplicable by reference to any normal sources of information open to the medium." Broad goes on to

---

10. Ducasse, *Paranormal Phenomena*, 35.

claim that no one who has made a careful study of the recorded facts and approaches the issue with a "reasonably open mind" would disagree, though he says it is "often dogmatically denied by persons who lack these qualifications."[11]

More recently, Edward Kelly, a distinguished research professor at the University of Virginia, echoes Broad's assessment when he comments on the evidence for psychic phenomena. He says bluntly, "Sufficient high-quality evidence has long . . . been available . . . to demonstrate beyond reasonable doubt the existence of basic 'paranormal' phenomena, at least for those willing to study that evidence with an open mind."[12] He repeats this assessment in a subsequent work where he describes the available evidence as "overwhelming . . . *for those who take the trouble to study it with an open mind,*" while acknowledging that it is denied by "professional skeptics . . . who conspicuously lack these credentials."[13] The problem that both Broad and Kelly allude to is that many of us cannot claim to have open minds with respect to this kind of thing, and few of us have really studied the evidence. Kelly characterizes the predominant attitude toward paranormal phenomena exhibited by mainstream science as "irrational incredulity."[14]

The Perspective of Disenchantment

Undoubtedly what Kelly calls irrational incredulity would be characterized differently by those who reject claims they regard as unscientific. They think of rejecting powers that are not recognized in our science as an inevitable result of a shift that has moved us away from prescientific ways of thinking about the world. Ancient people might have entertained ideas of magical powers, but these ways of thinking are viewed as no longer possible for people who have come to understand the world scientifically.

Some thinkers have characterized the world of modern experience as disenchanted, using a term popularized by Max Weber. One feature of a disenchanted world is the absence of nonhuman spirit beings such as fairies or angels or demons. But disenchantment means something

11. Broad, *Lectures on Psychical Research*, 259.
12. Kelly, "Introduction," xxvi.
13. Kelly, "Science and Spirituality," xv.
14. Kelly, "Introduction," xxvi.

more; it involves a rejection of results achieved by means other than those brought about by the physical forces science acknowledges. One of Weber's characterizations of the disenchanted world is "there are no mysterious incalculable forces that come into play but rather . . . one can in principle master all things by calculation."[15]

Unquestionably, modern people who have received a scientific education are less likely to explain what happens in terms of the activities of various nonhuman spirit beings. Scientific ways of conceiving things tend to replace some ways of construing events that our ancestors found natural and obvious.[16] But even if Weber's claim about this kind of disenchantment is accepted, it is more questionable to characterize the world of our contemporaries who accept science as limited to the calculable forces recognized by science. Admittedly, some modern people approximate the kind of disenchantment Weber describes. But the potential for experiences that include elements of mystery has not disappeared.

Many people in our time who are well informed about science take seriously the view that visionary experiences, such as near-death experiences, disclose truths about life beyond our earthly existence. Similarly, people with experience in meditation often think that in altered states of consciousness they get in touch with a level of reality that is more ultimate than anything ordinary experience discloses. A scientifically literate person in our era may accept the scientific privileging of ordinary sense experience as useful for learning about the world, but reject the claim that reflection on what this kind of experience reveals leads to the deepest understanding of things.

Similarly, people still experience the kinds of events that our ancestors sometimes took to be signs of a hidden reality breaking through. Not every well-informed person dismisses stories about becoming aware through some means other than ordinary sense perception of what is happening to a distant loved one facing trauma or death. Nor do scientifically literate people always deny that there are instances of healing that can't be explained in terms of our scientific understanding of physical causes.

---

15. Weber, "Science as a Vocation," 139.

16. It is not just science that led to this kind of disenchantment. Historians have noted that the questioning of belief in spirits and magical practices for dealing with these spirits was often motivated by theological concerns that such beliefs encroached on a proper recognition of the power of God. See Taylor, "Disenchantment-Reenchantment," 288. Such critiques played an important role in emptying of the world of spiritual powers other than those of the Creator, and in time many came to view the Creator's powers as like the powers that had already been rejected.

It is true that modern Western education tends to make us suspicious of reports of extraordinary events. We have learned a variety of debunking explanations that allow us to dismiss or to devalue claims that don't fit well with standard physicalist assumptions about the nature of things. But sometimes people are more confident that an event really happened than of assumptions that would lead to denying it could have happened.

Though it is possible to maintain an openness to signs that might point toward deeper realities than our science acknowledges, it is often easy in our culture to treat the disenchanted view as a kind of default assumption. Doing so means being skeptical about evidence of psychic powers. I have already said that my concern in this book is not to convince those who are most skeptical of the reality of psychic phenomena. For those who are undecided, I recommend studying some of the authors I cite. However, someone who has not undertaken a systematic study of the evidence, but is willing to grant that there is enough evidence to think that there could be genuine psychic phenomena, can consider much of what I say as a kind of hypothetical: What difference would it make if these phenomena are real?

My central concern is to explore what it would mean for Christian faith if extrasensory awareness and psychokinetic influence are understood as powers within the natural order that manifest themselves under the right conditions. It seems clear to me that accepting such phenomena would have significant consequences for Christian thinking, especially on topics such as miracles, prayer, and how God acts in the world. Subsequent chapters will explore why.

CHAPTER 5

Anomalous Phenomena

WE'VE ALL HEARD THEM: stories describing strange events that just don't fit with our usual ways of thinking about what is likely, or even possible. Some of these stories are told in ways that describe what happened as religiously significant, such as claims that God performed a miracle, perhaps in answer to a prayer request. But often reports of anomalous events don't suggest any kind of larger purpose that fits well into a religious narrative, and the accounts come from people who don't have religious beliefs as well as those who do.

These stories get our attention, often evoking a sense of fascination or even awe. But they can also leave us disoriented, unsure what to think. If they were presented as fictional portrayals, they might be entertaining or intriguing, but sometimes they are offered as factual accounts of real events. We can dismiss some of these stories immediately as unbelievable. But enough of them come to us from apparently credible sources to make us wonder: Do things of this kind really happen? Here is an example of the kind of story I am talking about.

A Lost Harp

Psychoanalyst Elizabeth Lloyd Mayer wrote a book that begins with an account of what happened after her daughter's harp was stolen. At the time, she was teaching in the psychology department at the University of

California at Berkeley and the psychiatry department at University Medical Center in San Francisco. Her daughter had been playing the harp since age six, and the particular instrument she played was an unusual and valuable type of harp that had been made by a master harp maker. After the theft, Mayer went through all the standard channels to try to locate it, even contacting the media, but nothing worked.

A close friend of hers suggested that if she really wanted to find the harp, she should contact a dowser. Not really expecting much and feeling ridiculous, Mayer called the president of the American Society of Dowsers, Harold McCoy, who lived in Arkansas, and explained her problem to him. Harold asked for a moment to check on the harp's location. After a pause, he told her that the harp was still in Oakland and asked her to send him a street map of the city. (These events predate a time when maps became readily available online.) Two days later, after receiving the map in the mail, he gave her a description of the specific street and the house where the harp was located. Mayer had never been to this neighborhood, but she went there and posted reward notices. Soon afterward, she received a phone call from someone who had seen the harp in a neighbor's house, enabling her to arrange for an exchange in which she picked up the harp and took it home.[1]

The day after the harp was returned, Mayer spoke on the phone with the dowser who had told her where to find it. He wasn't surprised that it had been returned. He had told her that she would get it back. But he asked what condition it was in. She told him that it was in superb condition, "not a scratch" and "barely out of tune." He replied with some relief that he had been working on that. Then he explained: "The guy who stole it—he's a crook but he's a coward. He got so scared havin' that harp, he was tempted to junk it every day. So I just went in every morning and said, 'You keep that harp safe; that harp's a precious instrument.'" Then Harold added casually, "You know thought forms can be very effective."[2]

The incident was the beginning for Mayer of a rethinking of deep assumptions about the nature of reality. Her book describes a journey toward a conception of the world that made room for things that had previously seemed impossible. It wasn't a straight-line journey, but she began to think about "a world where the barrier between mind and matter might be

---

1. Mayer, *Extraordinary Knowing*, 2–3.
2. Mayer, *Extraordinary Knowing*, 264.

permeable, where people might be able not only to find a harp from two thousand miles away, but to literally affect its material reality."[3]

Some people may find this story so hard to believe that they conclude that it just can't be true. I find the author entirely credible, and I have heard enough accounts of extraordinary knowing to see it as more than an isolated report. Nevertheless, the events seem incredible because what is reported conflicts with standard assumptions that we make about what can happen. We think of our knowledge of the world as coming through sense experience, either our own or reports of what others have experienced. Most of us find it obvious that we can't know what is happening halfway across the country just by going into our own minds and discovering the information. But according to the report, Harold is able to tell where the harp is located after a brief phone conversation in which he learns that it was stolen. Someone might suggest it was a lucky guess, but he is later able to give details about the location of the harp after looking at a street map. All of this sounds pretty spooky.

Dowsers understand themselves to be using techniques for focusing the mind in a way that reveals hidden information. They sometimes describe what they are doing as tapping into a plane of existence different from the material one by using intuitive powers of the mind. Most of us have heard of using a dowsing rod in a search for something that may be in the vicinity, such as underground water. But dowsers search for a variety of objects. They are sometimes called on by archeologists to aid in deciding where to dig for ancient ruins. Dowsing is also used to try to locate objects at a distance. In this case Harold apparently hones in on the location of the harp, perhaps as he holds a pointer device of some kind above a street map.

I make no assessments about the way dowsers understand what they do or about the effectiveness of dowsing generally, but the case Mayer describes suggests that something more than guessing is going on. We might notice that the techniques dowsers employ resemble other ways of focusing the mind, such as trance states or deep meditative states, through which unconscious awareness can be accessed. There are numerous credible reports of people in such states knowing things that they don't learn through ordinary sense experience. I'll give a few examples in subsequent chapters. However, my focus here is not so much about the particular

---

3. Mayer, *Extraordinary Knowing*, 264.

technique, but the oddness of the result. On standard ways of thinking, Harold cannot know what he appears to know.

Harold believes that his powers include not only determining the location of the harp, but discovering the thief's state of mind. More than that, he is convinced that his mental suggestions can potentially alter the thief's behavior. The story provides evidence that Harold can determine the location of the harp, but little evidence that he can do all that he thinks he can do. On the other hand, Harold's claims to such powers are not unique. In subsequent chapters I will be discussing other cases that suggest humans may have powers resembling those he describes. However, even if one is skeptical about some of his claims, his ability to locate the harp is striking enough to challenge our usual ways of thinking.

If the powers reported in this story were unlike anything we had ever heard about, we might decide that there is no need for serious consideration of whether this kind of thing can happen. But the extrasensory awareness it describes and the mental influence it suggests are reported in countless stories across many cultures and time periods. We may have good reasons for dismissing some of these accounts as unreliable, but that is different from concluding that all of them should be rejected. Furthermore, in addition to anecdotal accounts like this one, there is a growing body of observational evidence under controlled conditions of people with unusual powers as well as significant laboratory testing of abilities that may underlie this kind of phenomena.[4]

Even so, since events of this kind don't fit with standard scientific accounts of how the world works, many people think that whatever evidence is offered in support of such claims must be defective. Here I will just suggest that there is another possible response. When we find strong reasons to think that things happen that don't fit with our understanding of how the world works, we may decide that our understanding of what can happen needs to be expanded.

Things We Don't Talk About

After Mayer's experience with the missing harp, she began to reach out to colleagues to see if she could discover more about extraordinary knowing. One of her initiatives in collaboration with psychologist Carol Gilligan was to start a discussion group at meetings of the American

---

4. For excellent surveys of the experimental data, see the writings of Dean Radin.

Psychoanalytic Association. The group was called "Intuition, Unconscious Communication, and 'Thought Transference.'" People who wanted to participate in this group had to submit a written account of an anomalous experience. The response was overwhelming. The group was quickly filled to capacity and then expanded as more people insisted that they had to be included.[5]

Many of the stories that participants submitted were about experiences they had not previously disclosed to others. Highly educated professionals in our society learn early that expressing some views may lead to harsh judgments by colleagues. It can impede professional advancement to let it be known that you take seriously claims that don't fit with standard scientific accounts. But in a setting that is perceived as safe, stories of anomalous experiences may come out.

One psychoanalyst told of how he closed his eyes to prepare himself for the coming day's work and saw the image of a toddler putting a plastic bag over his head. Two hours later he was in a session where a patient described seeing his son with a plastic bag over his head and running away before the panicked parents could get the bag off. An early childhood specialist gave an account of a young patient suddenly turning to her and saying, "Your brother is drowning—you have to save him." The therapist said that she hadn't been thinking about it, but it was the anniversary of the day when her brother had drowned. A former head of the American Psychoanalytic Association told of a time when disseminated sarcoidosis had produced a large foreign mass in his lungs. He knew that the probability was that death would soon follow. He started meditating and running to calm himself down, and in his own words, "What started happening was that I literally *became* those cells and the lesions while I ran. And once that happened, the lesions started getting smaller." In time the mass totally disappeared.[6]

Mayer also tells of personal meetings with colleagues who opened up to her about matters they had previously kept to themselves. She did a psychological consultation with a neurosurgeon who had an astonishing record of success with the most difficult life-threatening surgeries. He told Mayer that he had to stop teaching. As she probed for the reason, he disclosed what he had never told anyone before. The reason his patients don't die is that when he learns of a potential surgery candidate, he sits

---

5. Mayer, *Extraordinary Knowing*, 14.
6. Mayer, *Extraordinary Knowing*, 14–16.

at the patient's bed and waits, sometimes for a long time, for a distinctive white light to appear around the patient's head. When it appears, he knows that the patient will survive the operation. He said that he couldn't possibly teach and not reveal such a thing, but he can't reveal it without having people thinking he is crazy.[7]

Trying and Not Trying

Mayer wanted to know more about how the kind of extraordinary knowing she was hearing about worked. So, she began to interview people who were said to have remarkable ability in this area. By getting recommendations from people she respected, she was able to weed out obvious frauds. As an experienced academic, she approached her research with a skeptical mindset, but her interviews convinced her that the people she was dealing with had genuine knowledge that was not attained through any ordinary channels. One of the people she spoke with was a woman named Deb. At the time of their first conversation, Mayer was in the process of deciding whom she would hire for a managing position at an arts organization. She had narrowed it down to two candidates who were very different, but had not made a decision. She told Deb her name, but told her nothing about why she was calling, except that she had heard of her and was curious.

Deb said, "Fine, I'll take a few seconds to be sure it's you I'm seeing. Then I'll say whatever comes to me. The whole session will be on tape, and I'll mail the tape when we're done."[8] Deb then described Mayer as in the middle of a decision between two women who were very different. She gave an uncannily accurate description of each of the candidates being considered, including quirky details that Mayer had noticed. Mayer had multiple conversations with Deb over the next two years. Even though she gave Deb hardly any information, she reports that "within minutes she would tell me things that made me feel she saw my life with a clarity my closest friends couldn't match, things I knew, but hadn't recognized I knew."[9]

After a few sessions, Mayer asked Deb about the state of mind in which she sees what she sees. Deb said that she didn't know how she

---

7. Mayer, *Extraordinary Knowing*, 11–12.
8. Mayer, *Extraordinary Knowing*, 43.
9. Mayer, *Extraordinary Knowing*, 44.

did what she did, but that often an image would cross her mind or the nugget of an idea. Deb said, "It's true that I try to see what I see, but then I stop trying. . . . It takes me over, . . . it's not me. . . . Except it is, because it's inside me."[10] Deb's experiences with extrasensory awareness started when she was a small child. She describes talking to a teacher in first grade, but responding to what the teacher was thinking instead of to what the teacher said. Over time, she learned to keep her mouth shut, but later in her work as a nurse, she used her non-ordinary channel to intuit danger to a patient.

Deb's ability to let her mind go sounds like both a natural aptitude and a cultivated skill of paying attention to impressions from the unconscious. She was aware that her powers of discernment were not infallible. She told Mayer, *"I'm pretty good, maybe 90 percent, but I gotta tell you. I'm not 100 percent."*[11] Nevertheless, there was enough accurate information to show that she wasn't just making lucky guesses, and Mayer was careful to avoid giving her clues that would reveal information. It is understandable why people hearing this kind of account might be doubtful, but for Mayer the detailed information she heard convinced her that she was dealing with a genuine case of extraordinary knowing.

Strange Connections

Mayer says that her experience with Harold pushed her to rethink her understanding of reality. What must reality be like for someone to locate a stolen harp from thousands of miles away in the days before the internet? The cases of extraordinary knowing she describes suggest that an individual's mind can somehow be linked to sources of information beyond what ordinary sensation and reflection provide. In the early days of thinking about telepathy, people often imagined that the linkage would be analogous to getting some kind of signal from a distant mind. But there is reason to think that extrasensory awareness doesn't work that way. What happens is more like tuning into a source of information to which you are already connected.

But how can we conceive such a strange connection? Thinkers who have reflected about psychic powers have sometimes used metaphors that allow us to picture how our minds can have their own

---

10. Mayer, *Extraordinary Knowing*, 46.
11. Mayer, *Extraordinary Knowing*, 45–46.

individuality but also be connected with a wider reality. Toward the end of his life, philosopher William James, reflecting on his study of psychic phenomena, compared individual minds to trees in the forest that have interlinked root systems. He posited a kind of continuum of consciousness in which our minds are rooted.[12] Another writer on the history of paranormal phenomena uses the metaphor of a "mental internet," comparing the way individual computers are linked to the worldwide web to the way human minds are linked to some mental network.[13] What exactly we might be connected to is conceived in different ways, but the various metaphors suggest that our sense of ourselves as cut-off from the rest of reality is a kind of illusion.

If we are connected somehow to some source of information that exceeds what we can learn through sense experience, how is it that we don't get more than fragments of what we potentially know? A general answer is that the linkage is through the unconscious mind and that most of what we know at an unconscious level does not make it into conscious awareness. Picture the unconscious mind as scanning a vast store of information that is mostly useless to us, but finding elements that touch our interests, such as danger to a distant loved one.[14]

We can think of this kind of radar as bringing the information to the threshold of conscious awareness, but there are barriers that can keep it hidden from us. One kind of barrier is that we erect defenses against anything that threatens our self-image or challenges beliefs that we are reluctant to give up. So, threatening material may not reach conscious awareness at all, or it might enter our consciousness only in a distorted form. Another barrier is that what comes from the unconscious mind is easily drowned out by a conscious mind that is dominated by sensory input. Material from the unconscious mind may not be able to slip into conscious awareness unless the "noise level" of our ordinary awareness is diminished. Some people may have a natural constitution that makes such a thing more likely. But even for those who don't, there are states of mind in which the noise level is reduced. In dreams or meditative states or conditions of sensory deprivation, the barriers blocking unconscious information are weaker. However, even when such information reaches consciousness, its significance may be unclear.

---

12. James, "Final Impressions," 324.
13. Simonsen, *Short History*, 28.
14. Radin, *Entangled Minds*, 265.

Fictional portrayals of psychic ability sometimes suggest people getting explicit and unambiguous information. But accounts from people purported to have psychic powers suggest that what is picked up through these channels typically requires interpretation that is fallible. Think of someone like Deb getting images and trying to guess what they mean. Or think of the psychiatrist whose image of the boy with the plastic bag over his head means nothing to him until he learns of an incident to which it corresponds. Or think of the neurosurgeon who sees a white light around a patient's head. Even if one is getting some kind of extrasensory information, it can be difficult to determine how it should be understood, or whether it is significant at all.

What Kind of Reality?

In our culture there is a bias toward thinking of what is ultimately real in physical terms. The standard view is that consciousness is a byproduct of physical processes in the brain. Given our usual assumptions about the nature of material things, it is hard to see how the kinds of anomalous phenomena Mayer describes could be genuine. Accepting that they do occur seems to call for significant revisions in the way we think about reality.

Some philosophers and religious thinkers advocate a reversal of the view that minds are derivatives of something physical. They posit a view called *idealism*, which takes mind to be the more fundamental reality and matter to be a derivative of mind. One contemporary defense of an idealist account can be found in Bernardo Kastrup's provocatively-titled book *Why Materialism Is Baloney*. Kastrup thinks that our experience of physical reality is a kind of construction of human consciousness. On his view there is no objective reality, but from our inner experiences, we talk ourselves into agreeing about what he calls a consensus reality. At a deeper level, he claims, only minds exist. He takes individual minds to be split-off versions of a Universal Consciousness. He thinks that psychic experiences occur under conditions that make our dissociation from the Universal Consciousness weaker.[15]

Some contemporary Christians may be attracted by this kind of view, but I suspect that most will find the account of physical reality implausible. However, idealism is not the only alternative to thinking of minds as

---

15. Kastrup, "Analytic Idealism and PSI," 274.

physical byproducts. A different approach is to question the characterization of matter as something totally different from mind. One form of it that some Christians have advocated is called *panpsychism or panexperientialism*, which claims that even at low levels of material organization, there is a mental or experiential aspect. The idea is sometimes ridiculed as saying that even rocks have minds, but philosophers defending this view distinguish between different forms of organizational structure. In some entities higher levels of experience (such as human minds) are built on lower levels that have more rudimentary experiential capacities. By contrast, entities such as a pile of sand are mere aggregates.

Philosopher David Ray Griffin argues extensively that his panexperientialist view fits with accepting psychic phenomena.[16] His account involves the claim that sensory perception is not our most basic form of perception. More fundamental is nonsensory perception, which he says goes on all the time, both in human beings and at lower levels of reality. The human capacity for sensory perception enables us to have clear awareness of some aspects of the world. However, a "side effect" of having intense sense perceptions is that most nonsensory perceptions are blocked from conscious awareness.[17] But he says that nonsensory perceptions of external realities can reach us at an unconscious level. These perceptions are a means by which we are influenced by other beings. By the same means, Griffin says, we also influence other beings who are capable of receiving nonsensory information.[18]

Another approach that challenges common ways of thinking about matter is inspired by accounts found in quantum physics, which deals with reality at the subatomic scale. Before the twentieth century, scientific accounts portrayed nature in mechanistic terms. One aspect of quantum reality that differs significantly from mechanistic accounts is the way entities separated by distance influence each other. Einstein derisively referred to these accounts as positing "spooky action at a distance." What physicists call *entanglement* is now supported by strong experimental evidence demonstrating that subatomic entities separated by distance are adjusted to each other. Their connection is not a matter of signals moving between them. It is rather that there are correlations that suggest they act more like parts of an interconnected whole than totally separate entities. At a commonsense level, we perceive things as separate,

---

16. Griffin, *Parapsychology, Philosophy, and Spirituality*, 128–46.
17. Griffin, *Parapsychology, Philosophy, and Spirituality*, 143.
18. Griffin, *Parapsychology, Philosophy, and Spirituality*, 144–45.

but physicist David Bohm theorizes that at a deeper level of reality, things are interconnected in ways that our concepts of space, time, matter, and energy do not allow us to conceive.

It is no accident that major figures in the development of quantum physics have entertained views of reality that take paranormal experiences seriously. The kind of interconnectedness that is empirically verifiable at the quantum level is suggestive with regard to what might be happening in cases of psychic phenomena. As religion scholar Jeffrey Kripal puts it, "most paranormal phenomena look like quantum phenomena scaled up into the macroworld."[19] Scientist Dean Radin says that quantum theory tells us that "*something unaccounted for is connecting otherwise isolated objects. And this is precisely what psi experiences and experiments are telling us. The parallels are so striking that it suggests that psi is—literally—the human experience of quantum interconnectedness.*"[20]

My concern here is not to settle on a particular approach to thinking about reality. It is rather to suggest that there are viable alternatives to materialistic views of reality that could accommodate anomalous events like the story of Harold and the harp and the other cases of extraordinary knowing that Mayer describes. Anomalous events may still evoke surprise, but if we can adjust our thinking about reality, we don't have to deny that they occur.

---

19. Kripal, *Flip*, 126.
20. Radin, *Entangled Minds*, 231–32.

CHAPTER 6

Crisis Revelations

THE RHINE RESEARCH CENTER in Durham, North Carolina, houses a large collection of submissions from people who describe their experiences of extrasensory perception. Here is one such report:

> One Sunday afternoon, several members of our family were eating dinner at my paternal grandfather's house. Suddenly, and for no apparent reason in the midst of pleasant family dinner chatter, my mother stood up and screamed "My mother! My mother! Something has happened to my mother!" We were all shocked. ... About fifteen minutes after her experience, the phone rang, and she received information from her father that her mother had indeed died fifteen minutes previously. My mother was not aware that her mother was ill, or even that she was in a hospital where she expired.[1]

Taken at face value, the account suggests that the woman who makes the sudden outburst was somehow aware of something unfortunate happening to her mother in another location. The story makes clear that this kind of outburst was not a typical occurrence. People were shocked when it happened. If she frequently screamed out this kind of concern for her mother, we might say that her fears were likely to coincide with bad news some of the time. But the apparent uniqueness of what occurred, along

---

1. Feather and Schmicker, *Gift*, 28.

with the timing of the news, suggests that she acquired information about her mother in some extraordinary way.

Of course, with a single account like this one, we can imagine alternative explanations that don't involve extrasensory awareness. We can think that the events are misremembered or intentionally distorted. We might postulate that details are left out that would suggest that the woman knew more about her mother's condition than the story claims. However, an examination of the Rhine collection, as well as other collections of this kind, makes it obvious that this story is one of many describing experiences that exhibit a common pattern. People sense that a loved one is in some kind of crisis, often involving a risk of serious injury or death. Soon after, they get confirmation of the event. This kind of pattern is displayed in reports from many time periods and various cultures. To explain away all such accounts by postulating mistakes or deliberate deception seems implausible, and in some instances, we hear this kind of story from people whom we have good reason to think are credible sources.

Examining accounts from the various databases where such stories are collected makes clear that reports of spontaneous extrasensory experiences are overwhelmingly about events that evoke strong emotion. In most cases the awareness involves someone with whom there is a close connection. In the Rhine collection, instances of sudden intuition like the one described in the case above are not the most common form. Around 60 percent of reports of extrasensory awareness in these accounts involve dreams. Sudden intuitions like this one constitute about 30 percent. The rest involve such things as bodily sensations of pain corresponding to someone else's injury or quasi-sensory awareness of distant events.[2]

In stories of this type involving dreams, the dream is often described as particularly vivid, leaving the dreamer unsettled. When there is a sudden intuition, the reports frequently suggest that the intuition evokes a strong sense of certainty. In the case described above there is a feeling of some unspecified danger, but many accounts of this type describe the concern in very specific terms. A man awakens from a nightmare at 3 a.m. with a feeling of alarm, saying that he just saw someone shoot his Uncle John. No one in the house can calm him down. In the morning the news comes that Uncle John was shot at around the time the nightmare occurred.[3] It is conceivable that people

2. Feather and Schmicker, *Gift*, 37.
3. Feather and Schmicker, *Gift*, 39.

have intuitions or dreams that seem just as convincing in cases where the anxiety-provoking event does not happen. However, since such experiences are typically not reported, it is hard to verify to what extent the kind of strong conviction that often accompanies these impressions is correlated with the event actually occurring.

Nevertheless, stories in which an intuition or a dream turns out to be correct give some idea of the type of persistent concern such an experience can evoke. In a remote area of Australia, a man's child had a slight fever. He and his wife suspected that the boy might have a touch of malaria, a disease that was not uncommon in the area. Close to daybreak, the man had a vivid dream in which a doctor examined the child and diagnosed diphtheria. He got up and checked on his son and found him breathing normally with a normal temperature. The man reports:

> I went back to my room, but not to sleep. The memory of the dream kept nagging at me. I reasoned with myself that isolated as we were, with no contacts between my children and other children, with no case of diphtheria anywhere within many miles reported, it was foolish of me to be disturbed by the dream.[4]

But he says, "After a while I could stand it no longer." With his wife, he examined the boy, who said that he had no pain. When he shined a light down the child's throat, he observed a tiny white spot, the size of a pinhead. He called the family doctor and asked whether it might be diphtheria. The doctor agreed to drive a considerable distance to check on the boy. By the time he arrived, the tiny white spot had become a patch. The doctor confirmed it was diphtheria and administered an antitoxin. After the treatment, he said that if he had arrived much later, it would have been too late to save the boy's life.[5]

Sensing What Isn't Present

Many of the accounts of spontaneous extrasensory experience involve a dream of something unexpected that turns out to be true. But there are also numerous accounts of people who are fully awake having sensations that don't come from any recognized physical cause. One form of this experience is a person feeling pain that corresponds to what is happening to a distant individual. A woman writing a letter feels a burning pain

---

4. Feather and Schmicker, *Gift*, 87.
5. Feather and Schmicker, *Gift*, 87–88.

in her right hand so severe that she can't hold the pen she was using. Soon she receives a call telling her that her daughter's right hand has been burned by acid in a laboratory accident.[6] A woman at work feels a terrible shooting pain in her right hip from which she can get no relief. A phone call reveals that her mother had fallen and broken her hip at the time the pain began.[7] These bodily experiences look like one of the forms an intuition of what is happening to a loved one can take.

In addition to this kind of experience, there are also many accounts of experiences of seeing, hearing, or smelling something that corresponds to what is happening elsewhere. Consider the following story from Alister Hardy's Religious Experience Research Unit collection. A woman has gone to the movies with her husband while a young girl babysits her six-month-old child. As soon as the couple take their seats, the woman feels a strong sense of uneasiness. She smells something burning, though there is no observable cause in the vicinity. At her insistence, she and her annoyed husband leave the theater. The burning smell for the woman gets stronger on the ride back. When they reach their room, they encounter dense smoke. A chair is in flames. The babysitter had dropped a lighted cigarette when she went to sleep. The woman gets the baby from the bedroom while the husband gets the unconscious babysitter out.[8]

Researchers in the nineteenth century used the term "hallucination," to refer to this kind of experience, since it involves having a sensory experience of something that is not physically present. In our time we often think of hallucinatory experiences as signs of mental illness, and there is no doubt that troubled individuals sometimes have sensations of what is not present. However, there is strong evidence that perfectly normal people have experiences of this type. One of the reasons we are not aware of the frequency of this kind of experience is that people are typically reluctant to disclose experiences that might lead others to question their judgment or their sanity.

The nineteenth-century researchers coined the term "veridical hallucinations" as a label for cases in which what is sensed provides correct information about distant events that wouldn't be available through ordinary means. In other words, they recognized that experiences not caused by ordinary sensation were not all just subjective projections. Some revealed objectively verifiable truths. A woman who

6. Feather and Schmicker, *Gift*, 78.
7. Feather and Schmicker, *Gift*, 48.
8. Hardy, *Spiritual Nature of Man*, 46.

had been estranged from her mother came home and was welcomed back. During the visit her mother described a terrifying vision she had four months earlier. While working at the kitchen table, she saw her daughter's face "and it was hideous—swollen and purple with . . . eyes popping out."[9] She was disturbed by the event, but the family convinced her it was just her imagination. The daughter had not told her mother about an experience four months prior when she was being strangled and nearly died. The daughter comments, "Her vision had shown what actually happened to me."[10]

Many people dismiss such stories with the thought that sometimes visionary experiences correlate with actual events and sometimes they do not. But some reports describe details that bear an uncanny resemblance to what happens far away. A young man had the experience of "seeing" his parents swerve off the road to avoid an oncoming car that was trying to pass. The tires on his parents' car caught on the edge of the road, resulting in a 180-degree turn and a roll-over onto the car's roof. He observed that his father had a bloody nose and had hurt his ankle. When the parents came home, their report of events corresponded to what he had "seen."[11]

In reports of this kind, it is sometimes difficult to tell whether what is reported is something someone dreamed or whether it was a waking experience. Sometimes the account comes from someone who describes it as occurring after waking up. In the vision of the car wreck, the man says he was "half asleep." In biblical times dreams and waking visions were regarded as similar experiences. A vision is a waking experience that is dreamlike. In either case, when the dream or the vision corresponds in striking ways to actual events, the correspondence suggests that there has been extrasensory awareness.

Mere Anecdotes?

Not every story of this kind provides strong reason to posit extrasensory awareness. In many cases we can think that there is likely to be an ordinary explanation of the seemingly anomalous knowledge. But some stories seem particularly impressive, and the cumulative effect of looking at numerous reports of this kind is often convincing for people who have not

---

9. Feather and Schmicker, *Gift*, 76.
10. Feather and Schmicker, *Gift*, 76.
11. Feather and Schmicker, *Gift*, 45.

ruled out the possibility of this kind of awareness. Some people, however, speak disparagingly of stories like these as anecdotal, contrasting such reports with scientific evidence. But even if there are limits to the kinds of conclusions we should draw from reports of extrasensory experience, testimonial evidence should be recognized as genuine evidence.

The distinguished physicist Freeman Dyson agrees with this assessment. While acknowledging that there is much of what he calls nonsense and fraud in reports of this kind, he finds the numerous accounts of extrasensory perception to provide convincing reason for accepting the reality of the phenomenon. He notes that a significant number of accounts have been investigated by competent researchers, such as members of the Society for Psychical Research. He observes, "The members of the society took great trouble to interview first-hand witnesses as soon as possible after the events, and to document the stories carefully."[12]

Nevertheless, even while accepting ESP as real, Dyson says that it is not likely to be provable on the basis of well-controlled scientific experiments. As he puts it,

> ESP only occurs, according to the anecdotal evidence, when a person is experiencing intense stress. Under the conditions of controlled scientific experiment intense stress and strong emotions are excluded; the person experiences boredom rather than excitement, and the evidence for ESP disappears.... The experiment excludes the human emotions that make ESP possible.[13]

While I think that Dyson underestimates what can be learned through controlled experiments in this area, his point that scientists cannot duplicate the conditions under which spontaneous extrasensory experience occurs is well taken. Hence, the experiments we can devise do not deal with the full range of this sort of experience.

Even so, there are two points to notice. One is that scientific investigation is not limited to controlled experiments. For some phenomena, careful observation is recognized as an appropriate scientific method. For example, scientists systematically observe what animals do in their natural habitat. Studies of this kind often reveal things that would not be learned by laboratory testing. There are numerous examples of careful observation of reported psychic phenomena. For example, anthropologists have studied shamans across the world who in altered states

---

12. Dyson quoted in Mayer, *Extraordinary Knowing*, 238.
13. Dyson, "Foreword," xi.

of consciousness are purported to display remarkable healing powers. Researchers have gone to séances in which trance mediums sometimes give evidence of knowing what they couldn't have known through ordinary means. This kind of investigation is sometimes valuable for distinguishing between cases in which the phenomenon is genuine and cases in which some kind of trickery is being used. It is also helpful in providing a richer understanding of what might be possible than controlled experimentation by itself would be likely to provide.

Second, even if there are limits to what controlled experiments can show, they have provided important statistical evidence that supports claims of the existence of extrasensory perception. One of the standard forms of testing in the early days of this sort of investigation involved experiments in which people try to get the correct answer with regard to some information where the chances of guessing correctly can be calculated precisely. For example, there are classic experiments that have been conducted with specialized cards in which chance would result in guessing correctly 20 percent of the time. Some of these experiments have yielded results far in excess of chance. In some cases, the odds against achieving the result by guessing alone are enormous. In an earlier era, such experiments were conducted using actual cards. Later experimenters substituted randomized machine-generated targets of various kinds. Procedures of this kind have been made increasingly sophisticated to rule out cheating.

When Dyson speaks of scientific tests as being boring, he no doubt has this kind of guessing experiment in mind. However, this experimental method is not the only form of investigation. Experimenters in this field recognized that ESP abilities were connected with a kind of awareness that occurs at the unconscious level. Even though we can't generally access this awareness by trying, there are states of mind in which unconscious awareness can reveal itself. There has been systematic experimental investigation of extrasensory abilities occurring in dreams.[14] There are also experiments of abilities displayed by people who are put in situations of sensory deprivation that have yielded impressive results.[15] In addition, there are studies with people who are experienced in putting their minds into altered states through meditation.[16] So, even though Dyson is correct in saying that science cannot

14. Ullman et al., *Dream Telepathy*.
15. Radin, *Conscious Universe*, 91.
16. See, e.g., Penberthy et al., "Impact of Meditation."

replicate the conditions under which ESP occurs spontaneously, he may underestimate the ingenuity of investigators in coming up with legitimate scientific ways to investigate the phenomena.

While I think that scientific investigation has produced important results that confirm the existence of extrasensory abilities, I find reports of spontaneous instances of extrasensory awareness indispensable for getting a richer picture of how these abilities work in context. I can imagine someone accepting the laboratory evidence, but not fully understanding its significance without becoming acquainted with the stories that led to this kind of investigation in the first place. Of course, we have to exercise critical judgment about the reliability of reports; they can be unreliable or misleading. But some reports seem well authenticated, and individual stories often fit into patterns that show similar experiences by many people. Philosopher C. D. Broad comments that even though we can raise questions about individual cases, the doubts become "less convincing when applied to the sum total of them taken collectively."[17] The confluence of this kind of anecdotal evidence and scientific evidence under controlled conditions can be mutually reinforcing.

Communication from God?

Stories of extrasensory experiences suggest unconscious sources that provide information that goes beyond what we could get through sense perception. This idea goes against the grain of what has become a standard way of thinking in scientific culture. But for someone who believes in God, it might raise the question of whether impressions from the unconscious might be a way to receive communication from God. The idea is not that everything that comes from the unconscious is a message from God. The suggestion is rather that the unconscious mind might sometimes be a channel through which God gives us access to truths we need to recognize.

Many Christians have experienced what they call divine guidance. Often these experiences involve a persistent impression of the need to do something. For example, I have heard numerous stories of someone getting a compelling urge to call or visit a particular person. One example comes from C. S. Lewis's report of an "unaccountable nagging" in his mind to go get his hair cut. When he went to the barber shop,

---

17. Broad, *Lectures on Psychical Research*, 15.

the barber greeted him by saying that he had been praying that Lewis would come in that day. Lewis had helped the man with various difficulties in the past. As they talked, Lewis realized that if he had come later, it would have been too late to help the man with the particular problem he was facing.[18] There is an obvious question of how to tell the difference between cases in which this kind of impression should be treated as authoritative and cases in which it is more like an obsessive urge to recheck the door to make sure it is locked. But even if our discernment of such things is not infallible, we can think that at least sometimes impressions of this sort provide guidance that goes beyond what our conscious reflection could give us. In retrospect, even if not at the time, we may be convinced that some impressions are from God.

I don't deny that people who think that they receive communication from God are often deluded. It understandable why we might be skeptical about people who report that they have a message directly from God. However, we can be too skeptical. Christianity was passed on to us by people who were convinced that they were in contact with a spiritual realm, and early Christians relied on this kind of contact for guidance. If we try to trim away what they say about their experience of the divine Spirit, we lose something that seems central to their understanding of God's revelation. They acknowledged that discernment was required to distinguish whether their sense of what God was saying was credible. Similarly, we can recognize that human efforts to correctly recognize whatever messages God might want to communicate are fallible, but we can also think that sometimes we get it right.

What stands out to me is that many of the most credible stories of divine guidance seem reminiscent of stories of people who get a persistent extrasensory impression. In the story of the man who worries that his child has diphtheria, there is no mention of any religious dimension, but we can easily imagine someone telling this kind of story in a way that represents the impression as coming from God. In my view, the question of whether we imagine God as doing something specific to send the impression or as just creating the kind of world in which we can get guidance that goes beyond what our ordinary reflective powers deliver is not particularly important. Either way of conceiving things could fit with Christian experience of God's guidance.

18. Lewis, "Efficacy of Prayer," 3.

I have been focusing on instances in which communication from God involves some kind of direction to do a particular act. But many of the stories told by people who describe contact with God convey something different. They portray a sense of God's presence that brings about a more hopeful understanding of some situation. Mark Fox has done a study of religious experience based on accounts submitted to the Religious Experience Research Centre. Many of the accounts he quotes describe a type of experience that involves being overwhelmed by a sense of love. One person writes,

> One night I was in great distress over a family situation and cried out to God to come to me if He existed.... Suddenly God came. Not with a clap of thunder or a flash of light, but gently and slowly and almost imperceptibly. He filled the room with His presence until he was everywhere. The comfort and warmth were indescribable. The room was Love.[19]

We might try to describe in propositional form the message that is received, but the message conveyed here is inseparable from an experience of God.

In another of the reports cited by Fox, a woman was in a depressed state during a period of grieving over the death of her husband. She says,

> Then one night . . . feeling lost and perhaps seeking comfort from a God who wasn't there, I suddenly knew that I was loved by something, and very tenderly loved too. I remember the feeling of utter incredulity that I could be loved by something which I can only characterize as "enfolding love." It was something outside myself, but at the same time within.[20]

In these reports, as well as many similar ones, the experience of God occurs for someone who is in an extreme emotional state. I am not suggesting that being in such a state is required for an experience of God or that everyone in such a state has this kind of experience. But if we read these accounts in the light of the instances of spontaneous extrasensory awareness I cited earlier, we might think that emotions are a factor in moving something one is aware of at an unconscious level into conscious awareness. Just as an impression of danger to loved ones produces a sense of urgency that evokes our attention, a feeling a

---

19. Fox, *Fifth Love*, 13.
20. Fox, *Fifth Love*, 66.

despair may be conducive to unlocking an awareness of God's presence that is mostly hidden from view.

Some of what moves into our conscious awareness is beyond our control. But if we think that the unconscious mind is a channel through which God can influence us, we can make an effort to attune ourselves to messages that God may want to send us through this channel. That does not have to mean seeking out striking paranormal experiences. Many of our impressions deal with things we know in ordinary ways, but have pushed out of conscious awareness, and often we cannot tell whether anything extrasensory is involved. Whether it is or not, being attuned to what God wants to tell us means cultivating capacities to pay attention to impressions that we can easily dismiss. The classical practices of prayer and meditation can be thought of as ways to become receptive to hearing the voice of God. God may speak even to those who have no belief in God. But some messages are likely to be received only by those who expect that some of what comes into our minds is purposeful communication from a divine source.

CHAPTER 7

Dream Messages

Psychologist Charles Tart reports that over the years many scientists he met discovered that he was a "safe person" to talk to about extraordinary experiences. Typically, scientists keep quiet about such things because of the risk to their professional reputation. After numerous conversations in which scientists would confide in him about experiences that they knew many of their colleagues would greet with skepticism or even ridicule, Tart decided to create a website where scholars from the natural and social sciences could tell their stories. Many of the stories on the website are posted anonymously with only a general indication of the individual's credentials. But there are also postings in which scientists with mystical or paranormal experiences offer accounts under their own name. The following account comes from psychologist Mark Schroll's report of a childhood dream.

In the dream he was on a field trip with his first-grade class. One of the girls in the class began to complain of stomach pains. She eventually collapsed and began to bleed from her stomach. None of his classmates seemed to recognize what was happening. When he tried to aid her, the other students acted as if the two were playing some odd game. When Schroll told his parents about the dream, they told him that dreams were not real, even if they sometimes seemed real. At school he told some of his classmates about the dream, and they made fun of him for having an overactive imagination. Schroll says he looked for the girl who had been in the dream, but she wasn't at school that day. As the day went on, he became increasingly agitated. His teachers tried to reassure him that nothing was wrong and told him to stop disturbing the class.

After lunch, Schroll's teacher reported to the class that the absent girl had been taken to the hospital for emergency surgery because of an appendicitis attack. When the girl returned to school, she told him about experiencing cramps during the day, but having her complaints dismissed by her mother and sister. However, her father, a surgeon, checked out her complaints when he came home for the evening and then rushed her to the hospital for emergency surgery. When Schroll told her about his dream, she initially accepted what he said, but later, under the influence of her peers, she became doubtful.[1]

Besides the uncanny premonition contained in the dream, one of the striking aspects of this story is the reluctance of people to think that the dream might reveal some unknown truth. The parents, the other children, and the teachers all pressure Schroll to recognize that it was only a dream. When the emergency surgery was announced, he took it as a vindication that he was right to be concerned. But according to his account, the teacher refused to say anything about the apparent verification of what he had dreamed. Everyone else seems to take a united front to enforce accepted cultural norms against thinking of the dream as anything more than a product of his imagination.

In many cultures the idea of dream revelations would not have been thought strange at all. Numerous cultures have taken for granted the idea that dreams can function as warnings or predictions that should be heeded. But for many of us, such an idea seems superstitious or maybe even mentally unbalanced. We don't have a problem in thinking that a dream may reveal something going on at an unconscious level. We can acknowledge that a dream might contain information that has been discerned in some ordinary way, but has not registered consciously. But in our culture treating dreams as a potential source of information about reality that has not come through the senses can lead to questions about our good sense. The authority figures whom Schroll encountered were quick to make sure that he understood that while a dream might seem real, it is only a dream.

---

1. Schroll, "Personal Encounter with Paranormal Dreaming."

Dreams in the Bible

One of the challenges involved in understanding ancient literature, including biblical writings, is realizing that the writers thought about some things in ways that are alien to our way of thinking. Sometimes this realization is surprising, but paying close attention to what a writer says can make it difficult to avoid. When we do look closely at biblical texts, we can notice clear indications that biblical writers thought differently about dreams than people in our culture typically do. They thought of dreams (or visions) as central ways that God communicates with human beings.

Stories of dream encounters with God are found throughout Hebrew Scripture. In Genesis 15 Abram's encounter with God is called a vision. Part of the experience occurs after Abram is put into a "deep sleep" (15:12). Accounts of learning truths through dreams or visions in biblical stories are found throughout these texts, and dream messages are not limited to Israelites. King Abimelech receives a dream warning that despite what Abraham has told him, Sarah is Abraham's wife (Gen 20:3). Jacob's dream at Bethel (Gen 28) and Samuel's dream at Shiloh (1 Sam 3) illustrate the widespread belief that dream messages from God are more likely to occur when someone is in a holy place.

The pattern of God speaking through dreams continues in the New Testament. In Matthew's version of the Christmas story, Joseph gets several instructions in dreams. One of these dream messages leads him to abandon his intention to dismiss Mary quietly when he discovers she is pregnant (Matt 1:19). Later there is a dream in which he is warned to flee the country (Matt 2:13). Paul has a dream that provides direction about where to go next on his missionary journey (Acts 16:9), and it was a vision of the risen Christ that turned his life around on the road to Damascus.

Dreams can be distinguished from visions; however, the distinction is not sharp. Biblical texts sometimes refer to dreams as "visions of the night." In Hebrew thought dreams and visions were viewed as forms of the same type of perception.[2] A vision involves dreamlike content that breaks into ordinary waking experience. Visions are not just an ancient phenomenon. People still report them today. These experiences can occur spontaneously, but the capacity for having visions can also be cultivated. It is often cultivated in cultures where visions are valued as ways of making contact with the spiritual realm. Hebrew prophets were thought

---

2. For a discussion of this issue, see Kelsey, *God, Dreams, and Revelation*, 33.

of as making this kind of contact in experiences that involved seeing and hearing things by means other than ordinary sensation.

When I first considered the idea that dreams might be communication from God, it seemed strange to me. I was used to thinking that dreams were constructions of the unconscious mind, and my own dreams seemed like jumbles of imagined perceptions that had been pieced together to produce bizarre scenarios. I didn't view dreams as a promising place to seek divine guidance. I could imagine the possibility of God sending a message through a dream, but how could such a message be distinguished from all the extraneous material that dreams contained? The possibility of making a significant life decision on the basis of what I had dreamed struck me as a foolhardy idea. Biblical writers clearly thought about dreams differently from the way I had learned to think about them. They thought that dreams should often be taken as providing divine instruction that needs to be heeded.

In that respect they weren't different from other ancient people. Virtually all ancient cultures, including the ancient Greeks, regarded dreams as a potential source of a wisdom from a higher realm. When I first started reading Plato, I noticed that the great thinker Socrates took seriously a dream he had that seemed prophetic of the time of his death.[3] This was the same Socrates whose defense at his trial includes an acknowledgement of receiving communication from a *daimonion*, a spirit being whose inner guidance took the form of prohibitions of some acts that Socrates considered doing.[4] Socrates was a master of reflective discourse, but he was apparently also receptive to revelation through means other than what people today typically regard as reasonable.

We could, of course, regard ancient ideas about treating dream experiences as messages from a higher realm as a superstition that should be discarded by people in our time. However, there is considerable tension in accepting what biblical authors say about God, while rejecting a central source they used to form their understanding. Saying that disclosures of God didn't really come through dreams or visionary experiences leads easily to a skepticism toward claims about God from those whose thinking was significantly shaped by these sources. But can we take seriously the idea that revelatory truth may be discovered through the unconscious processes that lead to dreams?

3. Plato, *Crito*, 44.
4. Plato, *Apology*, 39–40.

The Subliminal Realm

People in our culture tend to think of information reception as something that goes on in the kind of awareness that we have in ordinary waking states. We receive data through the senses, and by a conscious reflective process we formulate interpretations that we can then test by seeking verification through more sense experiences. We may admit that there are parts of the mind that are outside of our conscious awareness. But if we think of them at all, we tend to regard them as irrational aspects of our nature and not as potential sources of wisdom.

So, a first step toward considering the possibility that dreams might be revelatory is to reconsider these ideas about the unconscious mind. F. W. H. Myers in the late nineteenth century used the metaphor of a threshold to represent how only some mental states rise to a level needed for immediate awareness. He labels that which is below the threshold as *subliminal*.[5] Myers studied phenomena that provide evidence about the nature of the subliminal realm, including disintegrations of personality, striking instances of genius, dream states, hypnosis, visions of distant events, automatic writing, trances, ecstasies, and mystical states. These phenomena reveal centers of consciousness that operate below the threshold of ordinary awareness, but that nevertheless sometimes show signs of purposive intelligence.

The subliminal parts of our nature are a source of powers to do some things that we can't do through conscious effort. For example, we have a subliminal know-how that when activated can make physiological alterations to bodily processes that usually function automatically. There are well evidenced stories of people who have learned meditative techniques that allow them to exercise a degree of control over these automatic processes that seems incredible. Subliminal powers also enable some people to perform extraordinary cognitive tasks, such as complex arithmetical calculations that are done instantly or creative works that are produced in ways that bypass ordinary consciousness. My focus here is not on these abilities, but on whether subliminal awareness is a source of information that goes beyond what reflection on data from the senses provides.

There are numerous stories of discoveries that have occurred when a scientist has an insight in a dream that leads to the solution of what has previously been puzzling. There are also cases in which a creative project is advanced by ideas that come into awareness in a dream state. Many of

---

5. Myers, *Human Personality*, 22.

us have had dreams that gave us insight about something unrecognized that was going on in our relations with others. But it is possible to view such insights as a product of unconscious processing that arises when the subliminal mind puts together clues that we have become aware of in an ordinary way, but whose significance was unrecognized.

However, what if the subliminal mind has access to information that did not come through ordinary sensation? There is significant evidence that states of mind in which the control of ordinary consciousness is relaxed are conducive to extrasensory awareness. Dream states are a prime example. Louisa Rhine collected over fourteen thousand reports of spontaneous extrasensory experiences during her time at the Rhine Research Center at Duke University. She calculated that around 60 percent of the reports people submitted dealt with dreams that revealed extrasensory information.[6] In addition to such reports, there is a famous series of experiments conducted at the Maimonides Medical Center in New York in which people in the sleep lab were awakened when their EEG readings indicated dreaming had occurred. Their dream reports were then compared to randomly selected target images. Someone in a different room from the dreamer opens an envelope containing the target image and concentrates on it in a way that is intended to "send" it to the dreamer. Continuing over many years, the research provided impressive statistical evidence for correlations between the targets and dream content.[7]

Of course, none of this proves that God communicates with people in dreams. But recognizing that dreams might activate an ability to be aware of things we don't know about through the senses would mean that we can think of dreams as a potential channel through which there might be communication. People who believe in God can at least consider the idea that God uses this channel. I hasten to say that I am not suggesting that every extrasensory awareness is a divine communication. Rather I am suggesting that the idea that God could communicate through dreams is more worthy of consideration than my initial reaction to the idea allowed.

---

6. Schmicker, *Best Evidence*, 67.

7. Ullman et al., *Dream Telepathy*, 9–34.

The Strangeness of Dream Revelations

Even if we think that the unconscious mind is a potential channel for receiving information, we might find the idea of God communicating in this way strange. One reason is that we might contrast it with more straightforward ways of communicating. Dreams often strike us as random and meaningless products of the imagination. We don't remember most of them, and we can usually disregard the ones that we do remember. Furthermore, if dreams contain messages, those messages are often expressed in symbolic language that is difficult to understand. So, we might think that if God wants to communicate, the communication would take a form that minimizes the potential for misunderstanding. We might also think that this communication should be accompanied by signs that leave no doubt that the communication comes from God.

It may be too obvious to point out, but thinking that divine communication would be in a form that minimizes the potential for misunderstanding and leave no room for doubt about its divine source would disqualify biblical texts as divine revelation. When we look at the range of views people get from biblical writings, we can hardly attribute all the diversity to bad reading. There is, of course, plenty of bad reading, but there is also significant disagreement between people who are both well informed and capable interpreters about what messages we should get from these texts. Additionally, it is clearly possible for reasonable people to read the Bible without thinking that it is a communication from God. If we think that the Bible can be a vehicle of divine revelation, we will need to put aside some of the assumptions about what such revelation has to look like.

If we do entertain the idea of God communicating through dreams, there are several things to notice. One is that what comes into consciousness in a dream is partly our own construction. Jacob's dream of a ladder between earth and heaven may be a revelation from God, but it also looks like a creation built out of cultural ideas available to him. Whatever message comes from God seems to be shaped by human ways of thinking characteristic of a particular time period.

In addition to recognizing the human role in constructing dream content, we should notice that what comes into awareness in dreams is often what we resist allowing into the conscious mind. Some psychologists think of dream content as arising from thoughts we have suppressed during the day. The dream images can be thought of as coming across the threshold into consciousness in a disguised and sometimes distorted form that overcomes this resistance. Consider a paradigmatic biblical story in this light: Peter's dream (or vision) in Acts 10. Peter has accepted the standard Jewish food regulations as having the status of divine commands. In his vision he sees a sheet coming down from heaven with various animals that he regards as unclean and, therefore, not to be eaten. He hears a voice telling him to kill and eat what has been provided. Peter refuses to violate restrictions imposed by Hebrew Scripture. The voice tells him, "What God has made clean, you must not call profane" (10:15). The sequence is repeated three times.

Peter is puzzled about the meaning of the visionary experience. But he soon receives an invitation from a centurion named Cornelius who has had a vision telling him to seek out Peter. Peter goes to the house of Cornelius in violation of Jewish prohibitions about associating with gentiles. By this time, he has apparently discerned the meaning of his vision. He tells the gentiles, "God has shown me that I should not call anyone profane or unclean. So, when I was sent for, I came without objection" (Acts 10:28–29).

The text portrays Peter's vision as a revelation from God. It seems plausible to think of the communication as coming through Peter's subliminal awareness. Peter has been prepared to consider ideas to which he has some resistance. No doubt the willingness of Jesus to override Jewish regulations has played a role in opening him to thoughts that he is entertaining at a subliminal level. In the Acts account Peter has previously gone with Philip and accepted Samaritans into the Christian community, despite traditional Jewish antipathy toward this group. It is not much of a stretch to imagine that he is experiencing some cognitive dissonance about connecting his sense of Jewish identity with the apparent necessity of welcoming outsiders. What he is struggling with comes into awareness in the dreamlike experience through which he hears a message from God.

Is the Unconscious Mind Purposive?

Some Christians, influenced by the thought of Carl Jung, have found reason to think of dreams, not just in particular instances but generally, as purposive communication. Jungian analyst and Episcopal priest John Sanford says, "By showing situations symbolically in dreams, the unconscious communicates with consciousness and discloses its comments on the conditions of our life."⁸ He thinks of what he calls meaningful dreams as displaying a kind of intelligent purpose that is directed toward greater integration of disparate aspects of the self. Furthermore, Sanford says that he does not hesitate to call the intelligence we encounter in this way God. He writes, "God is the name we give to the purposeful numinous power that crosses our lives; our dreams are one of the manifestations of this power."⁹

Sanford calls the center of our conscious life the *ego*. When we ignore the unconscious aspects of the mind, we may assume that the ego is who we are. We may accept the purposes the ego pursues, such as striving for material goods and social recognition and power, as our purposes. However, Sanford calls the center of our unconscious lives the *self*. On his account the self is an active and energetic force that seeks integration of the total person, which would mean bringing the ego into alignment with the aims of the self. This psychic center he thinks of as Christlike. He sometimes calls it the God within, but also the image of God. The self in his view is our point of contact with God.

Sanford views dreams as a primary means by which the self seeks wholeness. On his account, dreams show us aspects of our nature that we don't recognize. For example, a dream might portray a character that we take to be an enemy. Following Jungian styles of interpretation, Sanford suggests that the enemy is actually an aspect of the self that has not been integrated into the larger whole. Sometimes the disliked features of the enemy are characteristics that might be turned into strengths. In dreams we encounter many forces, including forces that seem dark and demonic. But Sanford affirms, "Ultimately our dreams are in service of wholeness and of the psychic center of the personality. . . . Our dreams help to establish a conscious relationship to this inner image of God. In this way they are the Voice of God."¹⁰

This interpretation of the significance of dreams is not the only possible one. But I mention it to show that there are ways of thinking about dreams that provide alternatives to the standard cultural assumptions that tend to block the idea that dreams might connect us with the spiritual realm. F. W. H. Myers, whom I mentioned earlier in this chapter, suggests that ordinary consciousness is adapted to the needs of the

---

8. Sanford, *Dreams*, 7.
9. Sanford, *Dreams*, 13.
10. Sanford, *Dreams*, 179.

physical environment. But he postulates that *subliminal consciousness* is "adapted to the maintenance of our larger spiritual life during our confinement in the flesh."[11] Such an idea fits with the view that dreams might be a channel that could help put us in touch with realities that are mostly hidden from us in ordinary conscious states.

A Contemporary Dream Message

In an autobiographical account called *Girl Meets God* Lauren Winner describes a memorable dream that she took to be a divine message.[12] Winner's mother was from a Southern Baptist background. Her father was from a Reform Jewish household. When her parents divorced, she became more involved in Judaism, eventually officially converting to Orthodox Judaism. (She was considered a convert, since her mother was not Jewish.) Most of her friends were in the Orthodox community. She went to college at a place where there was a large Orthodox representation. But Winner had intellectual interests in history and religion that led to a significant amount of reading about Christianity. She was especially intrigued by the idea of the incarnation, even though she thought that Jesus couldn't be the Messiah.

The dream came in her sophomore year at Columbia University. In the dream she, along with a Jewish friend named Michelle, were among a group of women who were kidnapped by some mermaids. They lived underwater with the mermaids for a year or so. They could breathe, walk around, talk, eat good meals, go to the movies, and read classic literature. Things weren't really so bad, except for the fact that they were not allowed to return to life on land. In the dream they were rescued by a group of men. One of the rescuers was a man around thirty who reminded her of Daniel Day Lewis. Winner says that she knew somehow that the Lewis character had come specifically to rescue her.

She described the dream to some of her friends, who suggested various interpretations. One person thought that the rescuer was Elijah. Her boyfriend worried that her dream indicated interest in another man. But Winner says that as soon as she woke up, she was certain that the dream was about Jesus. He was the one who had come to rescue her. Nevertheless, she ignored this dream for a long time. It seemed to be directing her to do something that would greatly disrupt her life. It took years before she came to the point of publicly joining the Christian community.

11. Myers, *Human Personality*, 55.
12. Winner, *Girl Meets God*, 55–60.

There are several aspects to Winner's dream story that I find significant. One is that the dream is clearly shaped by her own creative imagination. She took it to be a communication from God, but if the central message of the dream is about Jesus rescuing her, that point is contained in a drama that shows evidence of her own artistry. Some of her composition utilizes idiosyncratic associations, such as a Daniel Day Lewis look-alike as the rescuer. The under-water environment might represent something stifling about the community she has identified with, but she pictures a kind of existence that allows her to lead an interesting and potentially fulfilling life. The only thing lacking is the ability to go to a different kind of life on the mainland, which she apparently views as her true home.

Winner says that the meaning of the dream was immediately obvious to her, though clearly it was not obvious to everyone else. One way to understand this difference is to think of the dream as a message she is sending to herself. At some level she knows what the dream means. She says that she was able to identify the rescuer with what she calls certainty. In saying that she is sending the message to herself, I mean that the strands she has woven together come from her subliminal awareness. We can postulate that God is speaking through that awareness, but that doesn't mean we can find a precise point where her creative imagination ends and divine influence begins. Whatever truth God has revealed is shaped by social and individual ways of understanding that are clearly human.[13]

The recognition that our subliminal awareness extends beyond what we can know through the senses makes it easier to entertain the idea that dreams can be communications from God. To think as much does not require us to imagine that we can always tell the difference between God's voice and our own. But sometimes we gain a degree of confidence that we have encountered a wisdom that comes from beyond us, and for a Christian it shouldn't seem strange to think of that wisdom as coming from God.

---

13. Winner takes the dream message to mean that she should become a Christian. Some will no doubt read this story as expressing a divine intention that everyone should become Christians, since Christianity is the true faith. However, one could accept that Winner is receiving a message from God, but think that it is an instruction that is particularly adapted to her. There is a path that *she* needs to take, and it will lead away from the Orthodox Judaism she has embraced toward Christianity. Of course, if she embraces this new path, she will affirm the truth of central Christian doctrines, but it is possible to be committed to the truth of your own faith while acknowledging that there are other doctrinal stances compatible with a way of life devoted to God.

CHAPTER 8

Revelatory Visions

ANGLICAN BISHOP HUGH MONTEFIORE offers the following account of an experience he had at age sixteen that resulted in his becoming a Christian:

> Sitting alone in my study, I saw a figure in white approach me, and I heard in my mind's ear the words "Follow me." I knew that this was Jesus. How did I know? I haven't the slightest idea. I had no knowledge of Christianity, . . . it had been intentionally kept from me. My parents were both Jewish—my father was president of his synagogue. I had never been to a church service. I had never read the New Testament. I had never discussed Christianity with my friends. . . . Yet I immediately recognized the figure I saw as Jesus. . . . The experience filled me, as conversions often do, with a deep and abiding sense of joy and happiness.[1]

Montefiore says that if someone had been present with a camcorder, he is sure that nothing would have registered. But even though he judged what he saw and heard to be in his mind, rather than a generally observable event, he says, "I couldn't doubt that it was divinely initiated."[2] While he believed that God gave him the vision, he thinks that what happened was "mediated through some unknown paranormal process."[3] Just as there

---

1. Montefiore, *Paranormal*, 234.
2. Montefiore, *Paranormal*, 235.
3. Montefiore, *Paranormal*, 235.

are regularities in nature involving physical causes, Montefiore thinks that there are also psychic regularities and that God can act through either kind of regularity. While he recognizes that others might doubt that what happened to him was an encounter with Christ, he found the experience so compelling that he did not think of becoming a Christian as something he chose, but rather something this experience had made his only option.

Though Montefiore says he had no knowledge of Christianity, we should probably suspect that in twentieth-century England, he had some awareness of it, even if what he knew was very limited. His account makes clear that Christianity was not something he had consciously been thinking about, but it seems plausible that an awareness he had entertained at a subconscious level came bursting to the surface in his vision. I say this not to devalue the experience. He says himself that it came about through some paranormal process, and in processes that lead to extrasensory awareness, subliminal material comes into conscious awareness. We might speculate about why such a thing happened in his case, but his account does not provide enough information to answer that question.

It might be surprising to discover that Montefiore refers to visionary experiences as hallucinations. By a hallucination he means "an apparent perception of an external object not physically present."[4] That is a fairly standard definition, though my dictionary adds that such things "may occur in certain mental disorders."[5] This addition reflects a widespread view of our culture that normal sensory experiences are caused by physical objects and that perceptions lacking this kind of cause are deficient. The usual assumption is that these deviant perceptions should be treated as projections of an individual's mind that might arise from being mentally unbalanced or from some physiological condition that compromises optimal functioning. Given this way of thinking, it is not surprising that the word "hallucination" has a negative connotation. Describing an experience as a hallucination, yet thinking of it as a genuine contact with reality, sounds odd to most people. But Montefiore thinks of his experience as an encounter with God.

The association of having perceptions of what is not physically present with mental problems presumably has much to do with why people in our culture are reluctant to talk about experiences that deviate from the

---

4. Montefiore, *Paranormal*, 213.
5. *Webster's New World College Dictionary*, 641.

paradigm of causation by a physical stimulus. When we see or hear things that we have reason to think are not present in the way that ordinary physical objects are present, we know enough to keep quiet about it. It is not that people in our time don't have these kinds of experience. David Hufford cites research establishing that the occurrence of visionary experiences among ordinary normal people has been greatly underestimated. He also claims that some classes of visionary experience that are known to be normal for human beings should be distinguished "from hallucinations as that term has been traditionally used."[6] He lists near-death experiences and after-death experiences of a loved one as examples.

We typically think of hallucinations as involving a confusion about what is physically present. But visionary experiences often involve no such confusion. As Morton Kelsey puts it, "True visionary experience is seldom mistaken for giving immediate knowledge of the physical world."[7] He characterizes visionary experiences as intrusions into waking consciousness that are "superimposed" on or "synchronized" with physical reality. Admittedly, someone who has had limited experience with visions might not recognize what is perceived as a vision, but reflection on what is experienced often leads to thinking that something other than ordinary seeing or hearing is involved.

Montefiore says that his experience was not of something that would be generally observable, but he regarded his vision to be so compelling that he became a Christian because of it. Visionary experiences often make people confident that they have made contact with a deeper level of reality. They could be wrong, of course. But thinking that they must be wrong is connected with assuming an overly simple dichotomy between ordinary sense experiences and perceptions that are merely projections of one's own mind. Assuming this dichotomy hides another possibility: We may have perceptions that arise from our capacity for receiving information about reality through extrasensory capacities.

Visionary Experiences in the Bible

We don't usually think of biblical experiences of something transcendent as instances of extrasensory perception, but consider an example. Isaiah 6 describes a remarkable experience of Isaiah that culminates in

---

6. Hufford, "Visionary Spiritual Experiences," 147.
7. Kelsey, *God, Dreams, and Revelation*, 23.

his call to a prophetic mission. The story is told in the first person. It begins with the statement, "In the year that King Uzziah died, I saw the Lord sitting on a throne, high and lofty; and the hem of his robe filled the Temple" (6:1). The account goes on to describe angelic beings around the throne praising Yahweh. The Temple shakes and is filled with smoke. The angelic beings do a cleansing ritual to assuage Isaiah's fears. Then Isaiah hears the voice of Yahweh asking who can be sent on a prophetic mission, and he volunteers for the job.

It is implausible to think of what Isaiah sees and hears as an ordinary perceptual experience in which his visual and auditory abilities are stimulated by the physical presence of a figure on a throne that he recognizes as Yahweh. It is more believable that what he sees and hears is in his mind in the way that a dream experience is in the mind. Someone influenced by our cultural patterns of thought might suggest that the events described are either occurrences that anyone who managed to come into the Temple at the same time would have perceived or they are merely a product of Isaiah's imagination. People in Isaiah's culture would have viewed things differently. They could have agreed that Isaiah was seeing and hearing what no one else in the vicinity would have seen or heard, and they would likely have acknowledged that there is something dreamlike about the experience. But they would have regarded such a visionary experience as a way for a human being to encounter God. In different terms, the vision could be an extrasensory awareness of a reality that is not accessible by ordinary sensation.

But understanding the vision as a kind of contact with reality doesn't mean that we should think of the events Isaiah perceives as caused by some scene occurring in a heavenly realm that Isaiah somehow witnesses. Imagine what happens to Isaiah as parallel to what happens in cases of crisis apparitions. The person experiencing the apparition receives information at an unconscious level about a danger to a loved one. The recipient then represents the information in a form that enables him or her to make sense of it, such as a visual appearance of the person in danger.

So, suppose we think of Isaiah as having a subliminal awareness of what Yahweh seeks to do in relation to the nation. Then imagine the mind of Isaiah taking this information and putting it into an intelligible form. Just as our dreams are sometimes dramatizations that convey a particular message, we can think that Isaiah's vision is a kind of dramatization of Yahweh's message to him that takes the form of an encounter with Yahweh in the Temple. Understood in this way, the vision makes use of images of Yahweh and the heavenly hosts that reflect ideas accepted in Isaiah's time. The point is that a visionary experience can be revelatory, even if there is a significant role of the recipient's mind in shaping how that revelation comes into human consciousness.

I don't mean to suggest that all visionary experiences are revelatory, and when a vision represents a transcendent reality, we don't have an independent way of determining whether extrasensory information is involved or, if it is involved, how reliably it is interpreted. We can imagine Isaiah's contemporaries doubting his story because they think it is fabricated or misreported or misinterpreted. But that kind of doubt is different from doubting that God communicates sometimes through visionary experiences. People in Isaiah's culture would have taken it for granted that dreams and visions were primary ways through which divine communications come.

Our culture biases us toward thinking of visionary experiences as nothing more than subjective projections. It can be startling to notice how different the biblical outlook was. Consider the New Testament example of Paul. Paul is portrayed in Acts as having visions that give him guidance about what to do. In Acts 16 he has a vision of a man of Macedonia who pleads for help. In Acts 18 he is assured by God in a vision that he can speak without fear of harm. In Acts 22 he is praying in the Temple when he falls into a trance that leads to a vision of Jesus telling him to leave Jerusalem. In Acts 23 he learns in a vision that he will go to Rome. In Acts 27 he sees and hears an angelic messenger telling him that his shipmates will be safe, despite a major storm, but he is to stand before the emperor in Rome. Paul makes plans and adopts attitudes that presume that the visions are messages from God.

There are references in the epistles to Paul's visionary experiences. In a particularly striking example, he tells of a person who fourteen years earlier was "caught up into paradise and heard things that are not to be told, that no mortal is permitted to repeat" (2 Cor 12:4). Commentators agree that Paul was referring to his own experience. He says that he does not know whether the experience was in the body or not. What he describes sounds very much like what we might refer to as an out-of-body experience in which a person has sensations of traveling to another realm. It is clear that neither Paul nor other Christians of his era would have been inclined to think that all such experiences were merely subjective hallucinations. They might not give credence to every report. But recognizing that an experience was not caused by the ordinary operation of the senses wouldn't by itself have been regarded as a reason to dismiss it.

Of course, the fact that people in biblical culture took visionary experiences to be ways of making contact with the spiritual realm doesn't establish that they were correct to do so. On the other hand, the fact that many people in our culture find it difficult to take visionary experiences seriously doesn't show that visions can't be revelatory. The famous theologian Wolfhart Pannenberg, like Montefiore, had a compelling visionary experience that was instrumental in his becoming a Christian. In later reflection he says, "The thesis that we must regard all visionary experiences as psychological projections with no basis in reality cannot be regarded ... as an adequately grounded philosophical postulate."[8] Our culture may incline us to accept such a view, but some things our culture inclines us to accept arise from assumptions that we don't have to adopt.

Stories of Encounters with God

When I was a teenager, I was puzzled about biblical stories that described people as getting messages from God. I wondered how God communicated with people. For example, when the biblical text said that God told Abraham to do something, should I imagine him hearing an audible voice from the sky? Surely, I thought, it wouldn't be like what people I knew in church were describing when they claimed that God told them to do something. That is, it wouldn't be thoughts in someone's mind that are taken to be a divine message. On the other hand, hearing voices suggested something uncomfortably like what happens to schizophrenic people. Even putting that concern aside, if you heard a voice, what would assure you that it was God's voice?

No one I knew back then was able to give me an answer that seemed satisfying, but when I began to consider biblical stories as an adult, I noticed something that now seems obvious to me. I noticed that many of the stories in which people are said to encounter God (or angelic beings) refer to dreams or visions. Furthermore, even in stories where these terms are not used, there is sometimes reason to wonder whether what is described might be some kind of visionary experience.

Once I began to consider this possibility, it wasn't difficult to find examples of what I had imagined as physical events that could be

---

8. Pannenberg, *Systematic Theology*, 2:354.

understood differently. Consider the story of the temptations of Jesus. It seemed plausible to me that this story was derived from an account that Jesus might have given to the disciples. But what was he describing? After a prolonged period of prayer and fasting, Jesus would presumably be in a condition that is conducive to having visionary experiences. So, we can suspect that as he is meditating on his messianic task, he has a vision of a tempter. Similarly, when I looked at events such as the voice from heaven at Jesus's baptism proclaiming his identity, it made sense to me to understand what happened as a visionary experience of Jesus' that was not perceivable by other people.

The idea that some events described in the Bible are visionary experiences rather than matters of ordinary physical perception is not new in Christian thought. The Christian theologian and philosopher Origen appealed to it in the third century in his responses to Celsus, an early critic of Christianity. He compares Jesus's experience of seeing the heavens opening and hearing a voice to visionary experiences of the prophets Ezekiel and Isaiah. In waking visions, he says, the mind receives impressions that resemble experiences we have in dreams:

> And as in a dream we fancy that we hear, and that the organs of hearing are actually impressed, and that we see with our eyes—although neither the bodily organs of sight nor hearing are affected, but it is the mind alone which has these sensations—so there is no absurdity in believing that similar things occurred to the prophets, when it is recorded that they witnessed occurrences of a rather wonderful kind, as when they either heard the words of the Lord or beheld the heavens opened.[9]

Origen connects such experiences with a "perceptive power" comparable to seeing or hearing. He is clearly claiming that we have ways of learning about reality other than the senses.

The stories of Abraham explicitly describe some of his most important encounters with God as coming through visions or dreams. Genesis 15:1 tells us that "the word of the Lord came to Abram in a vision." In the vision Abram has a dialogue with Yahweh in which he receives promises that he will have many descendants. In verse 12 Abram goes into a deep sleep in which he is given a preview of future events.

---

9. Origen, *Against Celsus*, 1:48.

Apparently, even a covenant ratification that responds to Abram's request for confirmation occurs in a vision.[10]

Scholars typically doubt the historical reliability of patriarchal narratives. But if we think that there was a historical figure who moved from his native land because of encounters with his deity, thinking of those encounters as visionary experiences has some appeal. Montefiore speaks of the compelling nature of his experience of Jesus calling him. People who have near-death experiences often speak in a similar way about having no doubt of the reality of what they have experienced. So, my earlier question about how people in biblical times could have become confident of encounters with God might be answered in relation to what we know about people in our own time who have visionary experiences of transcendent realities.

One kind of experience described in biblical texts that is still reported today involves perceiving angelic beings. There are numerous books that include accounts of contemporary encounters with angels.[11] In our disenchanted age, many people find stories about encounters with angels difficult to take seriously. But a skeptical response often presupposes that the stories are reporting physical events experienced through ordinary sensations. Even if we dismiss many of these stories as products of an overactive imagination, we might think some of them are rooted in visionary experiences.

Morton Kelsey points out that there are numerous passages in Hebrew Scripture in which an angel acting as God's agent appears as a character in a vision. Recall, for example, Isaiah's vision in the Temple. On the basis of his study of biblical texts, Kelsey concludes that accounts of angelic encounters, as well as other stories of transcendent experiences, are best understood as reports of visions. He says, "talking with God, angel, dream, vision, prophecy—express the same basic encounter with some reality that is not physical."[12]

Even if we think of visions as a way of getting communication from the spiritual realm, we can recognize that many of these experiences can be interpreted in more than one way. For example, there are more literal and less literal ways of understanding an experience of an angelic or demonic presence. Additionally, accounts of these experiences

---

10. Sweeney, *Jewish Mysticism*, 51.

11. Dale Allison has a helpful discussion of contemporary angel stories in *Encountering Mystery*, 73–98.

12. Kelsey, *God, Dreams, and Revelation*, 35.

are shaped by preexisting beliefs that are sometimes open to question. Religious traditions use their interpretive judgment over time to decide which experiences should be regarded as authoritative and how those experiences should be understood. Sometimes, for example, they conclude that an encounter with God is described in overly anthropomorphic ways that should not be taken literally. Or they might judge an account to be framed in terms of moral ideas that later revelation shows deficient. Accepting a religious tradition means accepting that over time this kind of process enables us to get closer to the truth.[13] On the other hand, there can be visions that lead people to question the version of religion they have been taught. For example, people who have near-death experiences often become supremely confident of life after death and their own existence as spiritual beings, but less confident of particular dogmas that have been presented to them as authoritative.

Continuing Glimpses of Transcendence

Visionary experiences are not limited to biblical times or to particularly holy people. Ordinary people in our own time report experiences of something transcending the physical order. Consider an account from the collection of the Religious Experience Research Centre, originally housed at Oxford University and now at the University of Wales:

> I was walking one night in the busy streets of Glasgow when, with slow majesty, at a corner where pedestrians were hurrying by, . . . the air was filled with heavenly music; and an all-encompassing light, that moved in waves of luminous colour, outshone the brightness of the lighted streets. I stood still, filled with a strange peace and joy, and the music beat on in its majesty and the traffic and the pedestrians moved through the light. They passed on their way, but the music and the light remained, pulsating, harmonious, more real than the streets. Then I too, lingeringly moved on, looking back at times till I found myself in the everyday world again with a strange access of gladness and of love.[14]

---

13. Sparks, *Divine Words in Human Words*, 279–328.
14. Fox, *Lightforms*, 137.

The man who had this experience said that he never had a repeat of anything similar, but he reflects, "It entered so deeply into my being that my mind rested in it all my days."[15]

The experience of unusual light is reported in numerous stories. In many cases the light is described as not just from without, but also flowing through a person's body. One man describes an experience he had years after a painful divorce initiated by his wife. He thought he had made peace with what had happened, but he began to feel rage about how she could have done this to him despite how much he loved her:

> Instantly a totally commanding voice spoke: "But did you love her totally?" So powerful was this voice that I felt I had been caught in sin on some cosmic scale. Instantly a radical surrender descended on me, a surrender of body, mind, and soul. It cleared the way for a river of living light and glorious emotion to race down through me. It is impossible to exaggerate the intensity of this feeling. It's like being electrocuted with joy. . . . After several minutes of light and outrageously glorious feeling, my being began to settle down to a state of mere bliss. . . . My emotional state now was one of what I then knew to be unconditional love. The love was coming toward me from everywhere. The room (probably the universe) was filled with love. It was like a force of nature just there for everyone.[16]

Experiences like these are often accompanied by significant life transformations. In discussing what he calls "extraordinary spiritual experiences," David Hufford points out that positive transformations that often accompany visionary experiences depend on the person who is having the experience accepting what is perceived as reality-based, and not just a sign of psychiatric problems. He claims that understanding an extraordinary experience in this way does not require thinking that what is experienced can be proven to be real and objective. It is sufficient, he says, for the person to have good reasons to believe that the experience is an encounter with reality.

In a culture like Isaiah's good reasons might come from a cultural acceptance of visionary experiences as a potential channel to truth. In our culture, Hufford says, it might call for "frequent confirmation of the veridicality of perceptions not explicable in ordinary physical terms

---

15. Fox, *Lightforms*, 137.
16. Clark, *Divine Moments*, 93.

... and the discovery that others have had very similar experiences."[17] Confirmations of the veridicality of visionary perceptions can be found in cases where what is perceived in some extrasensory way is subsequently verified by sense experience, such as determining that a vision of someone in danger at a distant location corresponds to an actual event. Recognizing that such experiences are common among people who are not mentally unbalanced is supported by empirical research. Claims about transcendent realities are open to doubt, but for someone like Montefiore who finds an experience of this kind compelling, the most reasonable option can be to trust in its genuineness.

---

17. Hufford, "Healing Power of Extraordinary Spiritual Experiences," 150.

CHAPTER 9

Glimpses of the Future

MARK TWAIN'S SKEPTICAL ATTITUDES toward Christianity are well known. His published writings contain many satirical and mocking accounts of biblical stories and of religious people. For him, Christianity falls into the category of superstition. What is less well known is that Twain had numerous experiences during his life that convinced him of the reality of what he called "mental telegraphy." He believed that one mind can communicate with another over great distances by some means that he thought of as comparable to sending a telegram, but without the physical medium of wires. He published two essays on the subject in 1891 and 1895 that described experiences that led him to think that this sort of mind-to-mind connection was real. He had written much of this material in 1878, but had delayed publishing it because he feared his reputation as a humorist might lead people to think he was joking.

Twain was completely serious. He was convinced that whatever process was involved had something to do with his literary success. One of his essays tells how he devised a detailed plotline for a book about some Nevada silver mines. The plot, he says, came suddenly into his mind, as if from nowhere. A few days later he received a letter from a friend on the other side of the country that contained a draft of the same plot Twain had written down. The friend, whom he had not seen in some time, had written the letter near the time the idea for the book had come to Twain. The plot descriptions were not word-for-word duplicates, but they were substantially the same. Twain thought of the divergence between them as a result of his "translating" ideas of his friend into his own linguistic style.[1]

Twain's experiences with paranormal phenomena go back much earlier in his life. One of his most striking experiences involved a dream that he had at the age of twenty-two. During his lifetime, he told people about the dream on multiple occasions, including in talks to various groups. He included a written account of it in his autobiography, which he dictated at the age of seventy. Twain had arranged a job for his younger brother Henry on a steamboat. While staying with his older sister and her family, he had a dream of Henry's death that was so vivid that when he woke up, he started preparing to go to the wake. It took him a while to realize that what he had seen had been in a dream. He writes, "In the dream I had seen Henry a corpse. He lay in a metallic burial case. He was dressed in a suit of my clothing, and on his breast lay a great bouquet of flowers, mainly white roses with a red rose in the centre."[2]

Twain told his sister about the dream, but though shaken by it, he reminded himself that it was only a dream. Three weeks later, news came that Henry had been badly injured in a boiler explosion on the ship. An overdose of pain medication led to his death. The standard practice was for burial to be in a pine box, but some women involved in the rescue efforts had raised money to put him in a metal coffin. Twain says that when he arrived, the scene was exactly what he had seen in his dream. Henry was in the casket wearing one of Twain's suits that he had borrowed on his last visit without Twain's knowledge. Only one detail was different from the dream. Twain saw the large bundle of white roses, but no red rose. Then an elderly nurse came in and put a red rose in the center of the bouquet.[3]

Stories about dreams that seem to foretell the future are common. They have been reported since ancient times, and they continue to be reported in our time. Not all of them involve a correspondence between the dream and specific details of future events. In some the dream appears to represent what will happen symbolically. Recall, for example, Pharaoh's dream described in the book of Genesis that Joseph interprets as predicting seven years of plenty followed by seven years of famine (Gen 41:25–32).

---

1. Twain, "Mental Telegraphy" paras. 15–20.
2. Twain, *Autobiography*, 274–76.
3. Twain, *Autobiography*, 274–76.

Consider a contemporary example of a dream that looks predictive even though it isn't a duplicate of what happens. In 2022 a man carrying a knife rushed onto a stage and attacked writer Salman Rushdie. The attack lasted for twenty-seven seconds, resulting in serious wounds to Rushdie's hand, neck, chest, thigh, and eye. Lying in blood, Rushdie believed he was going to die. He recovered, but lost sight in one of his eyes. Two days before the incident, he had a vivid dream of being in a Roman amphitheater, rolling on the ground while a gladiator stabbed him with a spear. The dream disturbed him enough that he had an impulse to cancel his upcoming appearance at the event where he would be attacked. But he reasoned that he shouldn't change his plans on the basis of a dream.[4]

Stories of predictive dreams can often be explained in ordinary terms. We can frequently treat the apparent similarities between the dream and what takes place as coincidental or as a product of putting together information we possess at an unconscious level that has been acquired through ordinary sensation. But for some stories such explanations seem inadequate. Even if we take into account that we notice it when our dreams are fulfilled and don't notice it when they are not, some accounts of dream fulfillments suggest what seems impossible: that we can sometimes get advanced information about what will happen in the future.

Premonitions of Death and Disaster

Stories of dreams about future events typically involve occurrences that evoke strong emotions. The emotions can be reactions to positive events, but many of these stories are about events that evoke our fears, such as death, disaster, or serious illness. Sometimes people alter their plans because of a vivid dream, but often they don't. A woman dreamed that her sister's new husband is shot on a hunting trip by a discharge of a boy's shotgun. She is frightened and tries to warn her sister. But the sister and her husband discount the dream. Two days later the husband is killed in the way she had dreamed it would happen.[5]

Some dreams are not viewed as predictive until they are seen in the light of later events. A woman dreamed about three men: her husband, her father-in-law, and another man whom she couldn't identify, standing

---

4. Gross, "Two Nights Before the Attack" paras. 1–10.
5. Feather and Schmicker, *Gift*, 148.

in a stairway having a serious conversation. She woke up from the dream, saying to her husband that his sister needed a blood transfusion. Both of them were puzzled about why she had said such a thing. A year later the woman was in a hospital stairway talking with her husband, father-in-law, and brother-in-law. She suddenly had the thought that the place and positions of the men matched what she had dreamed. Her husband had been called to the hospital to give blood for his sister's transfusion.[6]

Sometimes the ability to have predictive dreams seems to be triggered by a transformative experience. Elizabeth Krohn had a near-death experience after being struck by lightning in the parking lot of her synagogue. After this experience she began to have dreams of disasters and near-disasters before they happened. She decided to start sending herself dated emails that documented the dreams. One of the dreams verified in this fashion occurred six and a half hours before Captain "Sully" Sullenberger landed a commercial airliner in the Hudson River. She dreamed of a Southwest or US Airways plane crashing in the water in New York City. In the dream, the passengers survive and stand on the wings of the plane while waiting to be rescued. Media reports of the event showed pictures of people standing on the wings of a US Airways jet after its crash landing in the Hudson River.[7]

After almost every major disaster, there are reports of people who claim to have dreamed about it beforehand. For many of these reports, we have only the words of someone who claims to have dreamed about what happened, but in some cases, others confirm that they were told about the dreams before the incidents occurred. There is often reason to wonder whether memories of the dream have been altered after the fact, intentionally or unintentionally, and there is some subjectivity in judgments about how closely the dream corresponds to what happened. Reports of this kind are not usually examined critically by unbiased parties to determine the extent to which verifiable predictions come true. But even when we weed out cases where claims of advance information about the future lack strong evidential support, we are still left with numerous cases in which the usual explanations of lucky guesses or misreporting seem strained.

---

6. Feather and Schmicker, *Gift*, 157.
7. Krohn and Kripal, *Changed in a Flash*, 87–90.

Anecdotal and Experimental Evidence

Some people dismiss all reports of prophetic dreams or of premonitions as unbelievable. They sometimes argue that what these stories report conflicts with well-established presumptions about how the world works, which should be revised only if there is indisputable evidence to the contrary. They often point out that reports of what happened are not the same as scientific evidence. By "scientific evidence" they typically mean controlled experiments. They may admit that we unavoidably form some beliefs on the basis of testimonial evidence, but argue that we shouldn't accept reports that conflict with fundamental beliefs without the kind of stringent testing that scientific method calls for.

It is sometimes claimed that there is no scientific evidence of precognitive abilities. However, a significant number of controlled experiments have tested the possibility. Among the experiments are tests of precognitive dreaming in which participants are asked to dream about some target, such as a video clip that they will be shown the next day. The particular target is selected from a list by a process involving a random-number generator. This selection is made *after the dream report has been submitted to experimenters*. Independent judges who do not know the actual target rank similarities between the dream content and various targets. Some experiments of this type are inconclusive, but most of them have yielded statistically significant correlations between dreams and the targets.[8]

I won't try to list all the various types of the experimental tests of precognition, but they include experimental subjects choosing from multiple options and assessments of matches to an option randomly selected *after the choice has been made*. There are also experiments in which a subject is asked to describe a visual target that will be selected by machine-generated random selection process *after the participant's description has been recorded*. Overall, such experiments show statistically significant evidence of precognitive abilities. For some experimental subjects the rates of accuracy are astounding.[9]

One particularly intriguing type of experiment that has shown surprising results involves testing what is called *presentiment*. A basic form of the experiment involves measures of the autonomic nervous system of subjects who are shown images projected on a computer screen.

8. Mossbridge and Radin, "Precognition as a Form of Prospection," 79–80.
9. Mossbridge and Radin, "Precognition as a Form of Prospection," 78–93.

Some of the images are calming, and others are emotion-enhancing. The emotion-enhancing images include erotic or violent representations. Not surprisingly, viewing these images correlates with bodily reactions. But in presentiment experiments, the bodily reaction is measured *before an image chosen randomly by the computer is projected*. It turns out that there is strong statistical evidence that people exhibit bodily reactions to emotion-enhancing images *before* the images appear on the screen. Experimental replications include a variety of different measurements of bodily reactions, including brain scans. In these experiments, we are talking about an anticipatory reaction of seconds, not weeks or years. Nevertheless, the results confirm something that seems amazing: an unconscious reaction to a presumably unpredictable future occurrence.[10]

Should We Wait for a Scientific Consensus?

A policy of discounting anecdotal evidence until experimental evidence settles the issue is understandable, but it is problematic as a strategy for deciding about precognitive abilities. Even when there is strong evidence from controlled experiments, it won't necessarily convince scientists to change their minds about a phenomenon that seems counter-intuitive. One reason is that quality experiments can be ignored or discounted. Most scientists won't be motivated enough to spend the time or effort to study experimental evidence outside their field, especially if its results are out of step with mainstream views. Those who do study the experimental data will often do so with an assumption that conclusions that conflict with well-established paradigms must be flawed. As a result, they will approach experimental reports with a level of skepticism that is hard to overcome. Even if we think that given enough time the scientific method will lead to truth, waiting for scientific consensus on phenomena that clash with fundamental scientific assumptions may mean waiting for a long time.

Another reason not to rely exclusively on controlled experimentation is that not all phenomena are best investigated in this way. In the case of premonitions, the conditions under which spontaneous precognition is said to occur can't realistically be duplicated in the lab. We can learn something about those conditions from testimonial reports, but if we have decided that those reports have little evidential value, we may

---

10. Mossbridge et al., "Predicting the Unpredictable," 1–10.

just focus our attention on what can be tested under conditions that differ from those in which the phenomenon typically appears. Ironically, some scientists who begin with the assumption that anecdotal evidence cannot establish whether psychic phenomena occur have come to accept such phenomena as a result of their own experiences or the experiences of people close to them.

One example is Stuart Kauffman, a theoretical biologist who is well known for his work on complexity theory in relation to the origins of life. Early in his career, Kauffman assumed that there was no such thing as extrasensory perception, but two experiences led to alterations of his outlook. One occurred when he was driving his teenaged daughter Merit home from her boyfriend's house. As they passed a particular tree, visual images flashed in his mind that he compared to a "snippet of film." He saw Merit walking down the middle of the street with her back turned to oncoming traffic as a car struck her. He didn't mention the vision to Merit, but he made her promise never to walk back from her boyfriend's house, to always call for a ride. A month later after her boyfriend had broken up with her, Merit started walking home. From witness reports, she apparently put her purse down on the side of the road and then lay down in the street with her face toward oncoming traffic. A car coming around a curve slammed on the brakes, but struck and killed her. The place where the incident occurred was same spot where Kauffman had his vision.

The next day Kauffman received a call from a childhood friend with whom he a hadn't spoken in eight months. He told her about Merit's death, and she told him about a dream she had the previous night that prompted her call. In the dream, she had seen him sitting on the floor in agony while his wife embraced him. Kauffman found that he couldn't explain away his own vision or his friend's dream. He considered the idea that his vision had been a precognition of the future, but scientific views he found convincing led him to reject the idea that the future was predetermined in a way that made it knowable in advance. He decided that his experience must have been a result of a projection based on telepathic awareness of what was in his daughter's mind. The main point here is that it wasn't scientific testing that led him to believe that a phenomenon he had previously considered not worth investigating was genuine. It was a personal experience that he couldn't dismiss.[11]

---

11. See chapter 4 in Horgan, "Complexologist Tragedy and Telepathy."

Actual Future or Possible Future?

The objection that Kaufman raises about whether we can know the future is an important one. Other thinkers who are convinced that extrasensory perception occurs have considered the same issue. For example, philosopher David Ray Griffin accepts phenomena, including telepathy, clairvoyance, and psychokinesis, but does not accept precognitive forms of ESP. Two reasons are especially significant to him. One is that he thinks that knowing that a future event will occur would mean perceiving it, but he claims that such a perception would have to be caused by the future event, and he regards the idea of causation going from the future to the past to be incoherent. Another of his reasons is that knowing the future before it happens depends on the future already being settled. But our sense that we have freedom means thinking that what happens in the future depends on free choices. If what will happen is already fixed, then we don't have the power to bring about anything different from what is bound to occur.[12]

Griffin has no problem with someone having a premonition of a possible future, or even a probable one, but he thinks that we can't know what has not yet been determined. He says that some premonitions may be thought of as indicators of what will occur unless preventative action is taken. Knowledge of such a thing would not necessarily involve extrasensory information, but Griffin thinks that it sometimes does. On his view it could be based on telepathic awareness of what is planned or clairvoyant knowledge, along with unconscious inference of likely results. In other words, extrasensory information that is obtainable in the present may allow us to project a likely future. Griffin also suggests that in some cases there may be an unconscious exercise of psychokinetic influence that contributes to bringing about future events that have been predicted.

In contrast to Griffin's approach, some writers accept precognitive knowledge of an actual future, not just a possible one. Eric Wargo has written extensively about precognitive dreams.[13] His way of accounting for such dreams posits what some scientists have called a block universe in which the future is just as set as the past. In a block universe an individual's present existence can be thought of as a cross-section of a four-dimensional reality that includes past, present, and future. In Wargo's view, we can be affected by our future, as well as our past. He thinks of

12. Griffin, *Parapsychology, Philosophy, and Spirituality*, 90–95.
13. Wargo, *Time Loops*; *Precognitive Dreamwork*.

precognitions as glimpses of what will be perceived by one's future self. Though these glimpses can affect us in the present, he rejects thinking of them as warnings that can enable us to alter what will happen. In response to the claim that an already fixed future would conflict with free will, Wargo says that free will is an illusion.

Some Christians might be comfortable with Wargo's block universe in which the future is fixed. People on the Calvinistic end of the theological spectrum might think that it fits with the idea of divine knowledge and control. But there are also Christian thinkers called open theists who hold that the future is not entirely predictable, since what will happen depends on creaturely freedom.[14] On this view, even God does not fully know in advance details of a future that are not yet fixed.[15]

Premonitions and Preventative Action

It might be thought that knowing the future in advance would be very useful for planning a course of conduct. But suppose you have a premonition of some future event, say a train wreck. If what you have seen is the actual future, there is nothing you can do to prevent the train wreck from happening. To think of the premonition as supplying information you might use to prevent some bad event, you have to think of it as a representation of what *might* happen, a *possible* future.

There are stories that describe having a premonition, but being unable to prevent it. For example, a woman has a vivid dream about her husband dying in a plane crash. She begs her husband not to go on a planned trip, but he brushes her concerns aside and flies anyway. He is killed in the plane crash. There are also stories in which attempted preventative action actually contributes to bringing about an undesirable event. In one case a mother dreams of her young son being struck by a car. She takes her son to her own mother's house to keep him safe, but he slips out of her mother's house and is hit by a car in the location where she had brought him.[16] In

---

14. Pinnock et al., *Openness of God*; Sanders, *God Who Risks*.

15. Cases of biblical prophecy are sometimes thought to show that the actual future can be known. However, as biblical scholars point out, most instances of biblical prophecy do not involve predicting future events. In cases where there are predictions, they can usually be understood as projections of what will happen *if* present behavior does not change, e.g., if there is no repentance. Further, some events that are retrospectively described as prophetic predications are not best understood that way.

16. Feather and Schmicker, *Gift*, 197–98.

ancient times stories like this one were told to show that if something is fated to happen, trying to stop it is futile.

While cases of this kind can be striking, the fact that what is seen in advance is not prevented doesn't actually show that it had to happen. It shows that preventative efforts are not always successful. There are many reasons why they might not be successful in relation to what is seen in a dream about a future event. For one thing, dreams don't typically come with precise labels of time and place. If you don't know when or where an event will occur, it is hard to know how to prevent it. Furthermore, in some dreams about the future there is a combination of facts that match what happens and facts that don't. For example, what is dreamed may happen to a different person than the person in the dream, or it might happen at a different place or a different time. One man dreamed about his kitchen being on fire, but in the dream his house was on his parents' lot in another city. He called his wife, who told him there was no fire. He then checked with his parents, who also told him that nothing was on fire. A fire at the man's house did occur, but it was later in the day.[17]

There are, however, stories in which a dream about the future leads to preventative action that avoids something disastrous. Louisa Rhine calculated that in the stories about premonitions of disaster submitted to her, there was no attempt at preventative action in about two thirds of cases. No doubt in many of these cases no such action was viable. In cases where prevention was attempted, it failed in about a third of the cases.[18] Following is an example of a case from the Rhine collection where it was successful.

A woman wakes up around 2:30 a.m. after a terrifying dream that the chandelier above her baby's bed had fallen and crushed her baby. In the dream she heard rain and howling wind outside, and the clock read 4:35. Feeling foolish, she picked up the baby and brought her to her own bedroom. She looked outside, but the weather was calm. Two hours later the woman and her husband heard a crash and ran to the nursery. The chandelier had crashed into the baby's crib. Wind and rain could be heard outside, and the clock read 4:35.[19]

Stories in which a dream of some tragic event leads to preventing the tragedy suggest that the dream is of a possible rather than an actual future. However, those who take premonitions to be of an actual future

17. Feather and Schmicker, *Gift*, 43.
18. Feather and Schmicker, *Gift*, 195.
19. Feather and Schmicker, *Gift*, 2.

sometimes distinguish between the premonition itself and an imaginative filling in of details that might go with it. For example, in the dream of the chandelier dropping in the baby's room, the dreamer might imaginatively fill in the scene with the idea of the baby being killed. On their view, the core premonition occurs as it was perceived, but the imaginative details with which it has been combined may not occur.

Those who think that premonitions are of a future that is bound to occur are impressed by cases in which very specific and unlikely details are dreamed in advance. They argue that such things could not be predicted unless the future, or elements of the future, already exists in some fixed form. Those who think that the future is not set in advance can claim in some cases a premonition is misremembered after an event in a way that brings it closer to details of what actually happens. They may also suggest that facts in the present that aren't widely known can sometimes provide a basis for projections of what seems unlikely. For example, in the Mark Twain dream, the policy of putting a red rose at the center of a bouquet might have been a common practice in some places.

I don't know of a way to decisively establish whether or not there can be premonitions of future events that cannot fail to occur. Our judgments about whether there might be such premonitions depends on disputable assumptions, such as our assumptions about the nature of free will and physical causality. My own sympathies are with those who think that there is no actual future to know in advance, only possible futures. On this view, a premonition would be an extrapolation based on present information that makes some possibilities more likely than others. A dream about a plane crashing in the Hudson River might seem impossible to predict, but if you had extensive extrasensory information about things such as mechanical difficulties in the plane involved, where it would be flying, the skill and ingenuity of the pilot, the possible means of escape in a crash landing, that information might be a basis for dreaming about a scenario of survival. If such a story turns out to forecast actual events, it might seem remarkable, but perhaps that is because we are usually working with much more limited information. This kind of account doesn't deny that extrapolations of this kind might not correspond to reality, but in those cases, we wouldn't speak of seeing the future. Perhaps there are cases that can't be explained in this way, but I think the best strategy is to push the idea that premonitions are of a possible future as far as it can go.

Can the Future Influence the Past?

I mentioned earlier that one of Griffin's reasons for rejecting precognition of an actual future is his view that it is incoherent to think of a causal influence as going from the future to the past. But suppose we think of the future as existing in the present, not as a settled fact, but as a set of possibilities. In that case, having a premonition of the future could be thought of as awareness of some possible future that is projected on the basis of present facts. Even if we can't know what will actually happen, our present behavior can be influenced by awareness of a possible future. I am not just talking about tragedies that might be prevented. There might also be premonitions of desirable futures that attract us and motivate actions that contribute to making some possibility actual.

In chapter 1 I mentioned that Thomas Morris referred to what he called a personal epiphany of his mission in life that he described as powerful and unexpected. I don't know what form this epiphany took, but I can easily imagine it as a kind of awareness of a possible future that attracted him. Many people have given accounts of how they took a particular path in life that can be described in these terms. When he was a teenager, Bruce Damer during a walk saw a mariposa lily poking through the ground. He began to wonder how a complex flower had come from a simple seed or bulb. After posing the question, he had a vision in which he was having a conversation with a ball of small molecules. The molecules told him to figure out how they made copies of themselves. In response to his initial thoughts, the molecules told him, "Work on it." The vision of this task provided an impetus for a scientific project that became his life work.[20]

You get the point. Sometimes there are premonitions of future possibilities that direct us toward a particular path. We can think that God sometimes uses our capacity for getting an awareness of some future possibility to nudge us in a direction that may be personally fulfilling and also serve needs of the larger society. Such an awareness might be thought of as a hint God could give us about shaping our lives in a way that may be fruitful without forcing us to take a particular path.

---

20. Cheung and Mossbridge, *Premonition Code*, 60–61.

CHAPTER 10

Mind Over Matter

In 1967 the police in Miami were called in to investigate strange events at the warehouse of a company that sold novelty items. Objects had been inexplicably falling from the shelves and breaking. The police, of course, expected a normal explanation for the problem. Someone was intentionally doing it, or the shelves weren't sturdy enough to keep the items securely in place. Not only did the police fail to find a normal explanation; they observed things falling for no apparent reason from shelves that they had verified to be very secure. Additional outsiders who were called in to help also witnessed objects mysteriously moving from their positions, including one instance in which something moved twenty-two feet. They performed multiple tests to determine if any trickery was going on, but discovered no evidence of it.

The investigators noted that there were no strange incidents when a nineteen-year-old employee named Julio didn't come to work one day. They kept him under close observation when he returned and questioned him. His comments revealed that he experienced some emotional satisfaction when things did move, and he admitted that he became nervous when nothing happened. On multiple occasions the investigators observed that Julio was nearby when something unexplained occurred. Even though they didn't discover him doing anything to cause the anomalous movements, they suspected that he was somehow the source of the problem. When he took another job, incidents at the warehouse ceased, and there were reports of strange movements of objects at his new workplace.[1]

In the same year unexplained events began to occur in a law office in Rosenheim, Germany. The lights repeatedly went out. Sometimes bulbs would explode, and fuses would blow. Sometimes bulbs would unaccountably loosen in their sockets. Additionally, there were times when telephones in the office would ring even though no one was on the line. The disruptive ringing continued even from phones that were disconnected. The head of the office brought in electricians who thoroughly checked out the system, but their tests revealed no defects. Eventually, the office head called in the police to investigate, along with two physicists and Germany's foremost expert in psychic phenomena.

In addition to the electrical issues, the outside investigators began to observe other anomalous phenomena, including movement of decorative plates on the wall, paintings turning around on their hooks, drawers opening by themselves, lamps swinging, banging sounds, and a heavy filing cabinet moving about a foot. They quickly determined that the strange phenomena coincided with the presence of a relatively new employee, an eighteen-year-old secretary named Annemarie. Sometimes strange things happened when she walked by. They also noticed that she exhibited extreme nervousness. When she took a job elsewhere, the strange phenomena at the law office ceased. There were less intense phenomena at her next place of employment, and anomalous events there eventually stopped.[2]

These two cases are particularly well-investigated instances of what have been called *poltergeist phenomena*. The phenomena include various kinds of noises, movements of objects, and electrical anomalies that happen without discernible physical causes. There have been reports since ancient times of such occurrences, but often the evidence is insufficient to determine whether the reports are reliable, or the information in the stories is too sketchy to draw firm conclusions about what happened. Events like these are relatively rare, and they typically last for a period of less than two months before ceasing. Often the strange events have stopped entirely before outside investigators can check out reports. But there are a few cases like those described above in which skilled investigators have

---

1. One account of the Miami case can be found in Schmicker, *Best Evidence*, 227. See also the discussion in Griffin, *Parapsychology, Philosophy and Spirituality*, 74–77.

2. Schmicker, *Best Evidence*, 225–26; Griffin, *Parapsychology, Philosophy, and Spirituality*, 71–73.

been able to make careful observations and perform tests to try to determine what is causing the strange phenomena.

The term "poltergeist" is a German word with an etymological meaning of "noisy spirit." Imagine such things as the sound of rattling chains or explosive vibrations or raps, as well as unexplained movements of objects. The label reflects an assumption that such strange phenomena were caused by disembodied spirits, and sometimes accounts of this type are included in the category of ghost stories. However, poltergeist phenomena seem different from the occurrence of what we could call hauntings, which typically involve reports of apparitional appearances that may recur over a considerable period of time. Since the twentieth century, most researchers familiar with psychic phenomena have come to think of poltergeist cases as arising not from acts of mischievous ghosts, but as caused unintentionally by living human agents. It's not that they can prove that no disembodied agents are involved. It's more a matter of being reluctant to posit a disembodied agent when another kind of explanation is available.

People in the parapsychology lab at Duke University referred to cases of this kind as *recurrent spontaneous psychokinesis* (RSPK).[3] In contrast to ESP, in which the mind receives information that doesn't come through ordinary sensory means, psychokinesis (PK) involves influence by a mind on physical things that is not mediated by bodily acts. As the accounts above illustrate, the evidence in cases of this type tends to point toward a focal individual. When that person is no longer present, the phenomena cease. The individual is typically a teenager, in most cases a young teenager, who is having emotional difficulties. When it can be ruled out that this person is performing bodily acts to bring about the anomalous events, it is posited is that emotional disturbances leading to repressed aggression have resulted in mental states that cause the physical effects.

Many people, of course, reject the idea that what is going on in someone's mind could cause objects to move or electrical circuits to go haywire as an obvious nonstarter. They regard it a violation of common sense to imagine mental states as having powers to do things in the world apart from bodily acts. People who are convinced that psychokinetic influence does occur usually come to this view by considering particular cases in which other possibilities seem to be ruled out and

3. Horn, *Unbelievable*, 133.

laboratory investigations that provide statistical evidence of psychokinetic influence. They recognize that psychokinesis does not fit with pictures of reality that our scientific culture predisposes us to adopt, but they think that evidence of both ESP and PK gives us reason to reevaluate assumptions underlying those pictures.

Sometimes the impetus to reconsider assumptions arises not from hearing about what happens to other people, but from personal experiences we find difficult to explain. Stephen Braude described himself as a "hard-nosed materialist" when he had an experience of what he thought shouldn't occur.[4] He was in graduate school in philosophy when two friends he knew well invited him to participate in an "impromptu séance" in his own home. The friends described the activity as a game they called "table up," which they said they had played a few times before. Braude reports that during this "game" his own table began to tilt up and down without visible assistance. What happened was in daylight, and he claims that he was certain his friends weren't playing a trick on him. There was no concealed apparatus, and with everyone's hands resting lightly on the top of the table, he could also verify that no one's legs were causing the table to move. Even when they all stood up and kept their hands on the table, it still rose, and the movements continued when one of his friends temporarily left the room. Braude emphasizes that the table wasn't someone else's prop. It was his own table that he saw rising from the floor. Further, he assures us that he hadn't been drinking or doing drugs. The table-tipping was a prelude to using a cumbersome code to spell out "messages" from three unseen entities.

Braude says that what happened "scared the hell" out of him. In later reflection he realized that what frightened him wasn't the idea that they might be receiving communication from spirits of the dead. It was the thought that one or more of the people around the table might be causing the table to move, but not by any normal means. This thought was a challenge to assumptions about the world he had taken to be obviously true. Though he didn't forget the incident, he reports that he put consideration of it aside until he had completed his PhD, landed a respectable teaching position, and achieved tenure based on his published work in philosophy of science. Only then did he feel secure enough professionally to investigate matters that he knew most of his peers would view with contempt. In time he wrote numerous scholarly books and articles on

---

4. Braude, *Immortal Remains*, ix–xi.

psychic phenomena that even his critics recognized as models of high-level philosophical analysis. His study of the evidence convinced him that psychic phenomena, including powers of mind to produce direct physical effects, should be accepted as real.

Another prominent thinker who took psychokinetic phenomena seriously was quantum physicist Wolfgang Pauli.[5] Pauli had a dialogue with the famous psychologist Carl Jung for over twenty-five years that touched on quantum physics, paranormal phenomena, and the relationship between mind and matter. Jung's theory of synchronicity was one outgrowth of their dialogue. Pauli's reflections were motivated in part by personal experiences. Laboratory equipment that normally functioned perfectly would fail when he was around. It happened so often that fellow physicists termed it the "Pauli effect." One lab director was a close friend of Pauli's, but nevertheless refused to let Pauli visit his lab out of fear that his equipment would malfunction. Pauli describes how he would feel something build up inside himself and then things would break in the vicinity, which sounds very much like poltergeist phenomena. His reflections led him to the view that in the science of the future "reality will be neither 'psychic' or 'physical' but somehow both and somehow neither."[6]

A Psychokinetic Superstar

There are accounts of psychokinetic influence that suggest a control over this kind of power that we don't find in poltergeist stories. One problem with such accounts is that reports of amazing things people are alleged to have done are often tainted by the suspicion that some kind of trickery was involved. For example, many of the famous mediums from the nineteenth century who seemed to produce extraordinary physical effects in the séance room were caught using various techniques and props to create illusions. When their performances were examined by careful observers, such as members of the Society for Psychical Research, many of these physical mediums were exposed as frauds. It might be tempting to say that anyone who claims to produce anomalous physical phenomena is a fraud, but in addition to those who were carefully observed and found out, there were some individuals from the same era whose anomalous

---

5. Simonsen, *Short History*, 166–67.
6. Pauli quoted in Radin, *Supernormal*, 311.

physical effects were observed under strictly controlled conditions, and no indications of trickery were found.

The most noteworthy example was Daniel Dunglas Home (1833–1886)[7] (the surname is pronounced "Hume"). Home was a descendent of a Scottish Highland family that included relatives who were said to have "second sight." He had visions from an early age. In his teenage years various physical phenomena, such as loud raps and objects moving around the room began to occur. His religious family thought that what was happening must be demonic. After attempted exorcisms failed to stop these strange events, Daniel was turned out of the house at the age of eighteen. What others viewed as manifestations of the work of the devil, Home apparently took to be signs of God's power.

Home aspired to be a physician, but as word of strange physical effects associated with him spread, he became a kind of international celebrity who was widely sought out as a medium. There is a long list of anomalous phenomena that are reported to have occurred in his séances. They include raps or knocking sounds coming from various parts of the room, as well as levitation and movement of objects. According to reports, heavy tables would move sharply, while the objects on them would move or stay put in response to the commands of sitters. The reports tell of materialized forms in various parts of the room, along with auditory phenomena and odors. They also describe the playing of various musical instruments, while these instruments were completely untouched and sometimes levitated around the room.

The list of people attending Home's performances is a veritable who's who of prominent figures of the time, including numerous respected scientists. Many of these figures submitted written testimonials that offer detailed accounts of what they observed. Home typically conducted sessions in good light in locations other than his own home. He didn't bring along props or devices that might have been used for trickery. Further, he was willing to go along with demands of scientific observers who restricted his movements and set up equipment to assure that nothing questionable was going on.

In one session held at the home of the distinguished scientist William Crookes, Crookes had built a cage in which he placed an accordion he had purchased that Home had never seen before. There was room for Home to reach one hand into the cage to touch the instrument, but not enough

---

7. Braude, *Limits*, 70–108; Radin, *Real Magic*, 173–78.

room to manipulate it. When Home touched the accordion, it was seen to waver and to emit notes; then it began to expand and contract while Home's hand remained still. Home removed his hand from the accordion and placed his hand in the hand of the person next to him. Observers reported seeing the accordion floating in the cage with no visible support as it played a well-known melody. Crookes verified that Home was not moving a muscle and not touching the instrument at all.[8]

I realize that much of what is reported is hard to believe. But even if reports like these might be doubted, there is enough to suspect that Home was producing some strange phenomena through psychokinetic means. Peter Lamont, a University of Edinburgh historian, and also a master illusionist himself, published a biography of Home in 2005. He notes that there were, as expected, charges of fraud made against Home, but there was rarely any evidence put forward to support such claims. Unlike others, Home was never caught cheating, and he performed before witnesses that numbered in the thousands. He never hesitated to perform before the most skeptical audiences, and Lamont notes that none of the scientific or magical experts of the time were able to offer believable skeptical explanations of what they observed.[9]

Philosopher Stephen Braude has done careful studies of reports about numerous individuals said to have psychic powers, including Home. He writes,

> I started with the expectation that the received wisdom would be supported, and that my belief in the relative worthlessness of the material would be better informed. But the evidence bowled me over. The more I learned about it, the weaker the traditional skeptical counter-hypotheses seemed. . . . I was forced to confront the fact that I could find no decent reason for doubting a great deal of strange testimony. It became clear to me that the primary source of my reluctance to embrace the evidence was my discomfort with it. I knew that I had to accept the evidence, or else admit that my avowed philosophical commitment to truth was a sham.[10]

The kind of evidence Braude refers to is unlikely to convince everyone, though it should be pointed out that very few of those who reject it actually commit themselves to the extensive study he undertook. Furthermore,

---

8. Braude, *Limits*, 85–101.
9. Lamont, *First Psychic*, 260–61.
10. Braude, *Limits*, xi.

those who do study accounts of this kind can approach them with an unalterable conviction that such things can't happen. They often presume that regardless of what is reported, there has to be a normal explanation. But scholars like Braude, who are more than capable of looking at things skeptically and doing a close examination of relevant evidence, sometimes feel compelled to conclude that their only alternative is to admit that some reports of psychokinetic phenomena are credible.

PK in the Lab

There aren't many opportunities to investigate large-scale displays by people with the level of ability attributed to Home. When researchers try to investigate psychokinetic phenomena in laboratory tests, they are typically working with people who do not claim to have special abilities of this kind. The experimental tests that have been done do support the conclusion that consciously intending a result can increase the probability of the result. In relation to living systems, people have been able, for example, to change the rate at which bacteria in a laboratory dish grow by rates that exceed what we would expect to happen by chance.[11]

In addition to tests on living systems, there are also experiments in which people attempt to produce a change in machines that generate random numbers. In these cases, we can compare the intended result with what a random distribution should be. The most famous example involves tests done at the Princeton Engineering Anomalies Research project (PEAR). These tests provided convincing statistical evidence over a twelve-year period that an intention to produce an effect does cause a deviation from expectations. A striking result of these studies was that couples of the opposite sex were able to produce effects three and a half times stronger than individuals working alone, and couples who were in a relationship the experimenters labeled as "bonded pairs" had results that were six times stronger than those of single individuals.[12]

The changes involved are not on the grand scale of PK achievements ascribed to Home, but they do support the conclusion that mental states can produce physical effects. If we begin with the assumption that such a thing is possible, we can at least entertain the idea that some individuals are capable of producing very significant effects through psychokinesis.

11. Powell, *ESP Enigma*, 91–93.
12. McTaggart, *Field*, 118–19.

We should note that relatively minor physical effects can result in major changes. A fairly small alteration in the operation of someone's immune system might be enough to eliminate a large cancerous growth. A slight change in a mechanical system could cause a large machine to malfunction. Perhaps the difference between people who are able to produce large-scale changes and those who cannot is a matter of being able to direct psychokinetic influence to precisely the right place.

Large-Scale PK

Scientist Dean Radin suggests that psychokinetic effects would likely be influences on the physical indeterminacy in an object that exists at the subatomic level. If such influences could alter energetic equilibrium states to a miniscule degree, observable changes would occur:

> For example, if the mind could reduce the atmospheric pressure under a soda can just slightly, then using the same principle that makes airplane wings fly, the unbalanced pressure would shoot the can up a few dozen feet before equilibrium could be established. Likewise, if mind could momentarily alter the energetic equilibrium of the quantum zero-point field under a soda can, which is very roughly speaking the energetic equivalent of air pressure, then before the equilibrium state rebalanced it might launch the can into orbit.[13]

Of course, the ability to control such effects would depend on directing psychokinetic influence to precisely the right point. Such an ability is presumably rare. The anecdotal evidence suggests that it requires shifting into an altered state of consciousness conducive to accessing this kind of power. In Home this kind of state seems to have come on spontaneously, but altered states can also be brought about by meditative and ascetic practices. Some of the stories from religious traditions involving people who have engaged in extensive meditation sound very much like instances in which psychokinetic powers become available.

A central reason why reports of large-scale psychokinesis are hard to believe is that what is reported conflicts with assumptions about reality that shape our intuitions of what is possible. Our common sense tells us that physical change is produced by physical causes. The idea that mental influence could produce this kind of change doesn't fit with the way we

---

13. Radin, *Entangled Minds*, 270–71.

have learned to think. Most of us admit that mental states can produce physical effects in our own body, but people find it implausible to think that states of minds could have effects on other minds or on physical states beyond one's own body. This difficulty of conceiving such a thing depends on assumptions about reality that evidence of psychokinesis gives us reason to question.

Biblical Miracles

Some Christians insist that every miracle story in the Bible should be accepted as a literal account of what happened. But there are also Christians who find this kind of stance to be overly simple. In some cases, they judge that a miracle story is likely a way for a biblical author to make a theological point or is an example of pious exaggeration. Some Christians accept very few reports of extraordinary events described in biblical texts as historical. Others distinguish between reports that should be understood as representing historical events and those that should be interpreted in some other way.

While there are different reasons for being skeptical about understanding a miracle story as a historical event, an important general reason is connected with the thought that some events are physically impossible. Hence, there are Christians who accept some biblical reports of things like extraordinary healing, but find it more difficult to accept nature miracles such as stilling a storm or walking on water or increasing a small amount of food so that a large crowed can eat and be satisfied.

It might be suggested that when we are thinking about God's action, there is no reason to draw a line at what seems physically impossible. However, many theologians object to thinking of God's actions as overriding natural processes. Physicist and theologian John Polkinghorne says, "God may be properly said to interact with creation, but the word 'intervene' . . . would not be appropriate."[14] He thinks of God's interaction as occurring in the "open grain" of natural process and not "contrary to that process."[15] He identifies various ways in which the regularities of the natural order leave room for unpredictability, which allows God to influence what happens without producing results that are contrary to what nature could produced.

---

14. Polkinghorne, "Kenotic Creation and Divine Action," 100.
15. Polkinghorne, "Kenotic Creation and Divine Action," 100.

For someone who thinks of God as acting in ways consistent with natural processes, accepting psychic phenomena alters our expectations of what those processes can bring about. It seems incredible that a blind person could be made to see without medical intervention, but if telepathic powers could influence the individual's mind to activate healing processes or if psychokinetic powers could alter the person's physical condition, we can conceive of such a thing happening. It seems unlikely that someone could get a storm to cease on command, but in a chaotic system a minimal alteration by psychokinetic powers might produce major changes. It is relevant that in both of these cases there are testimonial accounts extending to our own era that describe relevantly similar phenomena occurring.[16]

Our intuitions about such things are connected with our experience. In our experience people can't control storms, axe heads don't float, the quantity of food doesn't expand to feed a crowd. But some things don't happen in our experience because the conditions under which they might happen are rare. Perhaps it is a very unusual individual who has sufficient control over psychokinetic powers to bring about targeted results. Perhaps it takes a combination of natural abilities and skills deriving from consistent contemplative practice. In that case the intuitions we start with about what might happen may be misleading. It doesn't follow automatically that every biblical report of something extraordinary happened as it is described. There can still be reasons for thinking that some biblical reports shouldn't be taken literally. However, expanding our concept of natural possibilities can make it less obvious that even things that strike us amazing couldn't have happened.

16. Keener, *Miracles Today*, 93–105, 177–90.

CHAPTER 11

Tales of Extraordinary Powers

I WAS FASCINATED AS a young boy with the story of Superman. The idea of someone with powers that greatly surpass ordinary human capabilities stimulated my imagination. I suspect that I wished I had powers like his, such as super strength and invulnerability. And wouldn't it be cool to be able to fly?

According to the story, Superman was from another planet. The powers he possessed were said to have something to do with differences between his home planet and earth. One explanation was that earth had a different kind of sun than the star of his home planet, which resulted in his cells receiving energy that gave him superpowers. It was also suggested that the difference between earth's gravity and the gravity of his home world had something to do with his ability to fly. There were other explanations, but none of them made much sense. The accounts that were offered sound like scientific gobbledygook. Nevertheless, these accounts were ways of suggesting that his superpowers should be thought of in natural rather than supernatural terms.

Are there real-life superpowers? There are numerous of accounts of people doing things that go beyond our expectations of human capabilities. Some of these stories are true, and some are not. But our assessment of which ones are true, or might be true, depends on such factors as what kind of evidence we take to be credible and how strongly we are attached to ideas about reality that would make some powers inconceivable. Our response in particular cases may be more nuanced than belief or disbelief. For some stories, we may decide that there is likely something extraordinary going on, even if we don't accept all that is claimed, and for some stories we may judge that we aren't sure of what happened or how what is reported should be interpreted. Some accounts we will likely reject as impossible, but there may also be stories that challenge our sense of what is possible.

A Story of Psychic Superpowers from the Bible

Stories of individuals with remarkable powers come from many time periods. Here is an example from biblical times. The events described are set in the context of a series of military conflicts between Israel and Aram. The prophet Elisha is portrayed as having advanced knowledge of where Aram plans to attack and repeatedly warns the king of Israel to avoid going to specific places. It's a kind of espionage story with a paranormal twist. The frustrated king of Aram learns of the prophet's involvement and sends a war party to Elisha's village. When Elisha's servant informs him that an enemy army with horses and chariots has surrounded his village, Elisha is untroubled. He replies, "Do not be afraid, for there are more with us than are with them" (2 Kgs 6:16).

Elisha then prays that the eyes of his servant will be opened. The prayer is granted, and the servant sees "the mountain was full of horses and chariots of fire all around Elisha" (6:17). At this point Elisha prays for the enemy troops to be struck blind. After his prayer is answered, he leads the blind men to the capital city and to the Israelite king. When Elisha prays again, the sight of the Arameans is restored, and they recognize the precariousness of their situation. The episode ends with Elisha advising the king of Israel not to kill the raiding party, but to prepare food for them. After they eat and drink, the Arameans return home, and according to the account, no longer conducted raids against Israel.

Elisha is portrayed in the story as seeing what is invisible to other people. In particular he sees horses and chariots of fire that apparently symbolize divine protection. His experience is not represented as hallucinatory, but as an apprehension of a deeper reality that is not apparent to physical sight. The story does not call Elisha's experience a vision, though that description seems to fit. The knowledge ascribed to Elisha about enemy troop movements, as well as his powers to bring about remarkable physical results, are presumably related to his connection with the unseen spiritual realm.

We don't get a specific account of how Elisha becomes aware of Aram's plans, but prophets are sometimes described in Hebrew Scripture as able to gain information about unknown things. For example, there is a story in 1 Samuel 9 about Saul seeking to find a seer who can help him discover a lost donkey's location. (The text informs us that prophets were formerly called seers.) The seer in this case turns out to be Samuel, who the previous day had received a revelation about meeting the man whom he should anoint to be king.

The power of seers to find lost things sounds something like Harold's power to locate a missing harp (described in chapter 5). We might suspect that in either case accessing the information is connected with entering into what we would call an altered state of consciousness. Accounts of early prophets in biblical texts portray them as sometimes getting caught up in ecstatic states in which they lose ordinary conscious control and utter prophetic words. Prophetic groups apparently had practices, including rhythmic music, facilitative to entering into a state of consciousness conducive to having visions and receiving auditory messages.

My concern here is not with drawing precise conclusions about how historically accurate the Elisha story is. I think that it is likely that there was a historical Elisha that the biblical stories are based on, but it shouldn't be surprising if there are embellishments like those that sometimes occur in the case of figures who become legendary. Regardless of what actually occurred, this story, along with others in Hebrew Scripture, gives us some idea of the beliefs people in biblical times had about some individuals possessing extraordinary powers.

Elisha in the story is described as knowing things about the enemy soldiers that go beyond what people are ordinarily able to know. On one interpretation, he has knowledge of what is yet to occur. But we could also take his knowledge to be more like a kind of telepathic awareness that taps into the plans of the enemy. The story seems to suggest something like infallibility in his predictions, but we could imagine that even if his predictions do not have a 100-percent level of accuracy, they may be accurate enough to give Israel a military advantage.

What should we make of this story? When I read it, I recognize similarities with stories from our own time and from other historical periods that portray people with remarkable powers to know what ordinarily can't be known and to perform awe-inspiring acts. As other chapters in this book make clear, I think that there are good reasons to believe that people sometimes do show signs of extraordinary powers resembling those the story describes. So, suppose we read the biblical story as an instance of this type of account. We could imagine Elisha by some combination of innate aptitude and training as able to achieve altered states of consciousness in which he becomes aware of information that is not available through ordinary sensory channels. The reports of his visions are suggestive with regard to Elisha's capacity to acquire this kind of knowledge.

However, in this story and others in the biblical text, Elisha is described not only as having extraordinary *knowledge*; he also *does* things that go beyond our ordinary expectations of human powers. For example, Elisha prays that the enemy soldiers will be struck blind, and they immediately become blind. One way of reading this story is to think that Elisha is much more effective in getting his prayers answered than most of us are. But if we are thinking of Elisha as having psychic powers, there is an alternative way to understand the account. We might say that in addition to having powers that enable him to obtain extraordinary knowledge, Elisha's powers of mind enable him to produce physical effects, either directly, or indirectly through affecting the minds of others. (The account sounds like a healing story in reverse.) Admittedly, the text suggests that all Elisha does is pray and that God brings about the extraordinary result. But given the well-known biblical tendency to ascribe to God what we would likely ascribe to secondary causes, we might think of Elisha's prayers as having a role in activating powers he possesses that he would undoubtedly regard as God-given.

Does this kind of account describe what actually happened? I have no way to say. I can't even say for sure whether this particular story is based on an actual incident. However, I can say that reading the story as an occasion in which someone has extraordinary powers that parallel other credible reports of people with similar powers may give us a plausible version of what might have happened.

Superpowers in Religious Contexts

Religious traditions have many stories about people who have amazing powers. These people are not labeled as superheroes. They are referred to by terms such as yogis or saints or Buddhas. These figures are thought of as more advanced in the ideals of their religion than the typical adherent. But along with whatever characteristics make them more advanced, they are sometimes portrayed as doing things that surpass ordinary human capabilities.

Many Christians don't presume a strong connection between being a saint and having extraordinary powers. Protestants typically follow the New Testament practice of calling all Christians saints. However, in Catholic tradition the conditions for being officially recognized as a saint include not only extraordinary piety or holiness but also evidence of having performed at least two miraculous acts. It might be said that if a saint does something miraculous, it is not through the saint's own power but is rather a kind of channeling of divine power. So, it could be claimed that we are not really talking about a power that should be ascribed to the saint. On the other hand, we could think of the saint as having the ability to do remarkable things because God has given the saint this ability. The New Testament, after all speaks of spiritual gifts, some of which seem to involve abilities to do what surpasses ordinary expectations.

Other religions besides Christianity speak of people who demonstrate abilities to do extraordinary things. Anthropologists who study tribal religions have used the term *shaman* to refer to a figure who is thought of as a kind of intermediary between the spirit realm and the human realm.[1] Shamans are especially valued in their communities for healing power, but stories from these groups tell of a wide range of extraordinary things that shamans are said to do. In Hindu tradition powers to do supranormal things are called *siddhis*. The *Yoga Sutras*, ascribed to Patanjali, includes accounts of remarkable attainments by those who achieve advanced levels of meditation. In the sacred texts of Theravada Buddhism, Buddha is described as having supranormal abilities and as expecting his disciples to have them as well.[2] In meditative traditions such attainments are often portrayed as an expected result of meditative practice, but not as the goal. In fact, people in these traditions are generally told that too much concern with extraordinary powers is a distraction from the central aim.

One of the difficulties of categorizing the kinds of powers described in religious traditions is that there may be multiple ways of understanding

---

1. Hunter, *Spirits, Gods and Magic*, 34–39.
2. Weddle, *Miracles*, 115.

what is said to occur. For example, there are stories of shamans traveling at extraordinary speeds and of disappearing. The stories also describe shamans as having the ability to project mental illusions into the minds of observers. So, should an alleged disappearance be understood as a physical event or as a kind of telepathic influence on observers? A related difficulty is deciding whether an event should be thought of as observable in an ordinary sensory way or apprehended only by those who are in an altered state of consciousness. For example, stories of what shamans can do, such as changing into an animal form, could be construed as accounts of visionary experiences of the shaman, or if we take claims of telepathic influence seriously, they might be understood as visions that the shaman projects into the minds of others.

Control Over One's Own Body

Some of the stories from religious traditions involve an extraordinary control over one's own body. We have a rough idea of the difference between things that we can control about our bodies and processes that operate automatically in a way that puts them beyond our control. The automatic control that operates most of the time can sometimes be overridden, such as holding your breath when diving under water. But there are also bodily processes that most of us don't think of as matters of choice, such as making your pancreas produce more or less insulin. Biofeedback has taught us that it is possible to learn how to control processes that are not normally under our control. So, the rough lines we might draw are subject to change. Still, some of the accounts of what people are described as controlling with regard to their own bodies seem astonishing.

There have been reports of yogis diminishing their pulse rates to zero. Scientific tests have shown that some individuals are able to alter their heartbeats to an extent that they can't be heard with a stethoscope, though they can still be detected on EKG readings.[3] One subject was able to cause an atrial flutter during which one section of his heart beat rapidly.[4] This same individual could produce an 11-degree temperature differential between the left and right side of his palm. Another Indian meditator was able to perspire from his forehead on command, even in freezing weather.

---

3. Murphy, *Future of the Body*, 529.
4. Murphy, *Future of the Body*, 532.

The ability to slow some bodily functions is presumably connected with dramatic reports of yogis surviving days of burial.

There are numerous stories in Christian tradition of saints who exhibit evidence of remarkable control over their body, though what happens is frequently described as an act of God, rather than something the saint does. It is well known that Saint Francis of Assisi developed marks on his hands and feet that looked as if nails had been driven through his flesh, apparently wounds resembling those Jesus suffered in his crucifixion. Since his time, there have been hundreds of reported instances of what are called *stigmata*.[5] People who develop such marks on the body are apparently those who have engaged in extended concentration on the suffering of Jesus.

There are hypnotic phenomena that seem to be related to stigmata. Some people under hypnosis who are asked to imagine vividly some kind of injury, such as a burn, later show signs of the injury on the skin.[6] It might seem counterintuitive that a person can produce significant marks on the body by some kind of mental process. But there are verifiable instances of such a thing happening. Francis presumably regarded his wounds as a divine gift, but I don't think that description precludes the possibility that they might have come about when powers of his mind to produce these marks were activated by his extraordinary identification with the suffering of Jesus.

There are many accounts in Christian tradition of bodily signs. Padre Pio, an Italian saint from the early twentieth century, reportedly said Mass for many years while wearing mittens covering blood-soaked hands that apparently became bloody through his concentration on the crucified Christ.[7] There are multiple reports of saintly women who regarded themselves as espoused to Christ developing a swelling of the finger in the appearance of a ring.[8] Some stories tell of odors like perfumes emanating from the bodies of saints. There are also strange reports of saints temporarily lengthening their bodies or some part of the body, such as an arm. Another remarkable ability reported in these stories is of fasting for periods of time that seem incredible. Some people are even described as no longer consuming any food at all, yet showing no ill effects.[9]

5. Kelly, "Psychophysiological Influence," 152.
6. Kelly, "View from the Mainstream," 31.
7. Grosso, *Smile of the Universe*, 20.
8. Grosso, *Smile of the Universe*, 21–22.
9. Grosso, *Smile of the Universe*, 24–31.

We don't have to believe all the stories to think that both in Christian contexts and in contexts outside of Christianity people sometimes develop powers of control over bodily processes that seem remarkable. Some saints are described as handling live coals or red-hot irons without being burnt. This kind of account seems reminiscent of multiple stories from various parts of the world of people being able to walk over burning coals without being hurt. American physician Andrew Weil reported that he tried to do this feat several times, but felt pain and had his feet burned. However, he says that he eventually slipped into a state of mind that allowed him to avoid pain or injury.[10]

Remarkable abilities of bodily control don't necessarily involve anything contrary to what our science could recognize, at least as long as science acknowledges that the changes described can arise when someone through mental disciplines develops abilities to activate unconscious processes that people don't normally control. But there are also stories from religious contexts of people doing things that go beyond what is explainable in terms of accounts offered in contemporary science.

Psychic Powers

Pantanjali's *Yoga Sutras* portray various kinds of psychic powers as an expected byproduct of entering into particular states of consciousness through meditation.[11] His account of kinds of knowledge that may be attained includes knowledge of other people's minds, of distant objects, of past and future events. Patanjali says that one may have detailed awareness of events in one's past, present, and future, including previous and future births. He represents potential knowledge as ranging from awareness of microscopic objects to large celestial phenomena. On his account, barriers of space and time that we ordinarily take for granted are overcome. While we can think that these claims are exaggerated, the idea that altered states of mind attained in meditation are conducive to extrasensory awareness is plausible. Research suggests that the lowering of sensory input, focused attention, and relaxation produced by meditative practice is conducive to becoming aware of extrasensory input from the unconscious mind.[12]

10. Weil, "Foreword," xviii–xxi.
11. Patanjali, *Yoga Sutras*, 3:16–46.
12. Kelly and Grosso, "Mystical Experience," 527–28.

In the Christian tradition, accounts of the saints contain a significant number of what can be considered as incidents of extrasensory awareness. Rhea White's analysis of Butler's *Lives of the Saints* cites reports of clairvoyance and telepathy, including the ability to "read hearts" telepathically.[13] The accounts White considered include fifty-five instances of saints accurately predicting specific future events, including destruction of a city by invasion, major fires, and in some cases the time of their own death. White notes that some saints seem to acquire psychic powers only later in life after they had engaged in contemplative practice for a considerable time.

Striking reports of telepathic powers can be found in stories about the legendary Padre Pio, who is described as being able to discern what is in the minds of people who came to the confessional.[14] One person who came to the confessional reported that after he had offered his own account of his sins, Pio reminded him of numerous actions and thoughts that he had long forgotten. In another report Pio is said to have discerned that someone who came to the confessional failed to mention that he intended to murder his wife. Pio threw him out, receiving him back only when the man had repented of his plans. As with other reports of spontaneous extrasensory perception, we can question whether what happened is accurately reported or properly interpreted. But the activation of extrasensory powers in people who practice the ascetic and contemplative life of many religious figures corresponds to what other research suggests about these powers.

Stories of religious figures include accounts of doing things that most people would say are physically impossible. One of the most striking cases involves the seventeenth-century Christian monk Joseph of Copertino. According to numerous witnesses, Joseph would sometimes levitate and fly through the air. These incidents were said to occur when he fell into an ecstatic trance state. On one occasion he was described as deep in prayer when he suddenly flew across the chapel to a high alter. Witnesses testify that on one occasion he was so awed by the presence of the pope that he floated to the ceiling. His biographer records seventy flights during the time he was in Copertino. The Vatican archive contains 150 sworn statements from those who observed Joseph's flights. During the canonization trial after his death, even the "devil's advocate," charged

---

13. White, "ESP Phenomena in the Saints," 15–18.
14. Grosso, *Smile of the Universe*, 89–102.

with arguing against sainthood, admitted that there were many credible witnesses. The witnesses included popes, princes, and admirals, in addition to ordinary citizens on the streets of the city.

No doubt many people are likely to say that they would not believe such a thing unless they saw it for themselves. I suspect that seeing it for yourself might not be enough. You might rub your eyes and start talking about optical illusions or some kind of trickery. Perhaps it will be surprising to learn that researchers in our time have taken the reports of Joseph's levitation seriously. Historian Carlos Eire and philosopher Michael Grosso have both written books showing how massively documented the reports about Joseph are.[15] Grosso, in addition to considering the strength of the testimonial evidence, considers virtually every conceivable alternative way to explain these accounts away and finds these explanations inadequate. He writes, "the historical case for Joseph's levitation is as strong as one could hope for in dealing with such a rare phenomenon as levitation."[16]

I am not concerned with deciding whether Joseph's levitation, or other stories of levitation where there is less evidence, actually occurred. If they did, it would presumably be a result of psychokinetic power to alter bodily composition or perhaps the surrounding environment. Some people who are convinced by these reports may prefer to say that the power of God could account for the levitations. But it seems a stretch to think that God would want Joseph to levitate. This kind of event fits less easily with our understanding of God's purposes than, say, stories of extraordinary healing. Levitation looks more like the kind of paranormal powers that Patanjali portrays as products of advanced meditative states. According to the accounts, Joseph's levitations were unpredictable and uncontrollable events that occurred when he shifted involuntarily into an altered state of consciousness.

Regardless of how we assess particular stories, I think that some stories of extraordinary powers challenge the assumption that we can confidently rely on our intuitions to determine what can happen. Our intuitions are useful for making judgments about situations where we don't have to consider possibilities such as psychic powers. But if such powers are real, some pretty surprising things can happen.

15. See Eire, *Good, the Bad and the Airborne*; Grosso, *Man Who Could Fly*
16. Grosso, "Evidence for St. Joseph," 6.

Though we shouldn't think that psychic powers make anything we can imagine possible, it is hard to say precisely what the limits of psychokinetic or extrasensory powers are. In some cases, the reasonable response to a claim about the extraordinary is to recognize that we don't know. But even if we are sometimes unsure about particular claims of extraordinary powers, we have strong reason to recognize that there are potentials of human nature to do things that seem incredible to those of us whose psychic potentials are less developed.

CHAPTER 12

Remarkable Rescues and Mysterious Helpers

MARTHA AND ROY WERE a couple in my church who regularly attended Wednesday evening services. That is an understatement. They almost never missed. But one Wednesday evening for no apparent reason they lingered at home until it was too late to go. A loud knock at the door got their attention. A frantic neighbor was shouting that her husband was choking and couldn't breathe. Martha and Roy rushed to her house. Roy had just the previous month completed a class in first aid that included instruction in the Heimlich maneuver. He performed the maneuver he had practiced in class on his neighbor, saving the man's life. Both Martha and Roy were convinced that their unusual behavior in remaining home that evening along with Roy's preparation to deal with the emergency were not accidental, but had been providentially arranged.

I don't recall whether Roy used the term "miracle" in describing what happened. He might have. It was clear that the event had left him awestruck. He saw a pattern in what happened that convinced him that things had been arranged to avert a tragedy, and he assumed that God must have done the arranging. Where Roy saw the hand of God in what happened, someone who doesn't believe in God is likely to see what happened as a beneficial coincidence. Such a person can admit that the events appear purposive, but insist that such an appearance doesn't provide strong reason to posit the work of a behind-the-scenes arranger.

I agree that the appearance of purposiveness sometimes arises by chance. But like Roy, I find that some instances in which a meaningful pattern seems apparent are difficult to think of as mere coincidences. Even if it is a matter of chance that Roy had recently learned the Heimlich maneuver at an opportune time, it strains credulity to say that the uncharacteristic behavior of staying home that Wednesday was just a coincidence. It is not impossible. But I wonder whether there could be some connection between the crisis and the puzzling delay. Given the evidence of extrasensory perception I have been discussing, might an extrasensory awareness that Roy would be needed account for why Martha and Roy stayed home that evening?

Someone could say that a psychic explanation of this kind makes it unnecessary to bring in God. A person who doesn't believe in God but accepts psychic phenomena might take that approach. But my guess is that if I had suggested to Roy that some telepathic power could be involved, he would have said that God might have used this kind of power to bring about the desired outcome. Just as someone might be convinced that an evolutionary process is the means by which God brings various kinds of things into existence, one might think that psychic powers are a means that God could use to influence events.

The idea of God working through nature can be understood in different ways. In discussing divine providence, philosopher Bruce Reichenbach contrasts God acting through miraculous interventions with God's maintenance of a predictable natural order. When he says that "God generally acts through nature and its laws to achieve his purposes,"[1] I understand him to mean that God's purposes can usually be achieved in noninterventionist ways by letting nature take its course. However, miraculously intervening to produce a specific outcome and just letting nature take its course are not the only possibilities. Some outcomes might be produced neither by a unilateral action on God's part to make nature do something nor through nature achieving an outcome on its own. They might involve God influencing what nature does without controlling the results.

But how can this kind of influence be conceived? Following John Polkinghorne, I conceive of it in terms of an informational flow that can potentially affect the behavior of created things. We can think of human beings as receiving informational input through the unconscious mind,

---

1. Reichenbach, *Divine Providence*, 10.

input to which they can be either receptive or unreceptive. We can also think that physical and biological systems can be sensitive to informational input.[2] Some people may imagine this kind of influence to involve God specifically sending some information that might lead to a desired behavior. But we could conceive of the availability of information conducive to achieving God's purposes as built into the natural order. When created things are "on the right wavelength," so to speak, they may behave in ways that would have been unlikely without such input.

When God acts through human agents, what those agents do will mostly involve human powers that we think of as ordinary. However, the motivation to act may involve powers that exceed our ordinary expectations. If Roy has an uneasiness generated by a dim awareness of danger to his neighbor, this uneasiness might be viewed as arising from a latent human capacity for extrasensory awareness. But thinking of his awareness in terms of natural capacities is not inconsistent with thinking that God might sometimes make an awareness coming from the unconscious mind particularly salient. If God works through nature, the dividing lines between what God does and what nature does are not easily distinguishable.

A Story of Surprising Survival

In the case of Martha and Roy what seems remarkable is not the means by which the next-door neighbor's life is saved. The Heimlich maneuver is known to be an effective way to deal with choking on food. What makes this case notable is that the conditions that resulted in the availability of a particular human agent able to perform the maneuver successfully seem unlikely. The rescue depended on Roy being home and knowing what to do. But it seems remarkable that he was home at the right time and that he had just learned what he needed to render aid.

However, sometimes the means by which a rescue occurs strikes us as remarkable. Psychologist Justin Barrett tells a story about a coworker of his wife named Doug who survived an explosion of propane gas while working on a farm.[3] Doug was inside a grain silo when an explosion occurred. The initial explosion didn't injure him, but it jammed the doors so that he couldn't get out of the silo. Realizing that he had no way to escape

---

2. Polkinghorne, *Belief in God*, 63.
3. Barrett, *Why Would Anyone Believe*, 34.

and expecting another explosion soon, Doug said in resignation, "Take me home, Lord." He then heard a voice say, "Not yet," and felt some "invisible hands lift him a dozen feet off the ground" through a second-story window. He dropped to the ground outside just before the silo and an attached barn exploded into rubble. Coworkers rushed Doug to the hospital where he told the doctors that God had sent angels to save him.

Assuming that things happened pretty much as they are described, I suspect that many people would call the events miraculous. Even people who are reluctant to use that term are likely to find what happened astonishing. Some will find the account unbelievable. A reasonable expectation for someone in Doug's situation is a violent death, but he somehow survives. Not only that, he hears a voice telling him that his time has not yet come, and when the silo doors are jammed, his body rises upwards to the only escape hatch. Doug doesn't report seeing any angels, but he was convinced that God had sent them to rescue him.

For some people, the central issue raised by this kind of story is whether what happened can be explained in scientific terms. They want to know whether we have to posit some power beyond nature. I don't know whether there is a plausible scientific explanation for Doug's rising off the ground to a second-story window, but I think it is possible that there could be. Perhaps the pre-explosion air pressure was conducive to propelling Doug upward. Even so, it still seems remarkable that it sent him to a window through which he escaped just in time. However, that might be chalked up to extraordinary luck.

What about the invisible hands and the voice Doug hears? It seems plausible that because the idea of angelic messengers fits his beliefs, Doug goes beyond the actual evidence to think in these terms. As for the voice, it is possible to think of it as a hallucination that is brought on by extreme stress. However, as will become clear in this chapter, the experience of hearing a voice in crisis situations is sometimes accompanied by instructions that enable a person to survive. A voice conveying extrasensory information that a person doesn't possess at a conscious level should surely be distinguished from the typical hallucination. Even though the evidence for anything extrasensory is not strong in Doug's case, looking at this case in the light of other crisis situations in which a voice is heard suggests that what Doug hears is more than just a product of his imagination.

A Benevolent Helper

Here is another case in which someone hears a voice during a crisis: Ron DeFrancisco was on the eighty-fourth floor of the South Tower of the World Trade Center in New York on 9/11.[4] After a plane hit the other tower, an announcement from the building's public address system told people in the South Tower that there was no need to evacuate that building. So, DeFrancisco took time to finish up some business. He was walking to the elevators when a second plane struck the South Tower, destroying the trading floor he had just left. He entered one of the emergency stairwells, but three flights down, he encountered people coming up who said that the smoke and flames made it impossible to go down. He turned around and climbed, but it was soon evident that there would be no escape to the roof. Turning around, he again sought to go down, but at the seventy-ninth floor, the way out was blocked by a collapsed wall. Smoke and flames were all around. People trying to escape that way were lying on the floor in panic.

Then DeFrancisco heard an insistent voice telling him to get up. In addition to the voice, he had a strong sense of a physical presence. He had the sense of someone lifting him up and leading him in a direction where he was able to resume his descent and fight his way through the debris. When the way was blocked by flames, something urged him on, and he was able to run through the fire. He was scorched, but eventually made it through to the seventy-sixth floor. At this point, he lost his sense of the benevolent helper. It took nearly an hour to make it to the ground. He was one of only four people who made it all the way from above the eighty-first floor, which was the center of the plane's impact.

Accounts of a benevolent helper in times of crisis differ, but some stories of this kind fit into a common pattern. T. S. Elliott's "The Waste Land" speaks of a "third who walks always beside you."[5] The reference was inspired by an account from Ernest Shackleton of an Antarctic expedition when under desperate conditions he sensed the presence of a fourth person in addition to his two companions. Elliott took poetic license in referring to a third person, and after him, the phenomenon came to be called "the third-man factor."

The extra person is sometimes seen, but is often an invisible presence. There are cases when this companion speaks, but in many accounts

---

4. Geiger, *Third Man Factor*, 1–7.
5. Elliott, "Waste Land" part v, line 359.

there is no audible communication. Almost invariably, the experience of this strange presence is felt as a comfort and an encouragement, but sometimes there is also guidance that results in deliverance. People have spoken of the presence as a guardian angel, though they often describe it in more neutral terms. During World War I three men who escaped from Turkish captivity all had an experience of an invisible presence. One of them wrote, "I cannot exaggerate how real his presence was, how content one felt—despite the mystery of it—that he should be there, what a strength and comfort his presence seemed to be."[6]

This phenomenon is most common when people are in extreme conditions. Stories of this kind often come from explorers in desolate regions, mountain-climbers, or people who are lost at sea. In the typical story the conditions have produced sensory deprivation, such as an environment where visibility is limited and everything is covered with snow. The sensory deprivation may be combined with physical injuries, as well as exhaustion and malnutrition. In many of these accounts, the odds against survival are great, and the temptation to give up is strong.

It is not surprising that many people think that the experience of a mysterious presence is a trick of the brain brought on by the stress of extreme conditions that have pushed people to their limits. But the "third-man" experience seems different from some types of hallucinatory experiences in extreme physiological states. Stories of shipwrecks sometimes include accounts of disorienting hallucinations, such as ships or shorelines that are never reached. There are also cases in which the person having such experiences has lost contact with reality. By contrast the "third-man" type of experience is described by people who typically recognize the strangeness of what they perceive. Sometimes they even think that the mysterious stranger is in their mind, but still find the experience to be a source of comfort and peace, and, in some cases, guidance that proves instrumental in survival.

James Sevigny was climbing in the Canadian Rockies in 1983 when an avalanche swept him and a companion down about two thousand feet. When he regained consciousness, he was severely injured. His back was broken, and he couldn't move one of his arms. He had cracked ribs, torn ligaments in his knees, internal bleeding, a broken nose, and open wounds. At first, he wasn't sure where he was. Only gradually did he

---

6. Geiger, *Third Man Factor*, 61.

remember. He found his dead companion nearby. He had an urge to just lie down beside him and wait to die himself.

Suddenly, he had a sense of an invisible being close by. The unseen presence communicated with him. He describes the experience as follows:

> It told me what to do. The only decision I had made at that point was to lie down next to Rick and to fall asleep and to accept death.... All decisions made subsequent to that were made by the presence. I was merely taking instructions.... I understood what it wanted me to do. It wanted me to live.[7]

The presence urged him to get up and told him which way to go. Because of his injuries, he could move only slowly; it took a day to go a distance of about a mile. As he struggled, the presence kept telling him to keep going. He finally reached his camp, and as he lay down in exhaustion, he thought he heard voices just before the presence left. He cried for help and was heard by cross-country skiers who called in a helicopter to take him to the hospital.

Other stories of strange guidance can be found in accounts from pilots. In 1932 Edith Stearns was off course and thought her only chance of survival would be to land on a railroad track she had been following. As she was preparing to land, she heard a voice saying, "No, no, Edie, don't." She leveled off and continued, coming upon a runway where she could land safely. On another occasion, flying in limited visibility, she heard a voice warning her to pull up. When she did, she realized that she had narrowly missed crashing into a hill.[8]

Other pilots have described similar experiences. Brian Shoemaker was lost while flying a helicopter in an Antarctic storm. He felt a presence beside him telling him to turn twenty degrees to the right. He was disoriented and didn't know what else to do, so he followed the instruction and made it back to the base just before his fuel would have run out. Shoemaker refrained from telling his copilot how he knew which way to go, but later he told a chaplain at the station and was assured that this kind of experience was not uncommon.[9]

---

7. Geiger, *Third Man Factor*, 7–8
8. Geiger, *Third Man Factor*, 92–93.
9. Geiger, *Third Man Factor*, 94–96.

What Is Going On?

Is the benevolent helper who is sensed really there? If what we mean by "really there" is that the benevolent helper could be perceived through ordinary seeing or hearing by anyone in the vicinity, then it seems doubtful. There are cases in which more than one person senses the mysterious presence, but the perceptions should probably be thought of as visionary experiences. In a visionary experience the cause of a perception is not a matter of light waves or sound waves being picked up by our senses. The input comes instead through the unconscious mind.

Noting that the third-man phenomenon is connected with extreme physiological conditions in which survival is at stake, some people have viewed the experience of a benevolent helper as a survival mechanism that is manufactured by the brain in extreme circumstances. Such perceptions can contribute to survival, they say, but should not be confused with experiencing something objectively real. That way of thinking goes with the assumption that only sense experiences give us genuine contact with reality.

That assumption can be questioned. Thinkers that I have mentioned earlier in this book have posited that the perceptions we have in ordinary sense experience are a result of filters that function to limit awareness. The idea is that the ordinary operation of our senses reveals only those aspects of reality that are needed for acting in ways conducive to surviving in a physical environment. But this idea raises the question of whether it might be possible to experience reality in a less filtered way. People with mystical or visionary experiences sometimes speak of encountering something more real than what they know through ordinary sense experience. More than one thinker has suggested that the key to experiencing reality in a less filtered way is through altered states of consciousness in which the filters are loosened. So, we could think of the extreme conditions in which a benevolent helper is experienced as conducive to a revelation of some feature of reality that is ordinarily hidden from us.

People who have experiences of a strange presence sometimes emphasize how real what they experienced seemed. Philosopher William James, in a chapter of *The Varieties of Religious Experience* called "The Reality of the Unseen," gives multiple examples of individuals who have sensed an anomalous presence. One person, whom he calls an intimate friend, says of an experience, "something was present with me, and I knew its presence far more surely than I have ever known the presence of any fleshly living creature. I was conscious of its departure as of its coming."[10] In this instance, the impression was one of dread or horror.[11] But the same man describes another instance in which the experience of a presence was accompanied by extreme joy. He speaks of "the close presence of a sort of mighty person." He says that "after it went, the memory persisted as the one perception of reality. Everything else might be a dream, but not that."[12]

We can call experiences of this kind hallucinations. But lumping together every instance in which a perception arises from something other than a physical stimulus makes it difficult to consider the possibility that dislodging the filters that govern ordinary sense experience may enable us to receive input about reality that we don't ordinarily have access to. Cases in which the benevolent helper is a source of extrasensory information conducive to survival suggest that we are getting this kind of input.

But if we don't take the benevolent helper to be merely a subjective projection, how can it be understood? There are several interpretive options. Some take the experience of this helpful companion to be an actual encounter with a being from another realm. Some explorers have thought that they were getting guidance from a deceased relative. People with a religious background have sometimes described it as an encounter with Christ or an angel. But taking the experience as real doesn't have to mean interpreting it this way.

Some have suggested that the benevolent helper is a kind of externalized version of oneself. But in cases where extrasensory information is received through the benevolent helper, the self that is experienced would have to be connected with reality in ways that go beyond commonsense pictures of the self. A person who thinks in these terms may

---

10. James, *Varieties of Religious Experience*, 62.

11. David Hufford has described a surprisingly common experience of utter terror that sometimes occurs on awakening from sleep (see Hufford, *Terror That Comes*). In the standard case, a person feels awake and can perceive the surrounding environment, but cannot move. The feelings of helplessness and fear connected with this sleep paralysis are often accompanied by the sense of an evil presence of a being who cannot be seen. Hufford has shown that there are many historical and contemporary accounts of this kind of experience. He remarks that such experiences make it understandable how normal people in both ancient and modern times could come to believe in evil spirits. In citing an example of someone who changed his mind about the reality of demonic beings after having this kind of experience, Dale Allison says, "I regard this change of mind as evidence for the proposition that some have believed in malevolent spirits because they have ostensibly run into them" (Allison, *Encountering Mystery*, 43).

12. James, *Varieties of Religious Experience*, 63.

waver between thinking that the information comes from within them and thinking that it comes from beyond them. In some cases, the sense of comfort provided by the experience depends on viewing the strange presence as a sign of a greater reality beyond the self. One mountain-climber who thought that the unseen presence was in his imagination reports, "During those hours of extreme tension I had an extraordinary feeling that I was not alone. I had a partner looking after me and taking care of me."[13]

How we understand the benevolent helper is likely to be connected with the way we conceive of what is ultimately real. People who believe in God may feel a resonance with thinking that the experience is a sign of God's presence. Believing that it is such a revelation doesn't rule out thinking that the channel through which it comes is one's own unconscious mind. Some may conceive of God as directly sending the perceptions. However, thinking that perceptions of this kind are a natural phenomenon that is activated when particular conditions are met is unlikely to reduce the sense of amazement that such perceptions tend to produce. Even those with few religious inclinations may wonder about what to make of their own impressions of a reality that seems more mysterious than they had imagined it to be.

---

13. Geiger, *Third Man Factor*, 126.

CHAPTER 13

Petitionary Prayer

IN PREPARING TO WRITE this chapter, I read numerous Christian stories about answered prayers. The stories I found were mostly inspirational accounts whose primary appeal is to people who already believe, or want to believe, that God grants prayer requests. When considered as evidence that would be convincing to those more skeptical about the power of prayer, such stories were less impressive. They described good outcomes that occurred after someone prayed, but the events often seemed like the kind of thing that might have happened with or without prayer. There were, however, some stories that told about very unlikely fulfillments of what someone prayed for. Even if these accounts left room for doubt, they provided some reason to wonder whether prayer had something to do with what happened. A few stories fell into the "knock your socks off" category.

A striking example of this kind of story can be found in an account given by traveling evangelist Ken Gaub in a book entitled *God's Got Your Number*.[1] I should say in advance that I cannot verify the truth of his account. What is described seems unlikely in the extreme, but it is not unique in that respect. There are many stories about events that don't line up with ordinary expectations of what is likely, including a significant number from credible sources. One could say that no such stories are

---

1. Gaub, *God's Got Your Number*, 11–15.

true, but for reasons that this book makes clear, I am not inclined to reject all such accounts. At any rate, let me recount the story.

Gaub tells about being in the parking lot of a pizza parlor in Dayton, Ohio near the church where the group of people he was traveling with had led services. While others in his group had gone in for dinner, he had gone off alone to wrestle with a personal issue that made him wonder whether he should continue his ministry. As he walked by himself, he heard a phone ringing in a phone booth at a gas station. (Yes, there used to be such things as phone booths.) Thinking that there might be some kind of emergency, he answered the phone. An operator said that there was a long-distance call for Ken Gaub. He expressed his incredulity as the operator asked him to confirm his identity. The thought crossed his mind that he might be in an episode of *Candid Camera*.

In the background, he heard the woman making the call from Pennsylvania tell the operator that she recognized Gaub's voice. After confirming his identity, the operator put the call through. The woman who placed the call had been contemplating suicide and crying out to God for help. In the midst of her struggles, she had the thought that Gaub, whom she had seen on television, might help her. A series of numbers appeared in her mind. She wrote them down and then placed a call to what looked like a phone number. The number turned out to be to this phone booth at a time when Gaub was passing by. Gaub was able to convince her not to commit suicide, and in the weeks that followed, he stayed in contact with her until he knew that her crisis was resolved.

I am sure that many people will immediately dismiss this story as a tall tale. At the other end of the spectrum, there are those who will believe the account because they are confident that God frequently answers prayer and can do anything. My response differs from both of these. My views on God's powers and answered prayer do not allow me to draw any conclusions about whether the report is likely to be true, but I am also unwilling to say that what is described couldn't have happened. What I notice about the account is that the seemingly magical revelation of the phone number at just the right time would be an instance of someone getting extrasensory information at a time of heightened emotions in a crisis situation. If I hadn't come across numerous credible accounts of extraordinary awareness, I might dismiss claims about it in this case. But since I think that there is good reason to believe that such a thing sometimes occurs in this type of situation, I am not willing to say that what is described couldn't have happened.[2] Nevertheless, even if the events occurred as they are described, I am not satisfied with the way people who believe in answered prayer are likely to interpret them.

The Standard Model

The standard way of conceiving petitionary prayer suggests to me a picture of God at the other end of a celestial phone line, receiving incoming requests and deciding to grant some, but not to grant others. Assumptions that go with this picture are typically that God can do all of this instantaneously, or perhaps timelessly, and that God is able to bring about whatever is requested. God's deciding not to do what someone requests is usually attributed to divine wisdom. That is, God knows better than we do what is needed.

Of course, thinking that God knows what is needed raises the question of why asking should make a difference at all. Presumably, God doesn't need to sift through a stack of requests to decide whether providing a particular benefit would be desirable. So, why doesn't God provide benefits when it would be good to do so, whether a request has been made or not? On the standard model, to think that requests are important, we have to imagine that God will withhold some needed aid just because someone hasn't asked for it, or maybe has not asked in the right way. Some have suggested reasons why God might operate in this fashion. However, none of the explanations I am aware of seem convincing to me.

The puzzle of why prayer requests should make a difference with regard to what God does may trouble some people, but I think that a different issue is more likely to make reflective Christians have doubts about the value of petitionary prayer. For every story about divine rescue or healing, there are cases where rescue doesn't come or where there is no healing, and many of those cases involve people who prayed just as hard. Some Christians are content to say that God's reasons for granting some requests

---

2. After discovering this story, I came across Larry Dossey's description of two other cases in which a string of numbers that pop into someone's mind turn out to be relevant phone numbers. In one a mother develops a powerful feeling that her son, who lives thousands of miles away, is in trouble. A string of numbers appears. When she calls, she reaches the emergency room of a distant hospital where her son was brought in after being seriously injured in an auto accident. In a very similar story, a woman becomes concerned about her young daughter; she sees a jumble of numbers and dials them. She reaches an emergency room where her daughter is undergoing treatment after an auto accident. See Dossey, *One Mind*, 20–21.

but rejecting others are beyond our understanding. However, there is a tension involved in thinking that God brought about a remarkable rescue of some people in a desperate situation, but didn't extend help to others who died or were severely injured in similar circumstances. It can be unsettling to try to praise God for providing help when things end well, while also being aware of a similar situation where things ended tragically and thinking that God could have helped. Christians who are troubled by cases in which people seek divine help but don't get it often find it difficult to believe that prayer requests make a real difference.[3]

It might be pointed out that the fact that prayers are not always answered does not imply that they are never answered. Admittedly so, but the experience of praying desperately for something and not getting it leads easily to doubts about whether apparent answers were illusory. We may be comfortable in thinking that sometimes prayer requests are not granted if we can think that there are good reasons for God to refuse some requests. But when the difference between successful petitions and unsuccessful ones looks arbitrary, it becomes more difficult to think that it reflects divine wisdom. Some Christians find it more plausible to think that claims of answered prayer are doubtful than to accept the kind of arbitrariness in which some receive help, but others whose needs were just as great are left to suffer their fates.

Reevaluating the Standard Model

I know Christians who have given up on making prayer requests or who offer such prayers only as a kind of ceremonial act in public contexts. But for someone who has doubts about the efficacy of petitionary prayer, there is another option. It is to find an alternative to the standard model. The standard understanding of what we are doing when we make prayer requests is that we are asking God to do something. We should note initially that it is more complicated than that. Some of our prayer requests, such as our requests for daily bread, are typically more like reminders to ourselves that we depend on God for our needs. Nevertheless, many prayer requests are pleas for help with what seems beyond our powers. But suppose that instead of conceiving such prayers as asking God to

---

3. Biblical scholar Dale Allison tells of praying for a pregnant young woman who had been struck by a drunk driver and was left comatose with serious head injuries. When she died, despite fervent prayers by many, he said that his confidence in prayer went away and never returned. See Allison, *Encountering Mystery*, 58–59.

do something, we think of God as having already provided resources that might help us and that prayer is sometimes a way to access these resources. In other words, instead of conceiving petitionary prayer on the model of a celestial hotline that leads to a divine act or a refusal to act, imagine it as more like a way of connecting with a power grid that God has made available.

Some of what is available to us could be described as psychological benefits that come from seeking God's help: a release from anxiety, a sense of God's comfort, a shift in perspective that leads to greater insight or altered attitudes. Even people who are skeptical about the value of petitionary prayer might acknowledge that the practice of prayer can help bring about results of this kind. But what about prayers that someone be healed or that some need that requires action by others be met? If we don't think of prayer as a way to get God to do something, how can our prayer requests make any difference in such cases? I will suggest here and explain more fully in due course that the kind of focused attention on a desired result that is characteristic of petitionary prayer can have causal consequences that extend beyond what happens in our own minds.

I recognize that thinking that the act of praying for something can have a causal influence on real-world results beyond potential effects on the one who prays sounds magical, or maybe superstitious. If I express a desire that someone be healed, how can my desiring by itself have physical effects on that person's body? What I desire may be connected with acts I am motivated to perform or get others to perform. For example, if my prayers motivate me to help a neighbor get medical assistance or to persuade someone else to help, the prayers might aid my neighbor. But it is a matter of common sense that wanting my neighbor to be well won't by itself bring about the neighbor's healing. I agree that it is a matter of common sense that wishing for something won't by itself make it happen. However, if we imagine a world in which the powers of mind that I have described in other chapters are real, we have to imagine that what happens in our minds is not as disconnected with what happens in the world as common sense might lead us to suppose.

Our common sense presupposes an understanding of our minds as separate from other minds and unable to influence what goes on in those other minds apart from some kind of physical mediation, such as vocal communication. But if psychic powers are genuine, this kind of separateness is not an ultimate truth. Accepting their reality allows us to conceive of ourselves as somehow connected at an unconscious level to other people and to the rest of the natural world in ways that are not apparent in ordinary experience, and this way of thinking opens a space in which we can imagine how prayer might have remarkable effects.

Philosopher John Hick offers an account of petitionary prayer that is derived from his reflection on evidence that convinces him of the reality of psychic phenomena. He says,

> We are all linked at a deep unconscious level in a universal network in which our thoughts, and even more our emotions, are all the time affecting others, as others are in turn affecting us. When in prayer or meditation, we direct our thought to a particular individual, this is intensified.... In the case of bodily healing, another's mind affects the patient's mind, which in turn affects the patient's body.... That prayer or meditation does sometimes make a tangible difference is a matter of experience.[4]

Lest someone think that this kind of idea is limited to philosophers, consider what Frank Laubach says in classic popular work on prayer:

> Every mind, it now seems probable, unconsciously receives more or less messages from other minds.... Like radios, we seem to be tuned into each other a part of the time and tuned off at other times. Our tuning-in buttons seem to be in the unconscious mind and nearly out of conscious control.... It is likely that every time we think intensely, some people near and far who happen to be tuned in to us get our thoughts without knowing where their ideas come from.[5]

Laubach thinks of the desires of the one who prays being communicated to someone else in a way that aids that person in tuning in to God.

In a workbook on prayer, Maxie Dugan articulates a recognizably similar idea. He cites research from physicists Harold Puthoff and Russell Targ of Stanford Research Institute in support of the conclusion that "all of us at the depths of our being, are linked, interrelated."[6] He understands their experimental evidence to show "that there can be communication (such as mental telepathy) among humans other than what we think of as normal channels."[7] Dugan suggests, "Meditative prayer

---

4. Hick, *Fifth Dimension*, 19.
5. Laubach, *Prayer*, 42.
6. Dugan, *Workbook of Intercessory Prayer*, 116.
7. Dugan, *Workbook of Intercessory Prayer*, 116.

... provides the channel through which we can send love, light and health-giving energy to others."[8]

Hick says that the picture of reality he describes shows us how prayer can be a "real force in the world" that operates by means other than God deciding to intervene miraculously in the course of nature to grant prayer requests.[9] On his account, the beneficial results of prayers of petition come about as a consequence of minds being connected at an unconscious level with the larger environment. He thinks that mental influence on others occurs to some degree all the time, but that focused attention can be a way of intensifying its strength.

The account offered by these writers about how petitionary prayer can affect others should be thought of as hypothesis rather than an established conclusion. However, there are some stories about prayer that make this sort of hypothesis seem worthy of consideration. One account from the collection of Alister Hardy's Religious Experience Research Centre is from a woman who learned of a man's distress and misery through a telephone conversation with him. She wanted to provide comfort to him, but she thought that it would be inappropriate for her, as a married woman, to go to see him. So instead, she expressed to God in prayer what she wanted to say to the man. Days later, when she unexpectedly met him, he was feeling better. In giving her an account of what had changed, she reported that he "proceeded to tell me almost word for word what I had said on my knees."[10] We don't have the exact words prayed or the words the man uses. But supposing that the correspondence is as striking as the woman takes it to be, and supposing that she hadn't said anything like this in the previous phone conversation, how should it be explained? We don't have to posit telepathic communication between human beings. Perhaps God relayed the words. But for someone who thinks that telepathic communication between human beings is an established fact, it may seem plausible to view the events as an instance of it.

Messages to the Unconscious

The writers I have referred to portray petitionary prayer as a way to communicate messages that may influence others at an unconscious level.

---

8. Dugan, *Workbook of Intercessory Prayer*, 116.
9. Hick, *Fifth Dimension*, 18.
10. Hardy, *Spiritual Nature of Man*, 45.

There is strong evidence that influences at the unconscious level can have significant effects. Research in hypnosis, for example, shows that suggestions given to a person's unconscious mind can produce physical effects, such as "changes in autonomic functions such as glucose level, gastrointestinal effects, skin temperature, salivation, and heart rate."[11] There are also verified cases of reducing or eliminating severe pain through hypnosis, as well as hypnotic healings of skin conditions.[12] Since I will be discussing healing in another chapter, I won't say much about it here except to suggest that it often involves a kind of activation of healing powers that we don't consciously control. Hick claims that such a thing can occur at a distance, and as it turns out, there is considerable research into attempts to heal at a distance that provides some support for this claim.[13]

The idea of influence on the unconscious minds of others is also suggestive in relation to some well-known stories about answered prayer that don't involve healing. For example, there are multiple stories about prayer from the life of the nineteenth-century Christian minister George Mueller. Mueller cared for thousands of orphans for many years, but had a policy of never asking anyone but God for help. In one of the best-known stories, he didn't have anything to feed three hundred orphans for breakfast. Though there was nothing at the table, he had the children sit down, while he thanked God for the food that would be provided. Soon there was a knock at the door by a baker who said that he couldn't sleep the night before and baked three batches of bread that he felt Mueller would need. Minutes later, there was another knock on the door. The milkman's cart had broken down near the orphanage. The milk on the cart would spoil before the wheel could be fixed, so the milkman offered ten large cans of milk, which was enough for all the children.

I have no way of knowing whether the events occurred exactly as they are described, and I can't help but wonder whether there were times when things didn't turn out so well. But supposing that something like what is described happened, how should it be understood? The standard way of conceiving it is just to say that God intervened supernaturally to provide breakfast for the orphans. But if we have become familiar with accounts of extrasensory awareness, it might occur to us to think of Mueller's need as being communicated by extraordinary means at an unconscious level to those in a position to help, leading to impulses to

---

11. Kelly, "Psychophysiological Influence," 181–82.
12. Kelly, "Psychophysiological Influence," 185–99.
13. Radin, *Supernormal*, 208–13.

provide what was needed.[14] There are other stories that suggest something similar, including accounts where someone with no ordinary way to know about a particular pressing financial need of a charitable organization has an impulse to send precisely the amount of money required just in time to avoid curtailing the organization's work.[15]

Cases of extraordinary answers to prayer are intriguing. However, most of the things we pray for don't yield the kind of spectacular results that show us that our prayers were a decisive factor in some outcome. If I pray for someone's safety on a trip, the fact that the person comes back safely doesn't provide strong evidence that my prayers contributed to this result. But thinking in terms of petitionary prayer as communication to the unconscious allows one who prays to postulate that prayer may affect what happens. It might, for example, contribute to an unconscious impulse to exercise caution. Viewing prayer in this way can also enable the one who prays to account for why praying does not guarantee the desired result. Prayers for someone's safety, for example, might not be enough to overcome the consequences of bad decisions by other drivers.

When Results Don't Come

If we think that when we pray for something, we are basically making requests and that it is up to God to decide whether to bring about what we have requested, it is hard to avoid being disturbed by cases in which we fervently ask for some needed aid and don't get it. It may not be a problem in cases where we recognize that our request was selfish or ill-conceived. But sometimes we are praying for what seems clearly in accord with what we think we know of God's intentions for the world. We can always say in such cases that there are things we don't know or that the ways of God are mysterious. But this line of thought often rings hollow.

On the revised way of thinking about petitionary prayer that I have described, there are plausible reasons why we don't always receive what we ask for, even if our request is in harmony with what God seeks. One kind of reason is connected with how we are praying. We might speculate that the kind of generalized prayer to "bless all the missionaries in the world" or to "bring about world peace" is less likely to be effective than requests

14. There is an additional issue in the Mueller story of why the milk wagon breaks down at just the right time. I won't speculate on it, though one could tell a story in which psychic factors played a role.
15. White, *Christian Life and the Unconscious*, 133–34.

where we can envision and passionately desire a specific outcome. We might also think that some ways of praying are ineffective because of our enmeshment in cultural assumptions that block our wholehearted participation in making petitions. Recall from an earlier chapter the story of the Choco Christians whose prayers for a woman's cure didn't work when they had skeptical Westerners present. Ways of thinking that we have learned to cultivate, which are valuable in many practical endeavors, can get in the way of entering states of mind conducive to connecting with the unconscious minds of others. To pray more effectively, we may need to unlearn habits that block these connections.

Skeptical ideas can also influence our behavior. In our culture people often have a difficulty thinking that spending much effort in praying is a wise use of time. I recall a story about a group of seminary students visiting the monastery where Thomas Merton lived. Merton spoke to these students and answered their questions about the monastic life. One student asked a question that was likely also on the minds of others. He recognized that Merton was someone who could have accomplished great things in the outside world. So, he asked him why he had chosen to isolate himself in the monastery. Merton's response was immediate and concise. He simply said, "I believe in intercessory prayer." The unspoken point of his remark is that the wider culture, including Christian culture, does not value intercessory prayer in a way that would incline many people to devote so much effort to the practice.[16]

However, we shouldn't attribute a lack of results just to ineffective praying or an unwillingness to put in enough time and effort. Even if we are praying well, there may be other forces in play. I might be praying for peace for a war-torn country, but others may be doing things that promote continued conflict. I might pray for someone's healing, but there may be something in that person that resists healing. In other words, even if prayer can achieve significant results, the effectiveness of our prayers may depend on what forces are aligned in opposition to those ends. Perhaps this is where New Testament instructions to be persistent in prayer make sense. They don't make much sense if we imagine that we have to keep praying to persuade God to grant a request, but they might be understandable if we think of prayer as aiming at results that may be opposed by individuals or systems supporting conflicting ends.[17]

---

16. I heard this story from Glenn Hinson who accompanied the students.

17. Wink, *Powers That Be*, 187–98.

Sources of Uneasiness

A possible source of uneasiness with the model of petitionary prayer I have been describing is that it makes answers to prayer a product of human action, rather than supernatural intervention. If we think of petitionary prayer in terms of communicating something from one human mind to another, that seems to cut God out of the process. So, does this model imply that God is not involved? I think that it implies is that God is not involved in the way people often picture it, i.e., frequently overriding the course of nature in response to specific prayers. However, God might be involved in a different way. We might think, for example, that the presence of the divine Mind is always a potential influence toward the good, but, as Laubach claims, telepathic communication from the prayers of others can help people to "tune in" to divine influence. So, a prayer for healing, for example, might make God's healing power available.

Some Christians may be reluctant to think that an answer to prayer can depend on human action. However, we should notice that much of what happens in the world depends on what humans do. God gives us significant control over what happens by giving us ordinary powers to do things such as plant and harvest crops. When we pray for our daily bread, we are not usually asking that the ordinary means by which we might achieve beneficial results should be circumvented. We can thank God for our food because we recognize God as the ultimate source of a created order that enables us to secure food. Admittedly, the powers by which we grow crops or repair our automobiles are different from the psychic powers described in the revised model. But those psychic powers can be viewed as an extension of our influence on what happens. We can influence events, not just through ordinary physical acts, but through mental acts as well.

Some may worry that saying that answers to prayer can depend on human action might lead to considerable guilt when our prayers don't work. If answers to prayer are entirely a matter of what God decides to do, we can say that once we have prayed, the matter is in God's hands, but if our powers don't lead to a good result, it looks as if we have only ourselves to blame? However, this way of putting the matter overlooks the way blame might arise under the standard model. We can always raise the question of whether the failure to receive a desired result is a product of not praying in the right way. People who believe that prayer requests are sometimes granted often think that things could have turned out differently if they had been more focused or more persistent or that their own frailties weren't blocking more effective praying.

Furthermore, the idea that we are to blame if the desired result is not obtained should be considered in the light of the fact that the relevant psychic powers are not easily controlled. You can't by applying extra effort guarantee that your unconscious desires will affect someone else's unconscious thoughts and desires in a positive way. You may be able to cultivate states of mind in which such a thing is more likely, but blaming yourself seems a little like blaming yourself for not having a skill, such as playing the violin that is attainable only through practice and the right kind of aptitude. Most of us can acknowledge that there are people who are better prayers than we are without beating themselves up over it. Our awareness of more accomplished prayers sometimes motivates efforts to improve our own praying.

A different worry about the revised model of petitionary prayer is that it may erase the difference between prayer and magic. We know that there are people who cast spells or engage in strange rituals in an effort to achieve particular results by methods that bypass ordinary physical causality. Some of these practices we label as witchcraft. When we condemn such practices, we are usually imagining that there are some forces that shouldn't be tampered with or that some ways of utilizing these forces are objectionable. Someone who believes that prayer can involve a form of telepathic communication is certainly thinking that there are real forces in the world that don't reduce to physical forces. In that respect the person is like the ancient Hebrews who regarded words that bless or curse as potentially achieving real-world results. Even if some of the same forces utilized in petitionary prayer also play a role in magical practices, Christian efforts to achieve desirable results through prayer requests are surely distinguishable from many attempts to bend reality to our will. For Christians, attempts to produce desirable results presuppose a submission to God's purposes. There are things we shouldn't pray for because we know that they are contrary to what God seeks. When we do ask for something, we are ideally attempting to align ourselves with what God seeks for the world.

Nevertheless, should we be alarmed by the thought that if we can use psychic powers for good, they might also be used for evil purposes? Admittedly, such a thought is scary, but that is not really a reason to conclude that such powers do not exist. Ordinary human powers can be used for both good and evil purposes. Some ordinary powers in the hands of demagogues who warp our thinking and prey on misdirected desires can lead to evil on a massive scale. Along with the potential for good in the use of psychic powers, there is likely to be a potential for causing significant damage.

It is important, however, to put our fears of these powers in perspective. Popular media that dramatize superpowers are likely to give us an overblown picture of how such things work. Even if there are powers to influence someone in a harmful way, most of us have significant mental defenses against such things. Perhaps some of the self-destructive ideas that bubble up from my unconscious are connected with others' ill wishes for me, but I presumably have some control over impulses these ideas might generate. Admittedly, we can be overconfident about the degree of control we have over what enters our minds at unconscious levels. Recognizing that there are forces that may threaten our mental health and stability is not unrealistic. But it need not be an occasion for despair. Perhaps it is an occasion for testing messages we become aware of "to see whether they are from God" (1 John 4:1).

I suspect that attachment to what I have called the standard model of petitionary prayer is strong enough for many Christians that they won't be ready to consider the alternative I have described. They are used to thinking of this kind of prayer in the way it is typically spoken of in Scripture. People ask God for benefits such as healing, and God grants or doesn't grant the request. It seems natural to think of how God grants prayer requests as involving some kind of direct action to produce the desired result. What I have suggested is that *how* God is involved may be more complicated than this simple picture represents it to be. But that suggestion is a reflective conclusion that might be compared to cases in which we replace anthropomorphic portrayals of God, which are clearly in biblical texts, with alternative ways of understanding what God does.

I don't expect all Christians to be convinced by my suggestions. My remarks are mostly directed toward those who have found standard ways of thinking about petitionary prayer troubling. I am suggesting a way of thinking that might enable some who have given up on petitionary prayer or who do it only halfheartedly to reconsider the practice. However, I don't want to create unrealistic expectations. We won't all have experiences like the one Ken Gaub describes. Even if we have experiences that give us confidence in the power of prayer, we will likely continue to have experiences that frustrate us. Nevertheless, praying for desirable outcomes seems to me a central part of the Christian faith that we should be reluctant to give up, especially if we have a model of petitionary prayer that motivates us better than the standard model.

CHAPTER 14

Extraordinary Healing

THERE IS A STORY in the book of Acts about Peter and John seeing a lame man at the Temple gate begging for alms. According to the account, Peter tells the man that he doesn't have money to give, but commands him in the name of Jesus of Nazareth to stand up and walk (Acts 3:6). Peter's act strikes me as pretty audacious. If I imagine myself having the impulse to tell a lame man to get up and walk, I am pretty sure that I would be thinking about what a dumb idea that is. I would realize that if he doesn't get up, I am going to look foolish. Of course, part of the background story is that Peter has already seen some extraordinary things, and his act is reminiscent of what he had observed in the healing ministry of Jesus. Even so, he knows that in commanding the man to walk, he is taking a risk. I suspect that in our time very few Christians, even among those confident of the reality of extraordinary healings, would be willing to go out on this kind of limb.

New Testament scholar Craig Keener, whose writings present evidence that miraculous healings still occur in our time, describes an experience he had as a young Christian. He says that while he "believed in miracles *in principle*," he didn't expect to actually see one. As a college student, he was assisting in a Bible study at a nursing home. An older woman in a wheel chair repeatedly spoke about how she wished she could walk. The leader of the Bible study, a middle-aged seminary student, finally tired of her lament. He walked toward her, grabbed her hand and said, "In the name of Jesus Christ, I command you to rise up and walk." Keener had a feeling of panic. He imagined the woman falling to the floor and the Bible study group being banned forever. He could see from the woman's face that she was horrified at what was happening. But with her hand held by the one who had told her to walk, she took a few steps around the room before coming back to her wheelchair. In subsequent Bible studies she moved around the room while holding onto a walker for security, but in time she was able to walk on her own.[1]

The idea of a lame person walking after being given a command to do so is bound to seem astonishing to people with our understanding of how the world works. We might not give it a second thought if we learned that someone who could not previously walk could do so now because of a medical procedure. We might make room for such a thing in a case where the inability to walk is psychosomatic. Perhaps we could think of the command as a kind of shock therapy that removes some mental block that is producing lameness. But to most people in our culture, it is hard to believe that major physical problems disappear in the way stories of remarkable healings suggest. Even people who pray for someone to be healed in a situation where physicians offer little hope of such a thing can be shocked if what they pray for actually happens.

Hearing a Voice

Pediatrician Melvin Morse tells the story of an infant patient of his named Teryn Hedlund.[2] At four months of age, Teryn was dying of Wolman's disease, a usually fatal liver disease caused by a genetic defect. After an initial diagnosis, metabolic and liver specialists who examined her all agreed that she was going to die soon. Morse struggled with giving the news to the baby's parents, but knew that he had to tell them. They were stunned that their child could have a disease for which there was no effective treatment. Against all expectations, Teryn survived the initial crisis. Even though she was growing normally, Morse wasn't able to offer much hope for the long term. But after a year had passed, a liver biopsy showed no indications of the disease.

When it was evident that Teryn was getting better, her mother told Morse how she believed her daughter had been healed. She said her brother-in-law had cured Teryn. To get a fuller account of what had happened,

---

1. Keener, *Miracles Today*, xi–xii.
2. Morse and Perry, *Parting Visions*, 124–27; *Where God Lives*, 112–14.

Morse contacted the brother-in-law who told him that on the night of the fatal diagnosis, he heard a voice telling him to go immediately and put his hands on Teryn's abdomen. He said, "The voice was loud and insistent, and I almost thought about getting up and doing what it told me to do, but I didn't. 'I'll do it tomorrow,' I said.... Then the voice spoke up again. It said, 'Go tonight. Tomorrow will be too late.'"[3]

The brother-in-law said that he was not a particularly spiritual or religious man, but with a sense of urgency, he went to the Hedlund house. The family assumed he had come to offer emotional support. He asked to hold the baby and to be alone with her. When this was allowed, he took her into another room and, though feeling ridiculous, put his hands on Teryn's abdomen as he had been instructed to do. He told Morse that he felt a warmth and a faint glow coming from his fingers.[4]

There are people who claim to have healing gifts who might describe such an experience. But the brother-in-law had no pretensions of having any healing powers. Nothing like this had ever happened to him before. He found these events to be as strange as they might sound to others. Some people having his experience might have said that the instructions about what to do came from God, but he spoke only of a voice. It seemed crazy to him to do what he did, but he felt a compelling urge to do it.

No doubt many people will question whether this account of events is accurate or claim that even if it happened as reported, there is not enough reason to connect the laying on of hands and the anomalous cure. However, stories of extraordinary healings are common, and even if we cannot draw firm conclusions from an individual case, looking at many cases of remarkable healings is conducive to thinking that there are healing powers beyond what we think of as ordinary.

I will return later to the question of how to conceive of such powers, but for now I want to focus on what sounds like an extrasensory awareness by the brother-in-law that tells him what needs to be done to cure Teryn. The awareness in this case comes through a voice giving him instructions. We have already seen examples in other chapters of people receiving extrasensory information in the form of an audible voice. Extrasensory information may also come through dreams or visions or persistent thoughts that some action is needed. We might think of the instructions the brother-in-law receives as coming from God, but

---

3. Morse and Perry, *Parting Visions*, 126.
4. Morse and Perry, *Where God Lives*, 112–13.

that interpretation is not inconsistent with thinking that God's message comes to him from his unconscious mind.

Here is another story of hearing a voice; this time the voice is heard in a dream. Jane Katra hadn't prayed since she was a child. Prayer had never made much sense to her. But she was driven to prayer one day by a debilitating headache from which she could get no relief. After praying, she was finally able to sleep. When she did, she had what she called a "vivid, startling, phenomenal dream." In the dream she was given instructions about doing healing with her hands. The message came from what she called "an extremely bright light." She resisted the instructions, having no desire to become a healer. She said, "You can't make me do it." The voice coming from the light told her that she wouldn't be forced, that it would be her choice. It talked to her in a way that she thought suggested compassion. However, she calls the experience an "interminably long tutorial."[5]

In the dream Katra was told about people she would meet and events that would occur. The voice said that two men would mentor her as she became a healer. She was given specific words they would say that would allow her to identify them. She was also told that on the next day she would put her hands on a stranger who would be healed. The voice said that she would not remember her dream until the healing had occurred. Toward the end of the dream, she was told to "hold out her hand." Then she says, "I was zapped with blinding light."

Katra says, "No one was more surprised than I when the events came to pass, when I met the people who had been described to me."[6] Those meetings came later. The encounter with a stranger occurred the next day. On her way to a meeting, she saw a woman lying on a couch in a hotel hallway. Hearing the woman groan, she asked her if she was alright. The woman said that she was in agony. She had been having a migraine headache for two days, and was so nauseated and dizzy that she couldn't walk. Her husband had gone to get a doctor. Katra offered to wait with her and asked if she could massage her scalp while they waited to see if that helped. She had barely started the massage when the woman thanked her. Katra said that she hadn't really done anything. The woman said, "Oh yes you did! I felt it when you brought your hands near. I felt the surge of energy! . . . It took the pain right away! . . . It felt

---

5. Targ and Katra, *Miracles of Mind*, 155–57.
6. Targ and Katra, *Miracles of Mind*, 156.

like your hands opened a dam and all the pain just poured out!"[7] It was only at this point that Katra remembered the dream.

One more story involving a mysterious voice—only in this case the voice is heard by a person who receives healing. Barbara Cummiskey was diagnosed as a teenager with multiple sclerosis.[8] From ages fifteen to thirty-one she was in the hospital most of the time. She had chronic pulmonary disease with frequent infections. One of her lungs was nonfunctional. The other operated at only 50-percent capacity. She was hooked up to devices that maintained her bodily functions. She hadn't been able to walk for seven years. Her feet were pointed in a way that made her unable to put them flat on the floor. Her arms were locked in a position against her body. In fact, her body was stuck in a kind of fetal position. She was blind except for a small area in each eye. After sixteen years of physical deterioration, the doctors sent her home from the hospital to die.

People from her church were visiting her when she heard a voice over her shoulder saying, "My child: Get up and walk." She was attached to a breathing tube and could speak only when someone plugged the hole in her neck. When those present saw her agitation, they plugged the hole, and she said, "God just told me to get up and walk." In her condition, it usually took several minutes for others to slide her out of bed and into a chair. But with a sense of urgency, she got herself out of bed and was able to stand. Her hands had moved to her side, and she realized that she was no longer blind. She extricated herself from the tubes enough to walk, even making her way down the wheelchair ramp and out of the house.

The next day she was examined by the doctors who had sent her home from the hospital to die. The x-rays showed that her lung was no longer collapsed, and other tests indicated normal functioning. The astonished doctors declared that what had happened was medically impossible: she was completely cured. When Craig Keener interviewed her many years later, she was living a normal life without any recurrence of multiple sclerosis. He confirmed details of the case with doctors who were involved.

---

7. Targ and Katra, *Miracles of Mind*, 159.
8. Keener, *Miracles Today*, xii–xvi.

Healing Power

Some healing stories describe a surge of energy flowing from one person to another. Healers often think of what they are doing as transmitting energy that has physical effects on the patient's body. Jane Katra says that she often feels something like an energy flow, but she also describes sensing a kind of mind-to-mind attunement with the patient. She came to believe that this connection between minds was the most important aspect of healing. She conceives of what occurs as a merging of minds through which healing information becomes available to the patient.

Most healers think of themselves as channels through which a power greater than their own becomes available. Christian healers emphasize that the power through which they heal comes from God. In the story mentioned at the beginning of this chapter Peter commands a man to walk in the name of Jesus. As in other New Testament narratives, he is following the example of Jesus who is confident of his ability to connect with divine power to heal. The teachings of Jesus have led Peter to believe that in continuing the mission of Jesus, he also has access to the kind of power by which Jesus healed. One way of acknowledging this access is to invoke the authority of Jesus.

Healers from traditions other than Christianity describe the source of their power in different ways, and some Christian healers have described their power in ways that suggest there can be healing outside of Christian contexts. The famed Christian healer Olga Worrall speaks of tuning her personal energy into harmonious relationship with what she calls "the universal field of energy." She describes the healer "as a conductor between the universal field of energy and the patient."[9] The tuning-in she speaks of appears to involve a withdrawal from an awareness of ordinary sensation to enter what Olga's husband Ambrose (also a healer) called a "realm of intuition." In a phrase that resonates with accounts from mystical literature, he says that the power to heal comes from "out of the silence."[10]

Katra characterizes the desired state of mind as different from controlling something, more like allowing something to happen. She calls it a "peaceful state of surrender."[11] But in addition to cultivating this state of mind for herself, she found it vital to try to get the patient into a relaxed

---

9. Olga Worrall quoted in Targ and Katra, *Miracles of Mind*, 258.
10. Ambrose Worrall quoted in Mayer, *Extraordinary Knowing*, 172.
11. Targ and Katra, *Miracles of Mind*, 174.

state without self-conscious thoughts. In her experience the connection with another person is sometimes severed by distracting thoughts or emotions, either from the healer or from the patient. Recall my suggestion in chapter 1 that healing can sometimes involve a kind of group consciousness that might be blocked.

In her early experiences, Katra would touch the patient, but she discovered that healing could occur without touch. She could put her hands near someone or be on the other side of the room or even in a distant location. We might postulate that touch is sometimes a vehicle for getting into the right state of mind. Harold (the dowser mentioned in chapter 5 who located the missing harp) suggested that the use of a dowsing rod is conducive to accessing a kind of knowledge that is in the body as much as in the mind:

> The rods let your body tell you what your subconscious mind knows. The rods free you up that way. They give you a way to stop your brain from stopping all the rest of you from knowing. But master dowsers, they've learned how to contact the knowing real directly. So for them the rods don't matter anymore. They don't need them.[12]

Self-Healing

We might conceive of the influence in healing as activating someone's capacity for self-healing. In other chapters I have pointed out that the subconscious mind knows how to do things that we cannot do by conscious effort. Skilled meditators use this knowledge when they learn to control bodily processes that ordinarily function automatically. There are also well confirmed examples of people given hypnotic suggestions, leading to changes in their bodies that alleviate physical problems such as inflammation, burns, skin disorders, and asthma. People in a hypnotic trance are in a state that makes the subconscious mind receptive to suggestions. But influence conducive to health can occur without a trance state. Consider, for example, the placebo effect.

In paradigm cases the placebo effect involves a medical professional doing something whose therapeutic benefit is achieved by influencing the patient's mind. It might be by giving a medication that in physical terms shouldn't be effective in lowering blood pressure or slowing the

---

12. Mayer, *Extraordinary Knowing*, 170.

progress of cancer, but nevertheless has those results. What a healthcare professional does might not even be a medical procedure at all. It might, for example, be a matter of soothing words that evoke a sense of confidence. The placebo effect occurs because what is done affects the mental state of the patient in a way that contributes to restoring health. Because we recognize that some therapeutic benefits come about this way, tests of the efficacy of new drugs or medical procedures are done using experimental designs to measure whether something in addition to the placebo effect accounts for positive outcomes.

The placebo effect works because a patient's belief that healing is occurring can help trigger the unconscious mind's capacity for self-healing. Things can work in the opposite way as well. Patients who are given a bleak diagnosis can take it to heart, resulting in negative health outcomes. (This phenomenon is sometimes called the nocebo effect.) A story that is well-known in social science literature shows how powerful the placebo effect can be: Psychologist Bruno Klopfer describes the case of a patient he calls Mr. Wright.[13] Mr. Wright had advanced cancer of the lymph nodes with tumors the size of oranges. Specialists thought he was near death. One day Mr. Wright overheard references to a new cancer drug called krebiozen, which was being tested at the hospital he was in. He asked to receive the drug. Even though his doctor thought the drug would not help him at a stage of the disease so advanced, he secured enough of it to give Mr. Wright an injection. Three days after injection of the drug Mr. Wright was able to get out of his hospital bed. His tumors gradually shrunk. Within ten days, he was released from the hospital cancer free.

Two months later Mr. Wright read news reports that the krebiozen trial had shown that the drug was not effective as a cancer treatment. Soon after, his tumors returned, and he was back in the hospital. At this point, his doctor lied to him, telling him that the news reports were wrong. He also told Mr. Wright that he had been given a dose from a weak batch of the drug and gave him an injection from a supposedly stronger batch. Again, the tumors shrunk, and Mr. Wright left the hospital. But after he heard another news report about the ineffectiveness of the drug, the tumors reappeared, and he was dead within a few days.

Several things about this story stand out. First, the remarkable cure from a condition for which no effective medical treatment was available apparently comes about entirely because of positive expectations of the

---

13. Klopfer, "Psychological Variables in Human Cancer," 331–40.

patient. His belief that he is getting a new wonder drug resulted in his cancer going away. Second, when he loses confidence that the treatment is medically effective, his disease returns. Remarkably, the process of gaining confidence and losing it is repeated. He gets better when he thinks something has been done that will cure him, and he gets worse when he no longer believes such a thing.

The placebo effect can work without anything paranormal occurring. But in addition to the patient observing and making inferences about the beneficial effects of some kind of therapy, we can posit in some cases what Katra called a merging of minds that stimulates the patient's mind in a way that is conducive to activating self-healing processes. Some people may be particularly skilled at providing this kind of influence, but acts of focused attention in prayer by those who have no specialized skills may also play a role in activating a patient's unconscious capacities for self-healing.

Self-healing can occur without another human agent. Physician Larry Dossey tells the story of a man from Tennessee named David Pack who injured his arm in an arm-wrestling match. Despite six months of medical treatment, the pain and disability were severe enough that he had to give up his job in the construction business. Before going to sleep one night, he suggested to himself that his arm would be healed. He dreamed that night of a man poking around his elbow, which caused him pain. In the dream he asked the man what he was doing and was told, "You have received two healings." On waking, he felt his arm tingling, as if it was asleep. When the tingling stopped, he found that the arm was "good as new." Later that week he learned about the second healing. A cyst on his back burst, relieving him of chronic pain that had troubled him for ten years.[14]

If we think of our unconscious minds as knowing how to harness bodily processes that can cure various diseases and disabilities, Pack's dream looks like a kind of enlistment of this knowledge. It is as if he invites his unconscious mind to heal him as he sleeps, and in response his mind sets in motion processes that fulfill the request. Surely, however, there are limits to what the body can do for itself. If we imagine Pack as having lost his arm, it would be hard to believe that he could have a dream that results in growing a new one.

---

14. Dossey, *Healing Words*, 74.

Even if we cannot specify precisely what the limits of self-healing powers might be, it is reasonable to be skeptical about some claims. For example, the story of Barbara Cummiskey mentioned earlier in this chapter includes a claim I didn't mention of instant restoration of muscles that have atrophied after years of disuse. Such a thing is rarely reported, even in stories of extraordinary healing. So, we might wonder whether there has been exaggeration. Nevertheless, there can be astonishing results that are not exaggerated. Some well substantiated stories suggest that the immune system can be activated to cure what we thought was incurable, and there are accounts that suggest a capacity of the body to do what seems like a reset to normal functioning, extending even to the genetic level.[15]

When Healing Doesn't Happen

New Testament scholar Craig Keener has written several books in which he gives accounts of healing miracles from all over the world. He wants to show that spectacular healings—including the blind receiving sight, the deaf hearing, lame people walking, and even the dead being raise—still happen in our time. However, Keener acknowledges that miraculous healings are the exception rather than the rule. He gives examples of people he knows who were not healed, but died in the prime of life. He says that he understands why people who work in places like cancer wards or hospice care, where they see suffering and death more often than miraculous recoveries, are likely to develop a cynical attitude toward the kinds of stories he tells.[16]

If extraordinary healing occurs sometimes, why doesn't it occur more often? The question is difficult to answer if we think that the decisive factor in who receives healing is God's decision that a particular individual be healed. We wonder why the power to bring about beneficial results is withheld most of the time. But suppose we think about extraordinary healings in a different way. Suppose that such healings occur when human beings connect with powers that are available in the natural order, but not ordinarily under our control.

One reason for the difficulty in accessing these powers is that our culture predisposes us to doubt about extraordinary events. Recall the story

15. Morse and Perry, *Where God Lives*, 115–16.
16. Keener, *Miracles Today*, 221.

in the first chapter in which indigenous Christians are able to participate in prayer for healing with the expectation that it can lead to the desired result, whereas westernized Christians find their participation hampered by a skeptical mindset connected with their scientific understanding. It is likely no accident that reports of extraordinary healing are more common in places where there are fewer cultural blocks to the possibility.

But even if we can get past our skeptical presumptions, another reason for the difficulty of using these powers is that the practices that might enable us to connect with them seem to involve a letting go of control, which contrasts with our usual thought patterns. Recall Katra's suggestion that the state of mind in which healing occurs involves a "peaceful state of surrender." No doubt there are individuals who are relatively adept at getting into such a state, but there is something paradoxical about being able to surrender, while also striving to achieve a particular result. The point here is not to deny that extraordinary healing sometimes occurs. It is instead to suggest that bringing about conditions conducive to it doesn't come easily to us. Stories of extraordinary healing that focus on successes can distract us from the fact that even gifted healers cannot heal on demand.

But if powers that might lead to extraordinary healing are difficult to connect with, why doesn't God make it easier? A complete answer to this question would likely call for a fuller understanding of the nature of psychic powers. However, even without such an understanding, one thing that seems evident is that greater control over powers of this kind is easily corrupted by the wrong motivations. There are hints in the New Testament that God's ultimate plan for the created order is to give human beings an enhanced ability to bring about results that seem to us extraordinary. But this step might be counterproductive without a greater degree of harmony between our aims and God's purposes that enables us to use these powers wisely. Until this kind of harmony is more fully realized, extraordinary healings can be thought of as previews of a time when human beings can assume a fuller role as co-creators.

Christians fall on a kind of spectrum with regard to their attitude toward extraordinary healing. In some Christian groups this kind of healing is believed to be a frequent occurrence. Expecting that it will occur functions as something like a default attitude. But there are problems with expecting too much. One is a tendency toward gullibility. If you are expecting miracles to be everywhere, you may find them even when there is little reason to think that anything extraordinary has happened.

Another problem is that in a community that celebrates frequent miraculous healings, there is often a pressure to manufacture instances of the extraordinary by questionable means. Even people with significant healing gifts can sometimes succumb to the pressure to perform.

At the opposite end of the spectrum, there are Christian groups where people are predisposed to treat claims about extraordinary healing with suspicion. The problem with expecting too little is twofold. First, it leads to attitudes that are in tension with entering into the states of mind conducive to healing. Second, it blocks our ability to recognize extraordinary outcomes when they do occur. What we are able to see is clouded by the habit of assuming that such things do not happen.

These two extremes are not the only possibilities. We can have a mindset that is open to recognizing extraordinary events without finding them everywhere. We can think that because such events are the exception to the rule, some degree of skepticism is called for. But it doesn't have to be a level of skepticism that is closed to the possibility of the unexpected. We can think that surprising occurrences are sometimes indications of a deeper reality than we are used to breaking through. If we view such occurrences in the light of the Christian story, we may see them as pointing toward a time when the exceptional will come closer to being the rule.

CHAPTER 15

Hauntings, Organ Transplants, and Past Lives

SOMETIMES OUR QUESTIONS ARE badly formed. For example, the question, "Do you believe in ghosts?" invites a yes or no answer. But answering yes or no calls for having a particular conception of what a ghost is. A popular idea is that a ghost would be a dead person who for some reason is still hanging around earthly sites. There are numerous stories describing some kind of "unfinished business" that needs to be taken care of before moving on to the next plane of existence. In many of these stories some living person who is able to make contact with these beings helps them on their way.

However, thinking that the issue is settled by deciding that there are or are not beings who meet some particular description of this type distracts us from other possibilities. It is like asking whether you believe in UFOs. Typically, when people ask this question, they want to know whether you think there are beings from another planet who have visited earth in space ships. But you might think that even if there are not such beings, UFO experiences shouldn't be written off as made-up stories or experiences of ordinary phenomena that have been misinterpreted. Similarly, you might reject some popular understanding of ghosts, but think that when people report seeing a ghost, there is a genuine question of how to understand the significance of the experience.

In considering the question of what a ghostly encounter might mean, it is important to notice that there is not just one kind of experience, but distinguishable types that might be described as experiencing a ghost. For example, the phenomenon that I earlier called *crisis apparitions* sometimes involve seeing an appearance of a person near the time of their death at a distant location. Another kind of experience, sometimes called *postmortem apparitions*, involves perceptions of an individual at a time that is clearly after that person's death. Additionally, there is the *poltergeist* ("noisy spirit") *phenomenon*. In cases of this type there are strange physical events that are sometimes attributed to unseen entities. Another type of case, which I will call *hauntings*, involves anomalous sensory phenomena at a particular location that are typically perceived on multiple occasions by different individuals. There can be overlap between these types, but lumping all such cases together as ghost stories can misleadingly suggest that there is a single kind of explanation for diverse phenomena.

I considered poltergeist phenomena in chapter 10. These cases involve physical effects that have been attributed to unseen entities, but the events center around the presence of a single living person who is likely to be unintentionally causing the phenomena by psychokinetic influence. Crisis apparitions involve extrasensory awareness through an impression or a vision that conveys information about what is happening to someone at a distant location. I am reserving a discussion of post-mortem apparitions for a later chapter. In this chapter I want to deal briefly with what I call hauntings, as well as some other phenomena that might be understood as having similar causes.

Hauntings

Hauntings involve anomalous visual or other kinds of sense experiences connected with a particular location. A person may see apparitions or hear sounds that suggest some ghostly presence, for example, at a house or a historical battlefield. In a typical case the phenomena recur for the same individual or others. Sometimes one person will have the experience when others in the same location do not. The apparitions typically engage in repetitive action and seem unaware of any living presences. In a common type of case what is seen or heard seems like a reenactment of some previous behavior. In some cases, investigation suggests a connection between what is reenacted and some traumatic event, such as a murder. For many of these stories there are plausible ordinary explanations of the experience in terms of physical causes or human suggestibility, and some accounts have been exposed as hoaxes. But there are also credible accounts of this kind of experience that seem difficult to explain without positing something beyond what we think of as ordinary.

Stories of ghostly hauntings have been reported for thousands of years by people in many different cultures. The reports come from educated and uneducated individuals, from those at the top of the social hierarchy as well as those at the bottom.[1] Many of the stories should be discounted for various reasons, but there are also some that have been investigated by competent researchers who have judged the reports credible and are unable to find plausible ordinary explanations. An important effort to investigate some accounts was made in the nineteenth century by members of the Society for Psychical Research. One of the most famous haunting cases they investigated involved the Cheltenham House in England.[2]

The first sightings there were by Rosina Despard in 1882. She was a nineteen-year-old medical student at the time who lived with her family. She wasn't seeking publicity. When the case was investigated, she used a pseudonym because she feared that the report might jeopardize her medical career and because her father thought that it might affect property values. Her experiences followed a common pattern. She would hear a noise suggesting a pushing of her bedroom door and footsteps outside. On opening the door, she would see a female figure. Here is an excerpt from her written account:

> The figure was that of a tall lady, dressed in black of a soft woolen material, judging from the slight sound in moving. The face was hidden in a handkerchief held in the right hand. . . . On further occasions I was able to observe her more closely. I saw the upper part of the left side of the forehead, and a little of the hair above. Her left hand was nearly hidden by her sleeve and a fold of the dress. . . . The whole impression was that of a lady in widow's weeds.[3]

---

1. Schmicker, *Best Evidence*, 212.
2. Society for Psychical Research, "Cheltenham Ghost."
3. Morton, "Record of a Haunted House," 313.

During a two-year period, she saw the figure about half a dozen times. Before she had told other people about her experiences, the figure was seen by three other individuals. Her sister saw the woman in black while coming down the stairs and asked whether the lady would be joining them for dinner. A housemaid who saw the figure was concerned that someone had broken into the house. Rosina's younger brother saw the lady while he was playing outside with a friend.

In subsequent years the figure was seen by around twenty people: family members, servants, and visitors. In a few cases a sighting was by two people at the same time. Most of the sightings were brief, but one lasted for around half an hour. Until 1886 the figure appeared solid and lifelike and was sometimes mistaken for a living person. After that, the appearances were less distinct, and after 1887 sounds were heard but no one was seen. Investigators confirmed that the descriptions of the figure were similar, even from those who had not previously heard of the phenomenon. They also noted that the family members were unusually free of fear and superstition.

Psychology professor Erlendur Haraldsson's research has led to a collection of more recent accounts of what he calls localized apparitions.[4] In one account, a woman arrives after midnight at a house to stay with some acquaintances. She thinks that everyone may be asleep, but sees a man inside pacing in the front room. She knocks and calls out, but he doesn't seem to notice. She ends up staying elsewhere. Later in a hotel some women are talking about the house where her acquaintances live. They ask her if she has seen the ghost that lives there. She says that she has not, but tells them about seeing the man pacing. One of the women pulls out a photo of a cousin who died when building the house. She recognizes the man that she saw pacing and is told that he had often been seen in the house.

Other stories in the collection describe similar experiences of seeing an apparitional figure associated with some place. One young lady is staying with her aunt when she sees a woman from the back who disappears when the light is switched on. When she tells her aunt what she saw, she is told that the figure has been seen by many people. In another account, a woman staying in a rented room frequently feels a presence and sometimes sees a man whom she thinks of as friendly and pleasant.

---

4. Haraldsson, *Departed Among the Living*, 145–52.

When she gives a description of the man, she is told that her description matches a man who had committed suicide there.

Sociologist Charles Emmons, who has done cross-cultural studies of ghostly encounters, notes that reports of these experiences in different cultures are very similar.[5] The similarities are apparent even when what is reported diverges from cultural expectations. For example, he notes that in Chinese culture people tend to be afraid of ghosts, typically assuming some violent intent. But in reports of such experiences in this culture, indications of evil intent are rare. Most often, the apparitions seem oblivious to the living.[6]

In many cases, it is hard to determine whether a story about a haunting should be judged credible, and often the details are not sufficient to rule out ordinary explanations. Some people think that all such stories should be written off as hoaxes or as due to confusion. Others take some of these stories as evidence that dead people sometimes remain attached to an earthly location. However, consider an alternative response to cases where ordinary explanations seem insufficient.

Psychologist Alan Gauld proposes that they should be thought of as instances of *retrocognition*, an extrasensory perception of past events.[7] The repetitive acts that occur in haunting cases suggest something like memories of past events that are somehow perceived as three-dimensional images that replay in a way that seems analogous to a video loop. Some stories describe perceptions of such things as historical battles in which soldiers dressed appropriately for the time period reenact the fighting. Generally, what is seen or heard is connected with events that had a strong emotional impact. In some reports, images that were previously more vivid seem to fade over time.

For people who are used to thinking of memories as stored in individual brains, the idea of a memory that might be picked up by someone in a particular location seems odd. But people who accept extrasensory perception often posit that what is perceived by such means becomes available when an individual's unconscious mind connects with some larger consciousness. Physician Melvin Morse suggests that accessing past memories involves a link to a universal mind in which the memories are stored.[8] He posits that some people have a sensitive right tem-

---

5. Emmons and Emmons, *Science and Spirit*, 102.
6. Emmons and Emmons, *Science and Spirit*, 109–10.
7. Gauld, *Mediumship and Survival*, 248–49.
8. Morse and Perry, *Where God Lives*, 85.

poral lobe of the brain that enables them to become aware of memories linked to particular places that they experience in an externalized three-dimensional form. He says, "The memory is usually perceived in the same way by all who tap into it."[9]

I am sure that many people will find such ideas far-fetched. But in the rest of the chapter, I will be describing several other types of puzzling phenomena that might make sense if we think that there is a human capacity for accessing memories that come from sources other than our individual experience. I am not suggesting that hauntings or the other phenomena I mention prove that such a thing occurs. But if we accept the reality of extrasensory capacities, thinking of apparently unrelated phenomena that we find puzzling as explainable in terms of extrasensory access to what others have remembered may seem worth considering.

Transplant Stories

Stories of hauntings strike most of us as bizarre. Another kind of story that has arisen in more recent times seems equally bizarre. There are now numerous reports of people who after an organ transplant take on characteristics that differ from those they had previously, but correspond to characteristics of the organ donor. I'll give only one example of this kind of story, but it should be noted that quite a few examples of this type have come to light.

In one case the donor of a heart was a seventeen-year-old black male. The heart recipient was a forty-seven-year-old white foundry worker. The donor loved classical music and aspired to play in Carnegie Hall someday. He was on his way to violin practice when he was shot and died. The recipient claimed not to be a racist, but was troubled when he heard that he had received a black person's heart. A surprising change after the operation was that the donor developed a love for classical music, something he previously had no interest in. He reasoned that this change had nothing to do with the operation because he thought that black people would not be into this kind of music.

According to the man's wife, her husband had raised the question before the operation of whether he could ask for a white person's heart. She described his attitudes as not quite Archie Bunker's, but as close to

---

9. Morse and Perry, *Where God Lives*, 85.

them. After the operation, she was shocked when he began to invite black people from his work to their house. She observed,

> He seems more comfortable and at ease with these black guys, but he is not aware of it. And one more thing I should say: he's driving me nuts with the classical music.... He never listened to it before. Now he sits for hours and listens to it.... You'd think he'd like rap music or something because of his black heart.[10]

This story is not an isolated case. There are numerous instances in which the transplant recipient seems to take on characteristics of the donor, even without much specific knowledge of the donor. These cases might be compared to cases in which someone seems to be possessed by an alien personality, but they don't involve a total takeover. What occurs is more like some kind of strange influence. If we ask how such influence occurs, ordinary explanations seem to fail. If the story had been about a brain transplant, we might have thought that the mind of the donor had been transferred to a different body. But it seems strange to think that particular features of the mental life of the donor could accompany a heart.

Suppose, however, that we think of what is going on in these cases as analogous to the way I have described haunting cases, i.e., in terms of accessing someone else's memories. In either case it is puzzling how such memories could be acquired. It is difficult to imagine houses or bodily organs as containing memory traces. Perhaps, however, that is the wrong way to think about how these memories might be accessed. If people in a particular location experience what I have likened to video replays of previous events in a haunting case, we could imagine the location acting as a kind of stimulus that unlocks an extrasensory capacity to sense phenomena connected with that location. In other words, the location might play a role in bringing to conscious awareness information that is accessible through the unconscious mind.

Think of the subliminal mind as having access to a large range of information that we do not possess at the level of ordinary consciousness. Our minds at an unconscious level might be thought of as scanning information we have access to and picking out items that are relevant to our concerns. So, for example, the death of a loved one at a distant location may emerge from this informational storehouse and then impinge on conscious awareness in a way that brings it to our attention. Similarly, we might think of the unconscious mind as picking

---

10. Braude, *Immortal Remains*, 238–39.

out as relevant information about the place where we are or about the donor of a heart that is now in our body.

In a haunting case the information seems to come into conscious awareness as sights and sounds. In a transplant case, it apparently shows itself through behaviors characteristic of the donor. We might imagine the unconscious mind as putting the various memories together in a way that leads to behavioral dispositions consistent with them. For example, memories of liking classical music might incline one to listen to it. Admittedly, this account is speculative, but remember that we are dealing with cases in which ordinary explanations seem to fail. If we have independent grounds for thinking that extrasensory perception is real, then we may find it plausible to view these cases in terms of extrasensory access to someone's else's memories.

Cases Suggestive of Reincarnation

Consider another kind of case that might seem unrelated to either hauntings or transplant cases. Ian Stevenson, a professor for many years at the University of Virginia, was a pioneer in modern research into cases that suggest reincarnation.[11] Much of his research involved cases in which a young child, typically between the ages of two and four, claims to be someone who has lived a previous life. In these cases, the child describes memories and exhibits behaviors and desires that seem to correspond to those of a particular individual who has died. Most of the cases come from countries in which reincarnation is widely accepted, however, there are a significant number of examples from countries in which the idea is less commonly believed.

When it is determined that the person the child talks about corresponds to an actual individual who died before the child's birth, Stevenson and subsequent investigators have attempted to determine whether information about the individual provided by the child could have been received through normal means. There are often strong reasons to rule out any connections between the families involved. In the strongest cases, information reported by the child includes unique and sometimes quirky facts about the life of the identified person that turn out to be true. In some of these cases the child is taken to visit the family

11. One of Stevenson's early works was *Twenty Cases Suggestive of Reincarnation*. His work has been carried on at the University of Virginia by Jim Tucker, whose writings include *Life Before Life*.

of the deceased person and immediately recognizes and knows details about these family members and about the location, while failing to recognize people that person didn't know.

In most of these cases, the person the child identifies with died a violent death. Often the child will have phobias that correspond to the way the person died, such as extreme fear of water or snakes or guns. In about a third of these cases the child has birthmarks or deformities that correspond to the person's death, such as marks resembling a gunshot wound in someone whose death came about that way. In addition, sometimes the child has cravings corresponding to interests of the individual, including cravings for distinctive foods, or for alcohol, cigarettes, or sex. The child may seek to dress as the person would have dressed, including cases where that person was of a different gender. There are also cases in which the child possesses skills the deceased person had that the child has not learned. These include such things as speaking in a different language or with a different dialect, or playing a musical instrument. The memories and behaviors associated with a past life tend to fade by the age of seven.

Some competent researchers who have studied the evidence think that some cases provide strong evidence in support of reincarnation. But looking at these cases in the light of the explanation I have considered in hauntings and transplant cases suggests another possibility. The primary evidence for reincarnation in these cases consists of memories that couldn't have been accessed in the ordinary way and behaviors associated with those memories. I have posited that hauntings and transplant cases might be explained in terms of memories accessed through extrasensory means. One thing that stands out about the cases in which a child seems to possess memories of someone who has died is that in most of these cases the individual had a violent death. Something similar is often suggested in haunting cases, and it is likely true in the relevant transplant cases. We might suspect that the emotional impact of memories of violent events makes them more likely to be accessible by extrasensory means.

But even if a child acquires memories of someone who has died, why does the child take himself or herself to be that person? A plausible answer is that having memories that don't fit with one's current life can be understood in only a limited number of ways. Someone might think that they are false memories, but a child who remembers particular events vividly is not likely to think in these terms. Another possibility would be to think that the memories are someone else's, but the vividness of the memories can make them difficult to distinguish from one's own. So, it may seem natural of think of the memories as being one's own, but from a previous time. Hence, the child comes think such things as, "I used to have a job in which I worked in a factory," or "I used to have children."

There is another piece of evidence, however, that is cited to show that the child is correct in his or her claims about a previous existence. In a significant number of cases there are birth defects or bodily abnormalities that correspond to the way someone died. Someone who accepts reincarnation could say that the consciousness of the deceased person produces physical effects on the body of the developing fetus. But if mental causation of physical effects is accepted, someone who is skeptical of reincarnation could say that the effects come from the mind of a mother who through some extrasensory process acquires an unconscious awareness of the deceased person's memories. Either claim about the birth defects sounds speculative. But someone who thinks that the mind of a deceased individual can have a causal influence on a child may find it hard to rule out the possibility that the mind of a living individual could have the same kind of influence on the child's physical and mental development.

Reincarnation and Possession

The idea that a child is a reincarnation of someone who previously died can seem like a plausible way to account for how the child has particular memories or behavioral traits. But suppose we investigate and discover that the person whose memories have been acquired didn't die until after the child was born. Stevenson himself cites two such cases in which there are verifiable memories like those in cases that he thinks suggest reincarnation, but the memories are of someone who was alive when the child was born.[12] He doesn't consider these cases as instances of reincarnation. He classifies them instead as possession cases. He also says that it can be unclear whether some cases should be described as reincarnation or possession.

Consider a well-known possession case from nineteenth-century Illinois. At the age of fourteen, Lurancy Vennum was subject to trances in which she seemed to be possessed by various spirits. Eventually, she declared that she was Mary Roof, the daughter of a neighbor family who

---

12. Stevenson, *Twenty Cases*, 376.

had died in an insane asylum nine years previously. She said things and behaved in ways that convinced others that she had Mary's memories and other traits. Mary's family came to believe that Mary had returned in Lurancy's body. For a time, she lived with the Roofs where she was accepted as their daughter. She fitted in well with her new family, and when Mr. and Mrs. Vennum visited her, she responded to them as strangers. Then, after a period of eight or nine weeks the Lurancy consciousness returned, intermittently at first, but then more fully. She returned home, claiming that what had happened seemed like a dream to her.[13]

It is not difficult to see why some people might conceive what happens in this case in terms of possession by an alien spirit.[14] Psychiatrists in our time would likely label what happened as an instance of dissociative identity disorder (what used to be called multiple personality

13. James, "On Mediumship," 52–53.

14 In the Gospels we find frequent references to possession by evil spirits. It is no secret that some Christians regard these accounts as teaching that evil spirits are real, but other Christians resist this kind of literal interpretation. In some groups it is taken for granted that encounters with angels or demons are frequent occurrences. However, I grew up in a very conservative branch of Christianity where I heard respected members of the congregation suggest that the accounts of demon possession in the New Testament should be understood as what we would call a form of mental illness. The idea was that biblical people were describing what they observed in terms of how they understood the phenomena. Some conservative biblical scholars have offered a more sophisticated version of the idea that not everything in biblical texts has to be taken as revelatory truth. John and Harvey Walton argue that in reading biblical accounts we should distinguish between biblical writers *referring to* beliefs commonly assumed in ancient times and *affirming the truth of* those beliefs (Walton and Walton, *Demons and Spirits*). They think that we misunderstand biblical revelation when we regard the framework used so speak to an ancient audience as revealed truth. Just as the Bible is not teaching us science, it is not giving us a course in demonology.

Some interpreters explicitly deny that there are evil spirits. Others, such as New Testament scholar Dale Allison, reject historical Christian mythology about Satan, but accept the possibility of nonhuman powers other than God who may not be friendly toward humans (*Encountering Mystery*, 43–44). Walter Wink thinks that even if the principalities and powers that Paul spoke of wrestling with are not actual spirit beings, biblical language describing personal powers functions as a reminder that we deal with powerful forces that are not easily controlled. He suggests that demonic evils arise from institutional forces that take on a life of their own, going beyond any individual human intentions. My inclination is to seek a place between the extremes of concluding that there are demons because the Bible refers to such beings and treating the biblical accounts of evil powers as ways of describing what would fit with our ordinary understanding of how the world works. It seems plausible to me that dysfunctions at the level of psychic powers play an important role in cases that suggest something beyond ordinary evils. (In the Lurancy case, it looks like extrasensory powers have run amok.) With regard to whether any nonhuman beings other than God intentionally or unintentionally contribute to such dysfunction, I withhold judgment.

disorder). They posit that aspects of the unconscious mind can acquire an independence from one's ordinary sense of self that sometimes approximates a distinct personality. Under some circumstances these alternate personalities can assume control. Usually, this kind of control is temporary. However, if we think of what happens to Lurancy as a case of dissociation, her ability to convince those who knew Mary best that she is Mary suggests that the alternate personality is constructed in part from materials acquired by extrasensory means. Laurancy's propensity to trance states gives us a clue about how such extrasensory information might have been acquired.

There are differences between Lurancy's case and cases in which young children seem to remember a previous life. One difference is that there is an overlap between Mary's life and Lurancy's, which makes it harder to think of it as a case of reincarnation. Another difference is that the Mary personality for a time replaces the previous personality, whereas in the standard reincarnation case the personality of the person who has died seems to coexist with the personality of the child. However, if we look at these seemingly different cases in terms of the acquisition of someone else's memories, they leave the impression of being different versions of the same type of phenomenon. Temporary displacement of a personality looks like a more extreme form of what awareness of alien memories could lead to, while the result in reincarnation cases (as well as transplant cases) is an influence that falls short of a takeover.

Our assessments of strange phenomena like those discussed in this chapter depend on our sense of what is plausible. Some people will be inclined to dismiss all stories like these as based on misleading reports or hoaxes, thinking that there must be some ordinary explanation. I think that while we should generally prefer ordinary explanations, some of these cases call for explanations that go beyond the ordinary. The alternatives for non-ordinary explanations that seem most relevant involve either extrasensory awareness or disembodied spirits. But even if we accept the continued existence of spirits of the dead, we can consider whether they are the best way of accounting for what happens in these kinds of cases.

Hauntings seem odd, but thinking of them as instances of dead people continually repeating acts signifying traumatic events seems less plausible to me than thinking that there are extrasensory powers of our mind capable of picking up memory traces connected with those events. Taking on the characteristics of a heart donor is difficult to understand, but the idea that the spirit of someone who died has accompanied the heart seems less likely to me than the idea of extrasensory awareness of donor memories triggered by the presence of the organ. Children who possess memories of someone who has died is puzzling, but positing that the dead person has come to inhibit a new body strikes me unneeded if we think that other cases give us convincing reasons to accept that extrasensory access to memories of the dead sometimes occurs.

CHAPTER 16

Mediums

RECENTLY I WATCHED A video in which people who represented themselves as able to establish contact with those who had died spoke to an audience composed of people who were grieving over the loss of a loved one. I felt a sense of disgust as I observed their techniques. They proceeded to engage in what is sometimes called fishing for information. Suggesting that they were sensing something from someone who had died, they offered descriptions that were likely to correspond to the circumstances of some people in the audience: "Is there anyone here who has recently lost someone after a lingering illness? . . . Did the person you lost have a name that begins with J? . . . Was it a father who passed away?" When receiving positive responses, they would hone in and try for more details, often replacing an initial suggestion with an alternative one, as if they were picking up something on a line that was a bit garbled. Most of what they said was general enough to apply to many people, but often people in the audience volunteered more specific information that the presenters picked up on, and the body language of those in the audience no doubt suggested when they were on a promising track. When the presenters did convey a message from a loved one, it was invariably a comforting one, the kind of message these people were eager to hear.

In interviews with audience members after the session, it was clear that some people were convinced they had received a message from beyond the grave. Others were not quite sure, but many of the doubters were still willing to try further sessions to see if they got stronger evidence. None of what I observed led me to conclude that there was genuine contact with the dead. A charitable interpretation is that these performers believed that they could accomplish what they claimed. I am in no position to assess their state of mind. But what stood out to me were their well-practiced skills of persuasion and the eagerness of the audience to hear comforting messages. The whole thing reminded me of what I already knew: there is often good reason to adopt a skeptical attitude toward those who can potentially profit from claims of extraordinary powers.

It is reasonable to suspect that many of those who represent themselves as able to make contact with the dead are pretenders who know that they are engaged in deception. After encountering such pretenders, it can be tempting to generalize that anyone who makes such claims is just a fraud. However, the full range of evidence suggests something more complex. It is likely that the vast majority of those who represent themselves as able to contact the dead know that they are using tricks to convince a credulous public. But in some cases, mediums (now often referred to as sensitives) provide specific information related to the dead person that they couldn't have acquired through any ordinary means. Mediums with extrasensory powers that enable them to acquire such information may understandably believe it comes through contact with someone who has died.

Others may believe it as well. It is impressive when a medium describes your Uncle Charlie riding a bicycle to work or playing the ukulele for family members or making a remark that seems exactly like Charlie's quirky sense of humor. But even when it can be determined that the medium didn't get this information from research into Charlie's life, that isn't enough to establish that the information came from Uncle Charlie. If the information is acquired through extrasensory channels, we may not know enough to be confident about where it came from.

Contacting the Dead

Attempts to establish contact with the dead are not new. They can be found in many cultures, including ancient Israel. There is a story in 1 Samuel 28 of King Saul seeking out a medium to put him in touch with the dead prophet Samuel. Saul had previously outlawed practices that included contacting the dead, but he is terrified by the strength of the enemy army he will soon be facing, and he is desperate for guidance about what to do. When none of the standard ways of seeking divine guidance are successful, he orders that a medium be found.

Saul puts on a disguise and travels to the house of a woman from the Israelite town of Endor. When he asks her to bring up a spirit for him, she is clearly suspicious, no doubt wondering if she is being set up. She points out that the king has expelled from the land all the mediums and wizards who are able to do such a thing. Saul assures her that she will not be punished if she does what he requests. Then he asks her to bring the prophet Samuel back from the dead. According to the account, she conjures up an appearance that Saul recognizes as Samuel. Saul asks the apparition how he should deal with the situation he faces, and he is rebuffed by a prophetic condemnation of his previous disobedience, along with a prediction that things are going to turn out badly in the coming battle with the Philistines.

Seeking wisdom from the spiritual realm has been a common practice in many cultures. It takes on a variety of forms. In ancient Greece there were oracles to which people could go to seek a message from the gods. The most famous was the oracle at Delphi where a priestess served as a medium to deliver messages from the god Apollo. The priestess, perhaps aided by drugs, would go into a trance state in which she was believed to speak the god's words. Often the message was cryptic and susceptible to multiple interpretations. The service likely required payment of a fee, but apparently people thought it was worth the cost to get messages from a higher realm.

Seeking contact with the spirit realm outside of sanctioned channels is rejected in Hebrew Scripture (e.g., Deut 18:9–13). It seems likely that the reason for the prohibition was not disbelief in the efficacy of practices that might produce this kind of contact, but concerns about corrupting influences on the worship of Yahweh that might come from adopting practices that were associated with the worship of other gods. But even though such practices were officially banned, the passage in 1 Samuel suggests that the prohibitions were not sufficient to eliminate them altogether.

In the later part of the nineteenth century in the United States attempts to make contact with the dead became very popular. The movement called spiritualism, which affirmed the reality of this kind of contact, is usually traced to the Fox sisters in New York, who devised a simple code to interpret rapping noises in their family home. They would ask questions and receive answers from the rapping sounds that were taken to come from departed spirits. The practice of conducting séances to communicate with the dead spread throughout the United States and Europe. What likely started as a form of entertainment became for many a serious pursuit.

This practice was influential enough that in the 1880s a group of leading scholars at Cambridge University set out to investigate it, along with related phenomena. Some of the most prestigious thinkers of the time were involved in the work of the Society for Psychical Research (SPR) in England. There was soon a corresponding organization in the United States. The early studies of these scholars included thought-transference, mediumship, apparitions, haunted houses, and séances. They investigated claims about these phenomena by doing careful observations under conditions where they could verify whether trickery was occurring. They also solicited reports from people who claimed to have experienced extraordinary phenomena and collected supporting testimony from others who could provide confirming evidence of the events described.[1]

One of the immediate consequences of their investigations was to expose a number of well-known mediums as engaging in fraud or trickery. Some of the SPR investigators gained a reputation for leaving no stone unturned to discover any efforts to deceive. Among these was Richard Hodgson who aroused considerable hostility from spiritualists because of his tough-minded skeptical investigations of mediums. But these same investigators, including Hodgson, determined that a few individuals convincingly demonstrated an ability to know things that they couldn't have known by ordinary means.

These mediums represented the information as coming from spirits of the dead. Some investigators judged that their extraordinary knowledge was convincing evidence that they were receiving communication from the dead. However, others believed that the information could have been acquired through telepathic means from the minds of living individuals. In other words, there was agreement among those who studied the phenomena carefully that a few of the mediums

---

1. One of the products of the Society's research was Gurney et al., *Phantasms of the Living*, published in 1886. An abridged edition of this work was published by Eleanor Sidgwick in 1918. It compiles a number of cases of experiences that suggest telepathic communication. The focus is on experiences of apparitions that seem to bring messages of distant events. Eyewitness reports are documented by investigators from the Society.

exhibited extraordinary knowledge, but disagreement about whether the knowledge was enough to posit contact with the dead.

Mediums and Séances

Mediums come in many varieties. Some relay messages that they represent as coming from the spirit realm without undergoing a significant change in their own state of consciousness. Some go into a light trance that doesn't interfere with other activity. Some go into a deeper trance in which their bodies become instruments for spirits to deliver messages from beyond. When mediums who enter a deep trance return to ordinary consciousness, they are typically unaware of what they said or did in the trance state. In addition to serving as a conduit for messages, some mediums have been known for producing anomalous physical phenomena that is represented as a manifestation of the spirits.

Mediums who go into a deep trance and those producing striking physical phenomena are much less common in our era than they were in the nineteenth century. Most mediums today, like the ones I saw in the video that I mentioned earlier, describe impressions they receive while remaining aware of what is going on around them. My focus initially will be on those mediums who go into the deepest trance states. I will use female pronouns in referring to trance mediums because the overwhelming majority of these mediums have been female.

Typically, a trance medium connects in the trance state with a being who is presented as her control. The control can be thought of as a point of contact between the medium and the spirit realm. The control is identified by name and has a personality that differs from the personality of the medium. The names and personalities of controls often seem fanciful and stereotypical, which leads many who have studied the phenomena to think of the control as a product of the medium's creative imagination. A medium may have a particular control for years, though over time a new control may emerge. When the medium is in a trance state, it is as if her body is taken over by her control. Typically, there are altered tones of voice and mannerisms that are distinct from those she usually displays.[2]

When the control puts the medium in touch with another personality, ostensibly of someone who has died, the medium begins to speak and

---

2. Some trance mediums get their messages through automatic writing. In such cases they write material that comes from unconscious sources by a process that bypasses conscious control.

behave in ways that resemble this person's behavior and speech during life. In contemporary terms, the medium channels the deceased. In the most impressive cases the medium in this state displays knowledge about a departed spirit and about other people connected with that person that could not have been acquired in ordinary fashion. The philosopher William James, who was involved in the work of the American Society for Psychical Research, reported on his experience with the medium Leonora Piper. He says that he was impressed by her knowledge of many specific details related to his family life, things that he characterizes as intimate and trivial. Included in his examples are the following:

> She said that we had recently lost a rug, and I a waistcoat.... She told of my killing a gray-and-white cat with ether and described how it had "spun round and round" before dying. She told how my New York aunt had written a letter to my wife warning her against all mediums.... She was strong on the events in our nursery, and gave striking advice during our first visit to her about the way to deal with certain "tantrums" of our second child, "little Billy-boy," as she called him, reproducing his nursery name. She told how the crib creaked at night, how a certain rocking chair creaked mysteriously, how my wife had heard footsteps on the stairs, etc., etc. Insignificant as these things sound when read, the accumulation of a large number of them has an irresistible effect.[3]

The effect, he says, was to "make me feel as absolutely certain as I am of any personal fact in the world that she knows things in her trances which she cannot possibly have heard in her waking state."[4]

It should be pointed out that mixed with verifiable information, there is often a great deal of what has been called rubbish. The transcripts of mediumistic sessions are often boring and meandering. James found that within the rubbish there was enough to convince him that paranormal knowledge was sometimes displayed, but he was not fully convinced that communications with the dead were occurring. One reason for his suspicion was his expectation that people who had passed to a higher realm would not be immersed in such tedious trivia.

There are serious discussions by philosophers who have studied this material about whether the kind of knowledge mediums display furnishes

---

3. James, "Certain Phenomena of Trance," 110.
4. James, "Certain Phenomena of Trance," 110.

significant evidence of life after death.[5] Some conclude that in some cases verifiable information possessed by the medium is best explained by positing contact with someone who has died. But others think that such information can be explained by accepting extrasensory powers of the medium without positing contact with the dead. Even those who think that some cases make it reasonable to posit that postmortem contact has occurred may acknowledge that the evidence is not sufficient to allow us to draw this conclusion with a high-level of certainty.[6]

Many mediums believe that they have made contact with people who have died. But some who practice mediumship have been puzzled about how to understand their experience. Eileen Garrett was one of the most famous mediums of the twentieth century. She had not sought her ability to go into a trance state. It was something that came to her spontaneously. When in a trance, she seemed to contact various spirits, but reflectively, she wondered whether she was encountering spirits of the dead or split-off parts of her own mind. Although she submitted herself for testing to scientists, including the famed researcher J. B. Rhine, and she personally funded a considerable amount of research into investigation of psychic phenomena, she never found a conclusive answer to her question. Toward the end of her life, she was inclined to believe that her apparent contact with spirits was genuine, but she also retained some doubts.[7]

Psychological Explanations

Garrett's question of whether the spirits she seemed to encounter might be split-off parts of her own mind presupposes an awareness of psychological thinking about parts of the mind that operate independently of conscious

---

5. For example, Braude, *Immortal Remains*; Griffin, *Parapsychology, Philosophy, and Spirituality*; Almeder, *Death and Personal Survival*.

6. Braude, *Immortal Remains*, 20.

7. Horn, *Unbelievable* 40–47; Montefiore, *Paranormal*, 45. Philosopher Phillip Wiebe argues in his book *God and Other Spirits* that certain experiences can make it reasonable to postulate the existence of invisible spirits, both evil and good. He gives numerous examples of strange phenomena that he says can be reasonably be interpreted as indications of demonic possession or influence. What is reasonable for a given individual can depend on preexisting beliefs. Wiebe's examples often come from Christian groups in which belief in the literal existence of angelic and demonic beings is assumed. But the point is that such beliefs perform a role in explaining strange phenomena for people who are able to entertain the possibility

awareness. Phenomena, such as hypnotism, reveal the existence of ordinarily inaccessible parts of the mind that can act independently of the conscious self. For example, a hypnotist might tell someone to open a window five minutes after being awakened from a hypnotic state. When the person follows the instruction and is asked why she opened the window, the typical response is to invent some reason that sounds plausible, such as claiming that the room was stuffy. The conscious self assumes that the behavior is under its control, and comes up with a possible reason for it. However, control has actually been assumed by some aspect of the subliminal mind that acts in obedience to the hypnotist's suggestion.

Control from the subliminal realm can also be recognized in what used to be called multiple personality disorder, and is now referred to as dissociative identity disorder. The condition involves parts of the self that have aims differing from those of the primary self. In some cases, these parts may be developed enough to constitute alternate personalities that can exercise control for extended periods of time. A person with alternate personalities might recognize that these personalities arise from his or her own mind. But given that they may act in ways that significantly differ from those of the primary self, it can seem like a kind of possession by an alien spirit when an alternate personality takes over.

So, when Garrett experiences spirits who seem to have a reality distinct from herself, she wonders whether the sense of a separate individual should be taken at face value. Could the spirits who seem to have their own life actually be parts of herself that are hidden from conscious awareness? It is hard to see how the possibility can be decisively ruled out, though it is understandable why someone who has a vivid awareness of spirits who behave in ways that suggest an independent existence and who have knowledge more extensive than the conscious self might be inclined to think of the spirits as existing independently.

But even if we think that what is experienced in mediumistic contexts are parts of the mind, these subliminal parts are sometimes channels through which information not accessible in an ordinary way is obtained. So, saying that the medium experiences parts of her own mind wouldn't preclude the possibility that these parts put her in contact with a reality beyond the individual self. However, even if there is such contact, the experience doesn't provide a strong basis for identifying the specific source of the information. She may take some communication to come from Aunt Sally, but that could be just a way her mind makes sense of having the information. The question of whether this way of interpreting what is going on is the most plausible one remains.

An Encounter with a Medium

Dianne Arcangel was a hospice worker and director of the Elisabeth Kübler-Ross Center. In the course of her work, she sometimes appeared on programs where professional mediums had also been invited. She was suspicious of the mediums she met, finding their various tricks to convince people that they could contact the dead all too obvious. Eventually, however, she was introduced to George Anderson, a medium who was held in high regard by people she worked with. Reluctantly, she agreed to allow Anderson to give her a private reading. She noticed that during the reading he sat in such a way that he could not observe her reactions, and he told her to limit her responses to yes or no without any elaboration, reducing the chance that she could be giving him clues. Then Anderson proceeded to give her very specific and detailed information about her life that contrasted sharply with the generalized messages she had come to associate with mediums.[8]

He appeared to be concentrating his attention on her dead relatives whom he described with uncanny accuracy. He spoke about her father and at a later point in the session, he referred to a female presence who he said claimed to be Arcangel's mother. Anderson was surprised, thinking he had made a mistake because he thought she didn't look old enough to him to have lost both parents. But she gives an affirmative answer to the question of whether both parents had died. Anderson asked on behalf of her mother whether she would deliver a message to someone named Helen. Arcangel replied that she didn't know any Helen. He told her that her mother had responded with, "Oh, you know, Dianne, Helen! Helen!" The inflection, pitch, and wording mirrored exactly the way her mother had spoken to her. It was only after the session that she discovered who Helen was. Her mother had never referred to the woman by her first name to Dianne, but she later found the full name in a journal that her mother had kept.

Anderson told Arcangel about spasms she had been having on her right side. At the time she denied this was the case, because she hadn't thought of them as spasms, but on reflection she later realized that he had

---

8. Arcangel, *Afterlife Encounters*, 176–98.

described them accurately. He described seeing someone giving white roses to Arcangel's daughter, which he interpreted to mean that she would be getting married soon. He referred to the ring used in the ceremony as a rare family heirloom. He also described a difficult pregnancy with serious complications, but said that she would have a healthy boy. Arcangel felt certain that these predictions were way off. She thought that her daughter might get married eventually, but it wouldn't be any time soon, and she didn't think her daughter would ever have children. But the events he had described occurred just as he said they would. The specially designed ring her daughter had planned for the ceremony wasn't ready in time, so instead she wore a ring her grandmother and mother had worn.

Anderson also spoke of a surgery for her father-in-law that would go badly, saying he wouldn't leave the hospital and would die at the beginning of the next year. During the session he qualified the claim by saying that the death was not inevitable. If her father-in-law is able to watch his diet carefully and keep on his medication, he may survive. In the coming months, after running multiple tests, a physician put her father-in-law on a very restricted diet and prescribed medication. But her father-in-law soon returned to his old habits. He ended up in the emergency room. After an unsuccessful surgery, he never left the hospital.

The details matter. I have described only some of the things mentioned in the session, but as in the case of William James's experience with a medium, there was enough to convince Arcangel that Anderson knew things that go beyond our usual assumptions of what it is possible to know. In later work with him involving other people, his powers were confirmed to her. Nevertheless, good reasons for concluding that a particular medium has impressive extrasensory powers is not enough to show that there has been contact with a dead person. And even if we posit that there is good evidence that a few mediums are able to establish this kind of contact, what are the odds of finding such a medium? In the overwhelming majority of cases, there are many reasons for doubt. So, the bottom line is that someone who goes to a medium to seek a message from deceased Uncle Charlie will almost always lack a strong basis for confidence that the message actually comes from Charlie.

CHAPTER 17

Near-Death Experiences

BRUCE GREYSON HAS FOR many years been one of the premier researchers of near-death experiences. His first encounter with the phenomenon occurred when he had never heard of such a thing. He had been out of medical school for only a few months when he was called to do a psychiatric consultation for a woman in the hospital emergency room who had overdosed on medication. When he got the call, he was eating a plate of spaghetti and had just spilled some sauce on his tie. Attempting to look professional, he tried with only partial success to make the blob less noticeable by applying a wet napkin. Before responding to the call, he put on a white lab coat that he hoped would hide the stain.

The patient, Holly, was unconscious in an exam room when he checked on her, but he was able to go down the hall to the family lounge and talk to her roommate Susan, who had brought her in. Greyson had an extended conversation with Susan about any factors that might have led to the incident, including her knowledge of any drugs Holly might have taken. His first interview with Holly was the next morning. When he introduced himself, Holly said that she remembered him from the previous night. Puzzled, he pointed out that she was asleep when he came in. Holly replied that it was not in the exam room that she had seen him, but sitting with Susan in the lounge. She said, "You were wearing a striped tie with a red stain on it." Then she went on to repeat the entire conversation he had had with Susan, all of his questions, along with her responses. Greyson found it unbelievable that she could know what happened while she was unconscious in another room of the hospital. When he later gave his report to the psychiatric consulting team, he omitted any mention of Holly knowing things that he saw no way she could have known.[1]

After the single interview with Holly, Greyson had no further contact with her. Even if he had, it would likely not have occurred to him to ask about other experiences she might have had after she lost consciousness. Such a question would have seemed bizarre. It was years later that Greyson learned that a significant number of patients had stories to tell about what they experienced during life-threatening situations. He was head of psychiatric emergency services at the University of Virginia when he met Raymond Moody, who was training there to be a physician. Moody's book *Life After Life*, which appeared in 1975, was the first book in English to use the term "near-death experience" and its acronym NDE. Greyson became interested enough in the strange stories that patients were telling to begin his own systematic investigation of the phenomenon that had shaken him as a young resident. He would pursue this interest for the rest of his career.

Awareness of What Is Happening When You Are Unconscious

The phenomenon that we call near-death experiences is now known to be reported in cultures all over the world, and stories of such experiences go back to ancient times. But widespread awareness of it in our time is connected with advances in medical technology that have resulted in resuscitations of people who would likely have died in previous eras. Not everyone who is brought back from the edge of death has a story to tell about it. But it has been estimated that somewhere between 10 and 20 percent of people who undergo cardiac resuscitation recall a near-death experience. It may be that other people have this kind of experience, but do not remember it after they regain consciousness.

We have become familiar with some of the features described in these stories.[2] They include a sense of leaving the body and looking at what is happening from an outside point of view, a transition to another realm where a Being of Light is encountered, a replay of events from your life, a

---

1. Greyson, *After*, 1–8.

2. Most of the features of what we call near-death experience can be found in experiences where there is no threat to life. See Fox, *Religion, Spirituality, and the Near-Death Experience*, 325.

meeting with loved ones who have died, and a return to the body. There are differences in what features are part of an individual's experience and in what order events occur, but there are enough similarities to allow us to recognize a common type of experience. The similarities are recognizable across cultures and in different eras. It is also noteworthy that these experiences are not limited to people who have religious beliefs about life after death. People who have no religious views have similar experiences.

I want to begin thinking about these experiences by considering the issue that troubled Greyson after his encounter with Holly. People who have near-death experiences sometimes report being aware of what was happening in the vicinity (and sometimes farther away) during a time when they were unconscious. They sometimes describe leaving their physical body during an operation and observing what was going on in the operating room from a viewpoint above the scene. It might be suggested that all of us have seen enough television shows with operating-room scenes to be able to make good guesses about what happens during a heart operation. Cardiologist Michael Sabom decided to test this hypothesis. He compared the descriptions of what happened in the operating room given by those who reported a near-death experience in which they said they observed the procedure to descriptions given by those who had a similar operation, but reported no such experience. The clear result was that people who didn't have this kind of experience almost always had major inaccuracies in their accounts. What they described included things that don't happen during this kind of operation. On the other hand, those who reported seeing what happened during their operation were able to provide accounts that were mostly correct about operating procedures.[3]

But it's not just a matter of statistical evidence. Some patients who have near-death experiences describe unusual events that couldn't have been guessed. For example, one patient who had bypass surgery said that he saw the surgeon "flapping his arms as if he was trying to fly." After the operation, the patient demonstrated the unusual motion he had seen. The surprised surgeon asked who had told him about such a thing. The patient insisted that he had seen it during the operation. It turned out that this surgeon had developed the unusual habit of holding his scrubbed hands on his chest to keep himself from touching anything that might contaminate his hands. During this time, he used his elbows

---

3. Sabom, *Recollections of Death*, 63–115.

to point out things to the team.[4] One account of this kind might be dismissed, but there are many cases in which patients give detailed and accurate accounts of procedures or conversations when they had no ordinary way of knowing about such things. Corroboration of events described by the patient is often supplied by medical professionals involved in the procedures who in many cases react to the patient's accounts with puzzled astonishment.

Patients say that they knew about such things because they observed them from a position outside their body. Out-of-body experiences are not unique to near-death situations. Most instances of this kind of experience are involuntary, but a few people have reported being able to produce such an experience intentionally by entering into a state of deep relaxation. During the experience a person seems to perceive things from a perspective outside of his or her body. Sometimes the experience includes viewing one's own body. Sometimes people report going to distant locations. It has been suggested that this sort of experience is like a fantasy, but in cases where it is connected with acquiring accurate information about what is happening that doesn't come from ordinary sensory observation, the fantasy explanation leaves us with a puzzle about how such information is obtained.

People have disputed about how to understand out-of-body experiences. Some say that the mind (or the soul or an astral body) separates from the physical organism and goes to another location where it has perceptions of what is happening. Others reject the idea of anything traveling to a different location. However, whether we think of something as separating from the body or not, accepting the anomalous knowledge reported in near-death experiences would require positing extrasensory awareness. And if the mind is capable of extrasensory awareness of events from a point of view outside the body, it becomes difficult to distinguish between the mind being at a different location from having an extrasensory awareness of how things would appear to an observer at that location.

The Mind and the Brain

People in our era often think of conscious awareness as a byproduct of brain activity. But the phenomenon of near-death experiences raises a

---

4. Greyson, *After*, 65–68.

problem for this view. In the typical near-death case, the brain would have to manufacture elaborate fantasies and memories while it is functioning at only a minimal level. However, when the brain is minimally functioning, it shouldn't be able to produce such fantasies or memories. Not only that, but one of the well supported findings of near-death research is that people describe their perceptions as more vivid than ordinary perceptions and their thinking as clearer and faster than in ordinary states. Even if the brain could produce some kind of experience under extreme conditions, it should be considerably less coherent than what is described.

Consider the well-known case of Eben Alexander. He was rushed to the hospital after a brain seizure. Initial exams showed that the cerebral cortex, the part of the brain associated with thinking, perceiving, and using language had shut down. Additionally, there was damage to the brain stem. The physicians who saw him expected that he was near death. Eventually, it was determined that he had a rare bacterial infection of the brain that had a 90-percent fatality rate (*E. coli* meningitis). If he survived at all, it would likely be only in a vegetative state. He lost consciousness in the emergency room and for the next seven days, he was in a deep coma. Doctors had no precedent for genuine recovery from a coma this long with brain damage this severe.

Alexander was a neurosurgeon who had operated on thousands of brains. After he did recover, he commented on his own case. He says that during his coma "my brain wasn't working improperly. *It hadn't been working at all.*"[5] Yet after he woke up, against all odds, he had detailed and vivid memories of a complex set of experiences of a higher realm. Medical experts agreed that he should not have had any experiences at all during his coma.

Alexander says that before his brain seizure, he held a view common among neuroscientists that "the brain gives rise to consciousness."[6] When patients told him about experiences they had while near death, he says that he never took the reports seriously.[7] But he describes the things he experienced while in a coma as more real to him than his perception of physical things. He eventually came to the conclusion that the brain is not the source of consciousness, but rather "a kind of filtering device through which a larger nonphysical consciousness is put into a form that we can

---

5. Alexander, *Proof of Heaven*, 129.
6. Alexander, *Proof of Heaven*, 34.
7. Alexander, *Proof of Heaven*, 127.

use in our earthly lives."[8] He describes the time when his neocortex was not functioning as an encounter with "the reality of a world of consciousness that existed *completely free of the limitations of my physical brain.*"[9]

People who have near-death experiences do not usually do the kind of reflection that Alexander did about the relation of between the brain and human consciousness. But they are almost always convinced by their experiences that there is life after death. It would be an overstatement to say that their experiences prove such a thing. However, they do provide evidence against a standard objection to life after death. The objection is that consciousness cannot continue without brain activity. Near-death experiences give evidence that people can continue to have vivid experiences, at least for a while, when brain activity ceases. It could be claimed that it doesn't cease completely, but there are cases of near-death experiences in which consciousness is reported despite the brain being shut down to a point where it is extremely implausible to think the experienced consciousness could be produced by the brain.

One of Michael Sabom's cases involved a procedure in which a woman's heart and respiration were completely stopped. Her brainwaves flattened, and blood was drained from the brain. Measures showed a shutdown of any metabolic activity. According to some definitions, she was brain dead. This radical technique was done to remove a basilar artery aneurysm from her brain. After the operation, she described having an out-of-body experience in which she observed particular details of the procedure, including descriptions of instruments she was unfamiliar with that were used and specifics of conversations by the medical personnel. Despite the condition of her brain, she described what she saw as "brighter and more focused and clearer than normal vision."[10] It is hard to see how this case can be understood on the view that consciousness is entirely dependent on brain activity.

The Life Review

One striking feature of many near-death stories is the life review. People who report a life review tend to say that their experience of time was different than it is in ordinary experience. Some accounts suggest that

---

8. Alexander, *Proof of Heaven*, 81.
9. Alexander, *Proof of Heaven*, 9.
10. Sabom, *Light and Death*, 41.

the review occurs rapidly, but a person is able to process what is being shown in a way that is unrushed and includes many details. Some people describe time as slowing down for them. Some speak of experiencing many things all at once. People say that the life review is unlike remembering something. It is more like reliving experiences, though some add that they experienced things not just from their own point of view, but from the point of view of others who were affected. The events relived include some things that have been forgotten, and the experiences are described as more detailed than ordinary experiences.

Here is one person's summary of the life review:

> In every scene of my life review I could feel again what I had felt at various times in my life. And I could feel everything everyone else felt as a consequence of my actions. Some of it felt good and some of it felt awful. . . . The information came in, and then love neutralized my judgments against myself.[11]

Another person reports,

> It *was* a re-experiencing of life, but from three different perspectives simultaneously. One perspective was my own version of my life. . . . However, I was also experiencing my life from the perspectives of those involved. I felt what they felt, I lived their emotions as they acted and reacted to me. . . . At exactly the same time I experienced a *third* view of my life. It was an unbiased view, free of the subjective and self-serving rationalizations. . . . To me . . . it can only be described as God's view of my life.[12]

The life review could be thought of as a kind of judgment scene, only it is not the scene we typically imagine of being in a courtroom and hearing a pronouncement of guilty or not guilty, followed by a punishment or reward. The judgment that occurs seems more like a judgment you make of yourself, but in the light of greater information and also with a more compassionate attitude toward yourself and others than people typically have. In contrast to the sort of retribution model that people often use to think of God's judgment, these stories suggest something closer to a concern that the persons learn from the experiences. There may be pain involved in facing up to unwelcome truths about yourself, but the pain might be thought of as having a therapeutic or redemptive

---

11. Greyson, *After*, 42.
12. Smith, "Intimations of Mortality," 14–15.

purpose. Most people who have the experience of a life review say that it changed their sense of what is important in life.

Other Realms

Many people who have near-death experiences speak of going to a realm beyond earthly life. Sometimes there is a kind of idyllic nature scene. Some people refer to it as heaven; some speak of being on the borders of the heavenly realm. In some stories there is a guide who helps the person understand the experience. People frequently describe their interactions with other beings as not coming through sounds, but rather through direct mental links. Some people talk about learning much about earthly life and the world beyond, but they often speak of losing some of this knowledge on return. They sometimes account for the difficulty of remembering what they learned as a result of this knowledge exceeding ordinary human capacities of comprehension. Nevertheless, people who return often offer summary accounts of what they learned.

Sometimes people describe meeting deceased friends or relatives. The most striking stories of this kind involve cases in which the person having the near-death experience was unaware that the relative had died or had never heard of the person. In one case, a nine-year-old boy woke up in the ICU unit and told his parents that he had seen his deceased grandfather, aunt, and uncle. But he also insisted that he had seen his sister Teresa, who was away at college. The parents were upset at what they considered to be delusional rants, but when they got home, they received a message that Teresa had been killed in an auto accident.[13] Eben Alexander, whom I mentioned earlier, had been adopted and had not met with his birth family before his seizure. After his recovery, he saw for the first time a photograph of a deceased sister from the birth family. He reports that he recognized the person in the photo as the woman who had been his guide in the celestial realm.

A significant percentage of people who have near-death experiences describe an encounter with a Being of Light. Sometimes people speak of going into the light or even becoming one with the light. Most people do not offer a definite account of who this godlike being is.[14] Some speak of a figure from their religious tradition, such as Jesus or an

---

13. Greyson, "Near Death Experiences," 42.
14. Greyson, *After*, 155.

angel. When people do use the term "God" they often suggest that there was something overwhelming about the experience that words can't convey. The most common feelings are peacefulness, thankfulness, and a sense of being loved.

Some of these experiences are described in very anthropomorphic terms. But some people suggest that what they experienced was in a form that fit with their own ways of conceiving such things. One woman says, "I was in front of this being, and I knew he was holy. I felt this was God appearing to me as I always imagined him: an old man with a large beard. He had taken on this persona so that I wouldn't be afraid."[15] Another person offers a more unusual account:

> Imagine a three-dimensional ball of intense energy made up of golden white light. In the center of the ball was the figure of a person—I couldn't tell whether it was male or female. Around the ball were smaller balls of energy traveling in different directions and made up of all different colors that circled the outside of the ball. . . . I knew who it was by recognizing and knowing the energy the form gives off.[16]

Negative Experiences

Even though a large majority of near-death experiences evoke positive emotions, there are cases of people who have horrifying experiences.[17] Researchers have proposed that these distressing experiences can be grouped into three categories. One is a type of experience that seems like what those who have positive reactions report, only it instead produces fear. There are a variety of reasons why a person might have such reactions. Some may be distressed by the disorienting feeling of being out of the body. Some are likely panic stricken by the loss of control over what is happening. A second kind of experience that evokes distress involves finding oneself in a vast emptiness, often utter darkness. The feelings associated with this kind of experience are loneliness, a sense of isolation, and a fear of annihilation. The third type of distressing experience is the least common of the three. It involves terrifying experiences that people sometimes associate with hell. Some accounts describe moving from a

---

15. Long and Perry, *God and the Afterlife*, 86.
16. Long and Perry, *God and the Afterlife*, 87.
17. The best book I have found on this subject is Evans, *Dancing Past the Dark*.

negative experience to a positive one; much less common is a movement from a positive experience to a negative one.

The available data give no indication that experiences evoking negative emotions happen only to people who are especially bad or who have the wrong religious beliefs. People can always speculate about whether an individual has done something that makes this kind of experience more likely, but most suggestions that have been made are not supported by the evidence. For example, some people who attempt suicide have frightening near-death experiences, but others who attempt suicide have blissful ones.

What should we make of the fact that while most near-death experiences evoke a very positive response, a small minority give rise to feelings of fear and panic? I think that any answer to this question is likely to be speculative. However, I have an impression and an observation that may be relevant. The impression is that these fearful experiences are stopped before reaching completion. We don't quite know what might have occurred if the experience had been longer.

If we think of what is happening as analogous to a therapeutic encounter, it may help to remember that in therapeutic contexts experiencing negative emotions can be a necessary prelude to a healing outcome. I can imagine many of these stories of distressing experiences as preludes that might lead to something more positive, only something stands in the way of getting past the fear and guilt that has overshadowed other possible responses. I hasten to say that I am not blaming the person who is overwhelmed with unpleasant emotions. Rather, I am suggesting that there is a way of viewing what is experienced that might make it less distressing.

In addition to this impression of a truncated experience, I want to add an observation. Near-death experiences are a type of mystical experience. If we look at the literature of mysticism, these encounters include not only blissful experiences, but fearful and disgusting ones as well. Some of the greatest saints have reported encounters that we might classify as hellish. The fearful forces described may not be the last word, but they may portray important truths about the kind of struggle that is involved in spiritual development. Perhaps the classic stories of descending into something hellish before rising above is a way of picturing such truths.

Previews of What Comes Next?

Some people want an unequivocal answer to the question of whether near-death reports tell us what happens after death. Do they or do they not give an accurate account of the matter? We should first note that when a report deals with such matters as what happened in the operating room, there is the possibility of independent verification. But when what is reported is about some realm beyond this one, we can't independently verify the report by means of sensory observation. Nor can we infer that if someone was right in observations about what was going on the operating room, that person is likely to be right in accounts of a transcendent realm.

We should also notice that to ask whether the accounts are accurate or not is too simplistic. People who tell about what they experienced are often quick to say that they don't have the words to adequately describe it. If we take the experience to be of a reality beyond the sensory realm, what is perceived may be unlike anything that fits into familiar categories. Reading these stories makes clear that people are describing things in terms that make sense to them, but we should expect that a great deal may be lost in efforts to translate what does not fit into familiar frames of reference into something understandable. In the various descriptions we may sometimes recognize different ways of speaking about recognizably similar things. But trying to piece these stories together into a single coherent account is likely futile.

Nevertheless, if we don't dismiss the possibility of visions of transcendent realities, these stories are impressive. For one thing, there is enough commonality to judge that the experiences are not purely subjective, nor do they sound like recitations of religious teachings. It is also noteworthy that people who have these experiences are virtually always fully convinced that they have encountered a level of reality beyond that which ordinary experience provides. One woman says, "Never did I think that it might be a dream. I knew that it was true and real, more real than any other thing I've ever known."[18] Another person says, "There was no sense of doubt whatsoever. Everything had a sense of being 'more real' than anything that would normally be experienced in the physical world as we know it."[19] Another says, "By comparison

---

18. Greyson, *After*, 96.
19. Greyson, *After*, 96.

my life in my body had been a dream."[20] It is hard to imagine how an experience of something transcending physical realities could be more convincing to the person who has the experience.

Furthermore, people tend to hold on to the sense of experiencing something more real than anything in ordinary experience years after the experience. Even when it has become a memory, they remain firmly convinced that they have encountered a level of reality more fundamental than anything given in the everyday world. Both immediately and in the long term, they display an unshakable certainty that there is a life beyond earthly existence. They lose their fear of death as a result of the experience, coming to view death as a transition to a desirable next stage.

Related to this new understanding of death is a conviction that the deeper order they have encountered is purposeful and benevolent. The stories show a compelling attraction to the life beyond. Even so, those who had attempted suicide are unlikely to try it again. They are not afraid of death, but their sense of having a place in a purposeful order greater than themselves leads them to think of their earthly lives as meaningful and precious. Those who come back to earthly existence often do so with a strong assurance that there are important things for them to accomplish.

There is much less research on the effects of frightening experiences, but it has been well documented that encountering an ultimate reality that evokes positive responses leads to significant shifts in attitudes and values. People develop greater concern for others and become more altruistic in their behavior. They become less concerned with material goods and with achieving competitive success. There is also a renewed appreciation for life and a desire to experience it to the fullest.[21] These changes are connected to a sense that the perspective from which they have previously viewed their lives is too limited and that their true identity is bound up with the larger spiritual order that the experience has revealed. The transformations they undergo seem in harmony with the teachings of the world's major spiritual traditions, though they can sometimes put them at odds with widely accepted versions of religious orthodoxy.[22]

---

20. Greyson, *After*, 96.

21. Not all of these changes are welcomed by close friends or relatives who do not undergo this kind of change. Sometimes there are conflicts that lead to the end of relationships that had been built around different values.

22. Some Christians are disturbed by the lack of a message of retribution and

It is obviously possible to reject these accounts of a spiritual realm as deluded. But it is not clear how anyone can be confident that they are. A less skeptical response would be to assess these experiences in the way William James responded to mystical experiences. He says, "It must always remain an open question whether mystical states may not possibly be ... windows through which the mind looks out upon a more extensive and inclusive world."[23] But even if it is an open question to those who don't have experiences like these, the question may not be open for someone who has a compelling sense of having encountered a deeper reality. And even for people who don't have a near-death experience, these experiences can, as James said of mystical experiences, "point in directions to which the religious sentiments even of non-mystical men may incline."[24] Many people, including some who have been skeptical about the possibility of life after death, find the testimony of those who have come to the brink of death persuasive reason to reevaluate their thinking.

---

punishment in these stories. In some circles these experiences are thought to be a work of the devil that contradicts what scripture teaches. However, some competent interpreters claim that the gospel message is fundamentally about achieving healing and wholeness, rather than on escaping a punishment that God is obliged to give. See, for example, Flood, *Healing the Gospel*. If we think that near-death experiences as revelatory, they may furnish an occasion to reconsider ways of thinking that come from reading the Bible through an Augustinian lens.

23. James, *Varieties of Religious Experience*, 327.
24. James, *Varieties of Religious Experience*, 328.

CHAPTER 18

Visits from Dead People

IN SOME CULTURES, SENSING spirits from another realm is not considered abnormal. In many of these cultures, being able to do so is regarded as a badge of honor. People even go through difficult training to learn to acquire altered states of consciousness that are conducive to this kind of perception. But in modern Western culture if you start claiming to see beings from the spirit world or to hear voices that don't come from a physical source, there are quite a few people who will at least look at you funny. They might also question your intelligence or your sanity. So, people in our culture learn to be cautious about sharing experiences that don't fit with commonly accepted ideas of normality. Even so, some of our contemporaries are willing to disclose having experiences that they know many of their peers will treat with suspicion or scorn. I begin with accounts from two prominent Christian writers, describing their encounters with people who have died.

J. B. Phillips is widely known for his biblical translations, as well as his other Christian writings. In one of his books, Phillips gives an account of a visit he had from C. S. Lewis after Lewis's death. Phillips says that he didn't know Lewis well. He had met him only once, though the two had corresponded a significant amount. He writes,

> A few days after his death, while I was watching television, he "appeared" sitting in a chair within a few feet of me, and spoke a few words which were particularly relevant to the difficult

circumstances through which I was passing. He was ruddier in complexion than ever, grinning all over his face and, as the old-fashioned saying has it, positively glowing with health.... He was just *there*—"large as life and twice as natural"! A week later, this time when I was in bed reading before going to sleep, he appeared again, even more rosily radiant than before, and repeated the same message, which was very important to me at the time.[1]

The difficult circumstances Phillips refers to apparently have to do with a type of depression that he struggled with throughout his life. The words from Lewis are reported in other sources as: "It's not so hard as you think, you know." Phillips says that he was puzzled by the experience and talked to a retired bishop about it. He says that the bishop assured him that this sort of thing happens all the time.

The other account comes from distinguished New Testament scholar Dale Allison. He tells of an encounter that occurred after one of his best friends was run over by a drunk driver. After several weeks in a coma, the woman died, along with her unborn child.

> About a week after this, I awakened in the middle of the night. There, standing at the end of my bed, was my friend Barbara. She said nothing; she simply was there. Her appearance did not match the traditional lore about ghosts. She was not faint or transparent or frightening. She was to the contrary beautiful and brightly luminous and intensely real. Her transfigured, triumphant presence, which lasted only a few seconds, gave me great comfort. Although she said nothing, this thought entered my mind: this sight is ineffably beautiful, and any person in that state would be ineffably beautiful.[2]

Several things stand out to me about these accounts. One is that the experienced apparition in each case is lifelike, not a stereotypical ghostly appearance. Another thing is that in both cases the appearance seems to meet some kind of individual need. Finally, I find it noteworthy that neither of these accounts suggests any doubt about what was experienced. Whatever their reflections on what the experience meant, both writers make clear that it was vivid, memorable, and personally significant.

---

1. Phillips, *Ring of Truth*, 89–90.
2. Allison, *Resurrecting Jesus*, 275.

Experiencing a Dead Person

Seeing a dead person who appears as very much alive is not an everyday occurrence. No doubt there are some people who would just rub their eyes and mumble something about a hallucination. But encounters of this kind usually produce a different reaction. Most often, people are convinced that they have had genuine contact with the deceased individual. Psychotherapist Edie Devers has done extensive research on what some have called after-death communications in which a survivor senses a deceased loved one. This experience sometimes takes the form of unusually vivid dreams, but often it involves a sensory awareness or a feeling of a presence that occurs when one is clearly awake. Devers found that this kind of experience is surprisingly common and she collected numerous accounts of it. An important impetus to beginning her research was an account she heard from her sister after the death of their mother.

Devers says that her sister's studies in behavioral science had led her to a firm conviction that whatever couldn't be proved through hard science didn't exist. Her sister reflexively dismissed anything mystical or paranormal. But her skeptical orientation was challenged by an experience two years after their mother's death when she saw a mysterious light. As Devers puts it,

> Within this shimmering light pattern my sister sensed a message, something she could only describe as a thought form. It said, "I'm doing fine. And so are you." . . . My sister knew in that instant it was our mother, and she had come to say goodbye again.[3]

The experience was enough to dramatically alter Edie Devers's sister's worldview. After this experience, she accepted the reality of an unseen world that she had previously dismissed, and this shift had transforming effects on her life.

In most of the stories about this kind of experience, what is seen is not just a light, but a definite visual appearance of the person who has died. Erlendur Haraldsson reports on an extensive study he made of what he calls afterlife encounters in which he verified that the most common type of encounter was a visual appearance.[4] Such appearances are often described as like seeing the person during life, except that the

---

3. Devers, *Goodbye Again*, 8.
4. Haraldsson, *Departed Among the Living*, 5–18.

apparition is typically visible for only a short time before disappearing. In some cases, other senses are involved: sounds, smells, and sensations of touch. In a minority of cases there are explicit words, as in the Phillips story mentioned above. But in most of the incidents, it is only a visual appearance, as in the Allison account.

The visual appearance is frequently described as remarkably real. Consider the account of a man whose wife had died after fifty-six years of marriage:

> I had gone up to our bedroom, preparing to lie down when she was there, so real I could reach out to her. She said, "I love you dear." In a few moments she had gone but I felt wonderful. . . . It was not simply a dream. I was holding my little cat who was with me at the time.[5]

Despite the vividness of this kind of experience and its personal significance, people are often reluctant to talk about what happened. One striking finding of a Swedish study involving widows or widowers was that when these people were asked whether they had sensed their spouse after death, hardly anyone answered in the affirmative. But after they were assured that experiences of the dead are a natural part of the grieving process, around half admitted that they had had this kind of experience.[6]

The sensation of touching is much less frequent, but there are multiple accounts that include such a thing. A widower reports, "I was in the dining room, she was there, I put my arms around her, she was as real and warm as I knew her. She smiled and was gone. . . . It was in the daytime. I have never before experienced any paranormal event"[7] A woman whose husband had died in the hospital described her encounter with him as follows:

> My husband just appeared at the side of the bed. He was in his usual undershorts and T-shirt. He looked so real, no different than you or me. . . . Then my husband got to laughing, and he hugged me and kissed me. He said, "I want you to know that I love you." It was just like he was living.[8]

In some of these stories there is no sensory experience of the other person, but instead a strong feeling of someone's presence. One person

---

5. Rees, *Pointers to Eternity*, 182.
6. Allison, *Encountering Mystery*, 12.
7. Rees, *Pointers to Eternity*, 182.
8. Devers, *Goodbye* Again, 42.

compares it to being in a darkened room, yet knowing that someone else is there. Others have spoken of discerning the presence in a particular part of the room.

Some of these stories involve dreams, but the dreams are described as different from ordinary dreams, more like a real-life meeting in their vividness. One woman describes an additional difference:

> Regular dreams seem to move a little faster.... But this was just a slow, everyday normal pace of living kind of thing.... We had a lengthy discussion, but it wasn't rushed.... When my husband and I were finished talking, we stood up, and he just put his arms around me.... It was so real.[9]

Apparitions of Living People

People can be convinced that they have had an encounter with someone who has died, yet find the experience puzzling. Reflective people are likely to wonder how such an encounter is possible and what it means. It seems relevant in thinking about such questions to consider the fact that apparitional experiences are not only of dead people; they also include experiences of people who are alive at the time, but sensed at a different location from their physical body. Furthermore, the stories of apparitions of someone who has died closely resemble accounts of apparitions of living people. Hornell Hart concluded after an extensive study that these two types of appearance were in most respects "essentially indistinguishable."[10]

Psychologist David Fontana describes a personal experience of an apparition of a living person that he knew well. He says that he had awakened early, as the room was becoming lighter:

> As I opened my eyes I saw a very dear friend of mine sitting on the left side of my bed, between me and the main bedroom window. She ... was sitting with her back against the bed-head a foot or so away from me, and with her legs stretched out in front of her. I ... said, "What on *earth* are you doing here?" She seemed not to hear, and I looked steadily at her. She was as solid as if in the body, and was looking with a thoughtful, serious, rather preoccupied expression toward the foot of the bed. As I gazed at her ... I saw that she was gradually becoming

9. Devers, *Goodbye Again*, 59–60.
10. Hart et al., "Six Theories About Apparitions," 235.

transparent ... then suddenly, like a light being switched off, she was gone.[11]

If this account had been about someone who had died, it would fit with similar stories of encounters with the dead, but the woman in question was very much alive. Fontana called the woman whom he had seen and described his experience to her. She had no awareness of being in his room. But she did remember having what she called a "psychic dream" that she couldn't fully recall. She had considered whether she should tell him about the dream, as she sat up in bed.

In Fontana's story, it is unclear whether the woman's "psychic dream" involved an awareness that she does not recall of being in another place. He suspected, based on his study of out-of-body experiences, that it might. He discusses some reported cases that include both an experience of being somewhere else and a corresponding awareness by someone else of an apparition in that location (often called reciprocal cases). In some stories of this type the person who appears is described as having mastered some kind of mental technique.[12] There is often room for doubt about the credibility of witnesses in cases like this. However, in some cases, the testimony of witnesses judged credible by experienced investigators is supported by written statements of the people involved. These cases include both contemporary incidents and historical ones.

One widely discussed earlier case from the files of the Society for Psychical Research took place in 1863 when Mr. Wilmot and his sister were on a ship traveling from England to New York. For much of the trip, the ship was in a severe storm. Concerned about the safety of her husband, Mrs. Wilmot (in Connecticut) awakened in the middle of the night and had a vivid awareness in her mind of going to her husband's room on the ship. As she came to the entrance to his room, she saw him sleeping on a lower bunk and also observed another man on an upper bunk. She hesitated to go in the room because the man in the upper bunk was staring at her. But she went to her husband's bunk, kissed and hugged him, and then went away. She said that the next day she had a strong sense of having visited her husband.

Mr. Wilmot reported that he dreamed toward morning about seeing his wife in her night-dress come into the room and then kiss and caress him for a few minutes. The next morning, Wilmot's roommate expressed

---

11. Fontana, *Is There an Afterlife?*, 423.
12. Osis and Haraldsson, "OOBEs in Indian Swamis," 147–50.

indignation about a woman being in the room on the previous night. When Wilmot pressed him for details, it became clear to him that what the man had seen corresponded to his dream. Later this man asked Wilmot's sister if she had come to the room. When she said no, he described seeing a woman coming into the room and going to Wilmot.

When Mr. Wilmot got home, almost the first thing his wife asked was whether he had had a visit from her the previous Tuesday. He replied that he had been over a thousand miles away at sea. She then told him about her experience of seeming to come to him and asked about whether his stateroom had upper bunks like the one she observed, extending farther back than the lower one. The SPR took statements from Mr. Wilmot, his sister, and his wife, confirming the details of the case.[13]

Alternative Explanations

People who have apparitional experiences of a dead person know that there is something anomalous about what occurs. They often speak of how real the experience seemed, but some of them wonder whether if another person had been present, that person would have sensed the same thing. In the case cited above in which a woman's husband appears at the side of the bed, he begins to laugh. She tells him not to make so much noise, since her mother in another part of the house will hear. He responds by telling her that she is the only one who can hear him.

A test of the reality of things in standard cases is whether others perceive what you perceive. When only one person sees or hears what others in the vicinity do not see and hear, we tend think that what is perceived is not real. We know that the mind is capable of producing vivid perceptions of what is not physically present. This ability shows itself, for example, in cases when a posthypnotic suggestion is given to a subject to perceive a particular person in the room who is in fact not there. After such a suggestion one may have perceptions of the individual that seem very real, but have been created by the mind in response to the hypnotic suggestion. So, we might think that experiencing someone who has died is a matter of the mind producing realistic perceptions, perhaps to meet some psychological need.

Early investigators of apparitional experiences at a distance tended to apply the term "hallucination" to these experiences, since they did

---

13. Sidgwick, "On the Evidence for Clairvoyance," 41–46.

not think they were produced by ordinary physical sensations. But they discovered that some of these experiences conveyed information that could not have been learned in an ordinary way, such as a danger to a loved one in another location. They coined the term "veridical hallucination" for this kind of experience, typically thinking that the conveyed information was received telepathically.

Louisa Rhine, who compiled numerous examples of crisis apparitions, thought that these apparitions should be understood as mental constructions of someone who learns by extrasensory means of a danger to a loved one and then represents this information as a perception of the person in danger. On this construal, what is perceived is a dramatization in the mind of the person having the apparitional experience, but more than just a fantasy, since it is based on information that comes from extrasensory input. So, on this model an extrasensory apprehension of some fact about a dead individual, such as a desire to assist a living person, might lead to a sensory experience of the deceased person.

That kind of account is not the only way of interpreting these experiences. Cases of apparitions of a living person that I have called reciprocal cases suggest some kind of linkage between minds. So, we might posit that a linkage with the (still existing) mind of a dead person could occur. There are different ways of conceiving such a thing. Bernardo Kastrup thinks that a living person might through a "shift in a state of consciousness" be able to connect with the mind of a dead person. He denies that the dead person can come into our space-time reality, and he thinks that whatever communication occurs would not be linguistic in nature. He characterizes it as a direct sharing of ideas and feelings.[14] Erlendur Haraldsson says that a possible interpretation of apparitional experiences of the dead is to think of the dead person as creating a sensory image in the mind of the living person.[15] He suggests that what is created might be a sense of an invisible presence, or it might be a perceptual appearance of a body.

Of course, to conceive of what occurs as a involving a connection between minds, we would need to think of the mind of the one who has died as continuing to exist. But most people who have this kind of experience find themselves thinking that they have made genuine contact with a loved one in another realm. So, they might treat the assumption of some

---

14. Kastrup, "Apparitions, Ghosts, and Mediumistic Communications."
15. Haraldsson, *Departed Among the Living*, 67–70.

kind of mind-to-mind connection as a reasonable starting point to be given up only if there is convincing evidence to the contrary.

How we understand what is happening in an after-death visit depends to a large extent on our preexisting assumptions. Someone who thinks that consciousness is dependent on a functioning brain will likely rule out possibilities that involve thinking that the consciousness of the deceased person continues to exist. Someone whose understanding of reality has no room for extrasensory perception will gravitate toward the subjective hallucination view. Admittedly, there are people who find this kind of experience convincing enough to alter their assumptions, such as Devers's sister in the story mentioned near the beginning of this chapter. But the urge to explain away what does not fit with your existing views can be hard to resist.

Even so, actually having this kind of experience is generally conducive to thinking that what is experienced is not just a subjective hallucination. Dale Allison says that the experience of his friend Barbara after her tragic death gave him great comfort. I understand him to mean that he took it to be revelatory of a wonderful transformation that had happened to her. But to think in that way means construing the apparition as more than just a fantasy. It would be comforting only if the message conveyed can be seen as a revelation of something that is true.

In modern Western culture, the difficulty of sustaining confidence in revelatory events involving strange experiences like seeing dead people is closely connected with a powerful tendency to think that anything other than what is perceived by ordinary physical means exists only in the mind. But thinking that something is in the mind doesn't show that it might not be revelatory. As J. K. Rowling's Dumbledore says to Harry Potter, "Of course it is happening inside your head, Harry, but why on earth should that mean it is not real?"[16]

Resurrection Appearances

After an extensive study in which he interviewed widows and widowers about their experiences of after-death visits by their spouses, physician Dewi Rees was struck by similarities between these experiences and New Testament accounts of resurrection appearances of Jesus. He recognized that there were differences as well as similarities, but he came to think that

---

16. Rowling, *Harry Potter and the Deathly Hallows*, 723.

contemporary after-death visitations had what he called a "special affinity with the Resurrection."[17] He sensed, however, that to suggest such a thing in Christian circles would be like violating a taboo.

There are multiple reasons why Christians might be reluctant to admit similarities between the accounts of resurrection appearances and contemporary stories of after-death visitations. But an important one is concern that thinking of these stories as at all comparable might undermine confidence in the resurrection of Jesus as *a fact*, rather than a purely subjective experience. There is reason to doubt that after-death visitations should be thought of as ordinary sense experiences, and in our culture, many people assume that the only alternative is to think of them as subjective hallucinations. So, acknowledging that these experiences resemble New Testament resurrection appearances could raise the question about how confident we can be that the resurrection appearances are objectively real.

It might be suggested that there is no analogy to be made because resurrection appearance accounts portray Jesus as solid and lifelike. For example, Luke 24:36–43 describes some of the disciples after the death of Jesus as thinking they are seeing a ghost. As proof that they are not, they are invited to touch Jesus and discover that he is a real flesh-and-bones person. The text also suggests that Jesus eats with the disciples. Some may assume that this kind of experience marks resurrection appearances as very different from after-death visits. However, contemporary accounts of experiencing a loved ones who has died are unlike stereotypical ghost encounters. A significant number of these experiences involve not only seeing, but touching and hearing as well. A common refrain in many of these accounts is that the experience was indistinguishable from the person who had died being physically present. There are features of these experiences that mark them as different from ordinary sense experiences, such as their limited duration and sudden appearances and disappearances. But those characteristics are features of the Jesus's resurrection appearances as well.

A significant number of biblical scholars have doubts about descriptions of resurrection appearances that portray Jesus as solid and real, rather than ethereal. They read accounts mentioning the physicality of his presence as additions to earlier stories that have been invented to reply to the claim that the disciples were seeing a ghost. Interestingly,

---

17. Rees, *Pointers to Eternity*, 180.

awareness of after-death experiences that frequently report lifelike perceptions provides a reason for thinking that these stories of experiencing Jesus as a physical reality may be based on something more than after-the-fact defenses.

One obvious difference between stories of post-mortem visits of loved ones and resurrection appearances is that people who have these visits do not conclude that the dead person has been resurrected. They tend to think of what happens as more like getting a visit from someone who continues to exist after death, but now inhabits a different plane of existence. By contrast the followers of Jesus concluded that Jesus has been raised from the dead. What might account for the difference? New Testament scholar N. T. Wright argues that resurrection appearances by themselves are not enough to lead to belief in the resurrection. But he suggests that those appearances were experienced in the context of having heard stories about Jesus's tomb being empty, which along with Jewish ideas of resurrection of the body was conducive to thinking of Jesus returning to earthly life.[18] By contrast, contemporary post-mortem experiences occur in situations when there is no reason to doubt the permanence of someone's death.

Another kind of experience that might be compared to resurrection appearances is visions of the risen Jesus after the time of the New Testament. Those who reject this comparison sometimes claim that resurrection appearances stop after a limited time. A common way of drawing the line is to follow the pronouncement in Acts 1:3 that Jesus's resurrection appearances lasted for forty days. Whatever Luke's reason for specifying this time limit, the claim raises questions even within the New Testament. In 1 Corinthians 15, Paul famously includes himself as a witness to the resurrection. While his wording does suggest something anomalous about his experience in comparison to the experiences of the original disciples, he refers to it in terms that suggest that his experience is on a par with theirs.

In addition to Paul, the book of Acts also describes an experience in which Stephen sees the risen Jesus. And people have continued to report experiences like this one after New Testament times. Philosopher Phillip Wiebe did an extensive study of visionary experiences of Jesus. He notes that many of the later accounts resemble those described in New Testament texts. His assessment was, "I don't think the evidence

---

18. Wright, *Resurrection of the Son of God*, 690–91.

supports the position that NT appearance accounts are *very* different from the post-biblical accounts."[19] It might be objected that these later reports are clearly visionary experiences whereas the New Testament resurrection appearances are not. However, Paul's Damascus Road experience, which he adds to an authoritative list of resurrection appearances, is a visionary experience. One of the strongest twentieth-century defenders of belief in the resurrection, Wolfhart Pannenberg, judged that other New Testament experiences of the risen Jesus, like Paul's, were also visionary experiences. He was not suggesting that they were purely subjective. He thought of these visionary experiences as messages revealing the truth about Jesus's continued existence.[20]

Some features of New Testament accounts of resurrection appearances seem puzzling when we think of them as ordinary sensory encounters. For example, those who have these experiences are sometimes described as failing to recognize Jesus or doubting that it is really Jesus. Additionally, in these stories Jesus suddenly appears and just as suddenly disappears. And he does things in some of the stories that suggest he is now free of material limitations. Some interpreters have attempted to explain particular anomalous features of these stories by saying that Jesus's body has been transformed. N. T. Wright speaks of what he calls transphysicality.[21] But reflection on the puzzling elements in the stories might suggest another possibility: that the experiences involve a form of perception that differs from ordinary sense perception. In commenting on the disciples' frequent failure to recognize Jesus, New Testament scholar Dale Allison says, "Something more than run-of-the-mill perception was involved. The appearances rather had uncanny features that suit visionary experiences better than everyday seeing."[22]

Even though our age is skeptical about visions as a source of truth concerning reality, people who have visionary experiences in our time often find them completely convincing. Recall, for example, how near-death experiences typically lead to altered understandings about reality and resultant life-transformation. We see that same kind of result in the first witnesses to the resurrection of Jesus. They were so convinced that Jesus had been raised from the dead that many of them were willing to do difficult and risky things because of this conviction.

19. Wiebe, *Visions of Jesus*, 31.
20. Pannenberg, *Jesus*, 92–93.
21. Wright, *Resurrection of the Son of God*, 609.
22. Allison, *Resurrection of Jesus*, 259.

We are in a different place from those early disciples. We receive their testimony about extraordinary encounters in the context of a culture that has taught us to view claims about the extraordinary with suspicion. We are especially suspicious about stories of remarkable events that don't fit with expectations that have been shaped by science. However, strong evidence that people sometimes receive information through extrasensory channels allows us be more receptive to testimony about experiences that our scientific habits of thought might lead us to dismiss, perhaps even to testimony about an event as extraordinary as the resurrection.

CHAPTER 19

Deathbed Phenomena

To A LARGE EXTENT, our culture has separated us from the experience of death. Unless we are in particular professions, such as police officer or ICU nurse, our experience may be limited to seeing a dead body at a funeral or being present when a relative dies in the hospital. When we see people in the hospital who are close to death, it is typically individuals who are heavily medicated, and in many cases kept alive by technological means. There is a significant contrast between the typical modern experience of death in a hospital and the classic historical scene of people gathered around the bed of a dying relative at home where family members exchange final words.

In recent years the hospice movement has provided an alternative way to die that is focused on offering comfort during the dying process to those who have refused life-prolonging treatments whose benefits they judge insufficient to outweigh predictable negative consequences. Patients in hospice treatment die at home or in facilities reserved for this kind of care. People experienced in hospice work come to know things about death that most of us are not aware of. Much of what they report was likely well known in cultures where people were closer to the experience of death, but their accounts can be eye-opening to those of us who are less familiar with such matters.

In this chapter I want to focus on two kinds of occurrences near the time of death that seem particularly striking. One phenomenon that has been repeatedly observed by those who care for the dying has been called *terminal lucidity*. Sometimes people who have been in states where their cognitive capacities are severely diminished suddenly become fully aware of their surroundings and exhibit normal or even enhanced mental functioning for a period before death. Given standard ways of thinking about the relation between our physical condition and mental states, this phenomenon is puzzling. The mind seems to emerge at greater strength when someone is in a physical state that we would expect to lead to diminished mental capacities. I will be providing some examples of the phenomenon in this chapter and reflecting on its significance.

Another phenomenon that hospice workers have described is visions by those who are dying. Typically, these visions involve encounters with people who have previously died, such as relatives of the patient. Sometimes there are also experiences of spiritual entities, such as angelic beings. Additionally, the visions may include awareness of a beautiful place to which the dying person is invited. People who are present and do not perceive what the dying person describes often call the reported experiences hallucinations. But while it can be tempting to dismiss these visions as products of a dying brain, we might wonder how confident we should be in that interpretation of what is going on. Even if we are skeptical about the idea that these experiences involve actual contact with dead relatives, might visions of people near the time of death be revelations of a level of reality that is ordinarily hidden from us?

Terminal Lucidity

Professor of Orthopedic Surgery Scott Haig offers a thought-provoking account of a patient of his named David who was dying of cancer.[1] He had been called in to take care of David's hip and pelvic bones. When Haig first met the patient, David was able to converse freely, and his demeanor was cheerful, though that appearance might have been primarily for the benefit of his family. But as the cancer progressed, David's speech became slurred, then incoherent. Finally, he stopped speaking and moving at all. The brain scans at this point showed that there was barely any brain left. David showed no expression or response to anything. It was as if he was no longer there. One Saturday when Haig came to check on David, he discovered that he had died the previous evening.

---

1. Haig, "Brain" paras. 1–12.

He met the nurse who had been with him at the time of his death. What the nurse said was shocking.

She reported that David had woken up the previous night just after Haig's visit. She said that he had said goodbye to the family. "Like I'm talkin' to you right here. Like a miracle. He talked to them and patted them and smiled for about five minutes. Then he went out again, and he passed in the hour."[2] Haig wrote,

> it wasn't David's brain that woke him up to say goodbye that Friday. His brain had already been destroyed. Tumor metastases don't simply occupy space and press on things, leaving a whole brain. The metastases actually replace tissue. Where that gray stuff grows, the brain is just not there.[3]

Haig says that what woke David up was his *mind*, a mind that, contrary to materialist dogma, is not simply a byproduct of the brain.

There are numerous accounts of cognitive faculties that have been lost, suddenly reappearing a short time before death. Accounts from physicians in the nineteenth century describe the phenomenon, though there is not much mention of it in twentieth-century medical literature before the experiences of hospice workers called it to the attention of physicians. Some of the case studies include schizophrenics and Alzheimer's patients suddenly recovering in a period before death. One case concerns a woman who had had Alzheimer's for nine years and no longer recognized friends or family members. However, she recognized them the day before she died, and she also was able to accurately tell people how old she was.[4] In another case a woman with Alzheimer's who had been unresponsive for five years, shortly before her death recognized her daughter and began to converse coherently about death, her church, and her family.[5]

The phenomenon of suddenly regaining mental capacities after a long period in which they were apparently lost is difficult to understand on the assumption that the mind is just a byproduct of brain activity. In earlier chapters I pointed out that some philosophers' reflection on psychic phenomena led them to posit that the brain is not the cause of mental functioning but acts as a kind of filter to reduce mental input to

---

2. Haig, "Brain" para. 5.
3. Haig, "Brain" para. 8.
4. Nahm and Greyson, "Terminal Lucidity, and Dementia," 942–43.
5. Nahm et al., "Terminal Lucidity," 140.

what is most useful for survival purposes. Thinking about terminal lucidity from the perspective of this view might suggest that as a person approaches death, the ordinary capacity of the brain to filter mental input is diminished, enabling the mind to operate briefly in a less constricted way. We might wonder whether the same reduction of filtering has something to do with reports in cases of near-death experiences of a sense of reality greater than what occurs in ordinary perception.

Transitional Visions

Hospice nurses Maggie Callanan and Patricia Kelley report that dying patients often interact with beings who are not perceived by others. These beings include people who have died, and sometimes figures with some religious significance, such as angelic beings. The nurses describe representative examples from their own patients.[6] A patient they call Fred was giving instructions to family members about practical matters that they needed to deal with after he died. "Periodically he'd break off the conversation to look across the room as if seeing someone we could not see. Once he turned his head again and said impatiently, 'Would you wait, I'm not ready yet!'"[7] Another patient, Martha, spoke to a nurse about the dead relatives she was seeing. When the nurse asked whether they were here at the moment, Martha replied that they had just left. She said that they come and go. The nurse asked what it was like. Martha replied, "Well, sometimes we talk, but usually I just know that they're here. . . . I know that they love me and that they'll be with me when it's time."[8]

Many cultures have stories about deathbed visions, but modern research on the topic is usually traced to the physicist William Barrett in the early twentieth century. Barrett's wife, a physician, sparked his interest in the topic when she told him about a vision one of her patients had. The woman had delivered a healthy baby, but she was dying. Here is Dr. Barrett's description:

> Suddenly she looked eagerly toward one part of the room, a radiant smile illuminating her whole countenance. "Oh lovely, lovely," she said. I asked, "What is lovely?" . . . "Lovely brightness—wonderful beings." Then seeming to focus her attention

---

6. Callanan and Kelley, *Final Gifts*, 85–97.
7. Callanan and Kelley, *Final Gifts*, 88.
8. Callanan and Kelley, *Final Gifts*, 89.

on one place for a moment—she exclaimed almost with a kind of joyous cry, "Why it's Father! Oh, he's so glad I'm coming."[9]

The woman's baby is brought to her. She looks at it with interest, asking whether she should stay for the baby's sake. Then she declares that she can't. She says, "If you could see what I do, you would know I can't stay."[10] As she returns to the vision, she is puzzled because her sister Vida is with her father. She hadn't been told because of her precarious health condition about her sister's death three weeks earlier.

In an earlier chapter I mentioned that there are cases of near-death experiences in which someone not known to be dead is encountered among dead relatives. There are multiple stories of deathbed visions in which this occurs as well. Callanan and Kelley describe a case involving a Chinese woman they call Su. As she nears death, Su has repeated dreams of her husband who had died years earlier. But she is confused because her husband comes to her with her sister, who she says lives in China. When the nurse discusses the matter with Su's daughter, the daughter says that the family decided not to tell Su of her sister's death for fear of upsetting her. When Su is told that her sister has died, she says, "Now I understand."[11]

In addition to experiences of people who have died or of spiritual beings, deathbed visions can include seeing some place beyond this world that evokes a sense of beauty, peacefulness, and joy. Sometimes the dying say that they are unable to put the experience into words. But when they try to do so, they use earthly images, such as a beautiful garden with flowers. It is also common also to speak of extraordinarily intense light and color. Sometimes people just fall back on saying how beautiful everything is. One woman who reported that she had visited heaven. After speaking of its beauty, she said, "If heaven is like that, then I'm ready."[12]

It is not surprising that visions of this sort are often treated as delusional. However, studies suggest that they are different from the ravings of someone who has lost contact with reality. In many cases people who have these visions are aware of their situation and able to converse coherently with relatives and healthcare workers. Sometimes they ask whether a relative or nurse can see what they see. They are almost always convinced that

9. Barrett, *Death Bed Visions*, 14.
10. Barrett, *Death Bed Visions*, 14.
11. Callanan and Kelley, *Final Gifts*, 93–94.
12. Osis and Haraldsson, *At the Hour of Death*, 165.

what they are encountering is real, not just hallucinatory. Sometimes they sound like mystics in saying that what the visions show is more real than what we experience through ordinary sensation.

It is noteworthy that people with no prior religious beliefs may have these visions. One woman reported that she had seen an angel, but reaffirmed her disbelief in God.[13] However, most people who had previously thought of themselves as atheists or agnostics apparently change their minds because of what they experience. One man who described himself as an atheist reported that the apparitions he was seeing, which included dead people and beings he called angels, were beyond his control and outside of his belief system. He said, "I am looking at life from a new perspective."[14]

These visions are marked by a notable absence of fear. The figures perceived are usually regarded as coming to aid in the transition to what comes next. Patients who have deathbed visions often show signs of delight at what they are experiencing. Recall the woman from an earlier example whose attraction to what she had seen in her vision was so strong that she couldn't bring herself to stay on earth, even for the sake of the baby she had just delivered.

Shared Visions

Most cases of deathbed visions are experienced only by the person who is dying. However, there are now numerous reports of cases in which people other than the dying patient get caught up in the experience. When Raymond Moody went to medical school, he was already well known for his pioneering work in near-death experiences. However, he hadn't heard of a shared deathbed vision until one of his professors in medical school told him about her experience.

Dr. Jamieson, a respected faculty member, had attempted CPR when her mother had a heart attack. She ceased her efforts only when it became evident that continuing them would be futile. At this point Dr. Jamieson felt herself lifted out of her body. She was looking down on her own body and her mother's dead body from above. Then she realized that her mother was hovering next to her in spirit form. She said goodbye to her mother, who was now smiling. Next, she noticed what she called a

---

13. Callanan and Kelley, *Final Gifts*, 91.
14. Lerma, *Into the Light*, 186–90.

"breach in the universe." Light was pouring into the room, and she could see people she identified as deceased friends of her mother, as well as others she didn't know. Then the light was gone, and she found herself back in her body next to her dead mother.[15]

In time Moody discovered multiple accounts of shared visions at someone's deathbed, and he even had a shared vision of his own. He, along with five other family members, were at his mother's bedside as she died. His account of what happened is as follows:

> As we held hands around the bed, the room seemed to change shape and four of the six of us felt as though we were being lifted off the ground. I had the feeling that the room had turned into the shape of an hourglass. I had a strong pull, like a riptide that was pulling me out to sea, only the pull was upward.[16]

Moody's sister pointed to the end of the bed and said, "Dad's here! He's come back to get her!" Everyone who was present said that the light in the room changed to a soft texture. There was also a shared sense of great joy. Moody's brother-in-law said later, "I felt like I left my physical body and went into another plane with her."[17]

Shared visions at someone's death include some features characteristic of near-death experiences that are not commonly part of deathbed visions. The Jamieson story, for example, involves an out-of-body experience. Another remarkable phenomenon that sometimes occurs in these experiences is awareness of a life review of the person who is dying. The adult son of a woman named Susan was dying of cancer. Susan was "swept up in a cloud" with him when he died. During this time, she witnessed many scenes from his life, some of which were familiar and some she didn't know about. The life review was so specific that she was later able to recognize friends of his she had never met and places she had never been.[18]

Another woman at her mother's deathbed described the light changing intensity, becoming much brighter, along with what she called a "rocking motion" going through her body. She said that she began to see the room from different angles, from above and from the other side of the bed. As she puts it,

---

15. Moody, *Glimpses of Eternity*, 8–9.
16. Moody, *Glimpses of Eternity*, 49.
17. Moody, *Glimpses of Eternity*, 50.
18. Moody, *Glimpses of Eternity*, 9–10.

> I don't know whether I was out of my body or not. . . . I was just glued to scenes from my mother's life that were flashing throughout the room. . . . The scenes . . . contained things that had happened to my mother, some of which I remembered but others I didn't. I could see her looking at the scenes too. . . . By the time the flashes of light were going on, she was out of her body. I saw my father, who passed seven years before, standing there . . . coaching my mother out of her body. . . . A part of her that was transparent just stood right up . . . and she and my father glided off into the light and disappeared.[19]

Some of the accounts, including Moody's own experience, involve more than one person at the deathbed sharing a vision. A woman was gathered with two brothers, a sister, and her sister-in-law as her mother was dying. Suddenly, they all saw a bright light that she described as "not any kind of light on this earth." At the point when her mother died, she says,

> we saw vivid bright lights that seemed to gather around and shape up into . . . I don't know what to call it except an entranceway. . . . We saw my mother lift up out of her body and go through that entranceway. Being by the entranceway, incidentally, was a feeling of complete joy. My brother called it a chorus of joyful feelings, and my sister heard beautiful music, although none of the rest of us did.[20]

When strange phenomena are experienced only by the patient who is dying, the hypothesis that the dying brain has produced a fantasy can seem plausible. But in cases of shared visions something more is needed to explain why people whose health is not in a compromised condition have the visionary experience. Someone could say that the emotional situation is conducive to fantasies. In cases where multiple people seem to have a similar kind of visionary experience, it is possible to posit some kind of group hallucination. But we can also ask whether that possibility is more plausible than thinking that the shared vision might be a kind of disclosure of a level of reality that is not ordinarily perceived.

Our culture predisposes us to think that some subjective interpretation of visionary experiences is preferable to the idea that visions might expand our awareness of reality. For us, talk of realities that surpass what we can perceive by means of the senses seems problematic. Some deathbed

---

19. Moody, *Glimpses of Eternity*, 37–38.
20. Moody, *Glimpses of Eternity*, 13–14.

visions, like near-death visions, apparently lead to knowing things that are not learned in ordinary ways, such as the fact that someone not previously known to be dead has died. But when the vision involves meeting dead people or perceiving otherworldly locations or angelic beings, what is experienced goes beyond what can be checked by ordinary sensory observations. We may assume that we should dismiss reports that we can't verify by ordinary empirical means. But people who have extraordinary visions, and some who hear about them, are often convinced that they show us things about reality that the senses do not reveal.

Even if a deathbed vision might disclose deep truths about reality, there can be questions about how it should be interpreted. For example, should the experience be understood as a literal encounter, or is it more like a dramatization of truths that have been discerned by extrasensory means? If extrasensory content is involved, is there a reliable way separating that content from imaginative constructions of the visionary?

There are also questions about how we should understand the continued existence these visions suggest. For example, is it some kind of extension of earthly time, or might it involve an experience of time we are unable to conceive? And how should we think about someone's identity in the afterlife? Does it persist in pretty much the way that we think of it as continuing in earthly existence? Or might some aspects of the kind of individual identity we are familiar with drop off? If it is true that our minds are connected with other people's minds in ways that are not apparent in this life, a fuller experience of that connection might radically alter our understanding of who we are. Perhaps life after death is different enough from earthly experience that we can only represent it in symbolic fashion. That might be one way of understanding Paul's claim, "For now we see in a mirror dimly, but then we will see face to face" (1 Cor 13:12).

The point is that even if we take deathbed visions and near-death experiences to reveal to us a wider reality, we might think that the descriptions involve a considerable amount of creative imagination. That is not to suggest that these disclosures are useless. They seem to have a transforming effect on people who experience them. If we are looking for a message conveyed by these visions, I suspect we should think of it as closely related to central ideas that give people a sense of comfort and joy. They are convinced that death is not something to fear, that the next stage is something they can joyfully welcome, that it involves a kind of fulfillment beyond what is available in earthly life.

CHAPTER 20

God Moves in Paranormal Ways

A COMMONLY HELD VIEW among Christians is that God allows nature to take its course most of the time, but occasionally steps in to override finite control. However, observation of what happens in the world makes it difficult to believe that God is regularly intervening in this way. Disastrous events occur often when there is no indication that God is doing much to prevent them. If we think of God as deciding when to override the natural order, it appears that God is biased toward inaction in cases where we think action is needed. Reflection on the terrible things that God seems to allow leads some people to a adopt a deistic picture of God as uninvolved in the created order and others to conclude that God doesn't exist.

However, it is a picture of God as managing what happens by selectively taking control that underlies these doubts about God's involvement in the world. There is another way to think about the matter. We could think that creating our kind of world involves God letting go of control so that finite beings can operate independently of God. Some believers are uncomfortable with the idea of a world in which God is not maintaining control over what happens. But the idea that God lets go of control need not imply that God stands back and does nothing. Even if God is not stepping in to take over, God might still influence created things in ways that don't override the powers they have been given. On this view, what God seeks for the world can be thwarted by created beings who are unreceptive to God's influence. But when these beings respond positively, God's purposes can be accomplished through them.

This way of understanding things puts a significant amount of responsibility on us. A poem attributed to St. Teresa of Avila contains the line, "Christ has no body on earth now but yours. No hands, no feet on earth but yours."[1] The poem takes the New Testament statement that Christians are the body of Christ to mean that what God can do in the world is limited to what created beings aligned with God's purposes bring about. No doubt the words are intended as an encouragement to accept our role as God's agents. But implicit in the idea that God's work is done through willing agents is the thought that there are things that God won't be able to accomplish because human beings are unwilling to align themselves with God's purposes or because people pursing God's will are opposed by created powers that are resisting what God seeks.

The idea that what God does is limited to what creaturely powers bring about might be taken as a denial that there can be outcomes that we recognize as extraordinary. However, as I have been suggesting throughout this book, in addition to ordinary human powers there are powers that go beyond what our standard ways of thinking about the world would lead us to expect. The use of these powers can sometimes achieve the kind of results that people typically describe as miraculous.

Divine-Human Encounters

Christians agree that God sometimes works through human powers. The powers involved are typically what we think of as ordinary human capabilities. We use ordinary knowledge or skills when we bring food to the hungry or solace to the brokenhearted. Sometimes we may speak a truth that someone needs to hear or give support to an organization providing housing for the homeless. We are unlikely to think of such actions as involving anything paranormal. However, if we think of God as involved, we may be picturing God as communicating with us by some extrasensory means to make us aware of what needs to be done in a way that enhances our motivation to do it.

Some biblical accounts of divine-human encounters suggest that interacting with God resembles conversing with another human being. However, there is reason to suspect that these accounts are

---

1. Teresa of Avila, "Christ Has No Body."

dramatizations of something that differs significantly from ordinary conversational exchanges. A key to understanding what encounters underlying these accounts might have been like is noticing how often biblical accounts describe God as communicating through dreams or visions.[2] We can describe a dream or a visionary experience in ways that make it sound like ordinary sense experience, but if God uses dreams or visions to communicate, the input comes through the unconscious mind rather than through sensory channels. In other words, the communication we receive is extrasensory.

In some of the most dramatic stories of extrasensory perception, someone has an impression or a dream with a clear message that is hard to ignore. Similarly, we can conceive of cases in which a person gets an unmistakable instruction from God. But most often, what comes from the unconscious mind will be like the biblical "still small voice" that is easily drowned out by noisier things that distract our attention from it. In the most common cases, a Christian may think that she is receiving God's guidance, but have doubts about whether it is God's voice or her own. Even when a message comes from God, our ability to receive it can be distorted by our preconceptions and biases. Nevertheless, we can sometimes be nudged toward productive action.

People typically think of extrasensory perception as a rare thing. It is true that dramatic instances in which a person receives clear and verifiable information that we recognize could not have been acquired in an ordinary way may not be frequent. But these dramatic cases are likely to be just the tip of the iceberg. We can be influenced by what comes through extrasensory channels even when we are unaware that such a thing is happening. If extrasensory perception is real, it is likely to be a hidden factor that potentially affects many of our choices.

If you make a choice to take a particular job or to avoid a particular person, there may be nothing that you later discover to confirm that extrasensory information affected your decision. But if the unconscious mind has a linkage to information that goes beyond what we get from the senses, it seems plausible that our behavior is sometimes affected by information that we possess, but don't know we possess. To put this idea in the context of divine guidance, our decisions may sometimes be influenced by information that God makes available, even when we have no way of recognizing that this information had any effect on what

---

2. Kelsey, *God, Dreams and Revelation*, 31–49, 81–98.

we did. We might, for example, act to avoid a danger because of a vague feeling of uneasiness.

There is a story from the Rhine collection in which a fifteen-year-old girl accepts a date from a young man she had met while hitchhiking. When he arrived at her house, he made a good impression on the girl's parents. They liked him better than the kind of boys she had been dating. But when she came out of her room, she took one look at him and immediately retreated to her room. Her parents took her breach of etiquette to be a sign of immaturity. Her father went to her room and implored her to go on the date. She was adamant in her refusal, even though she couldn't explain why in a way that made sense. Several years later a newspaper story revealed that the man she had refused to go out with was a serial killer who had murdered four young women.[3] Without this additional information about the man, we would be unlikely to entertain the idea of anything extrasensory going on. But cases like this give us reason to suspect that extrasensory information may often play a role in what we do, even when we don't realize it.

I suggested earlier that we can think of God as attempting to influence us without controlling us. If we accept that human beings can receive extrasensory input, we can think of God's influence as supplying us with information at an unconscious level that might motivate action in harmony with God's purposes. We should notice, however, that while this kind of information might affect what we do, we can resist it. Psychotherapists speak of defenses against truths we don't want to acknowledge. Such defenses can block what we are aware of at an unconscious level from coming to our conscious attention at all. Even when something from the unconscious mind makes it through our defenses into consciousness, it can be in a disguised form. Hence, we can typically avoid recognizing God's communication or direct our attention away from it. If we do respond positively, it may be because we have made efforts to weaken some of our resistance to attending to these messages. The practice of prayer is an important way of becoming more receptive to God. At its best, prayer redirects our attention toward something wider than self-centered concerns that might block divine guidance.

---

3. Feather and Schmicker, *Gift*, 126–27.

Meaningful Coincidences

Suppose you go to a park and meet a stranger who becomes a lifelong friend. Or you narrowly escape serious injury because of an impulse to do something unusual. Or you select a college course because it fits into a time slot you have available, and the course evokes a passionate interest that leads to a career choice. Some people have an urge to think of events like these as more than just coincidences. An extreme version of this tendency is the view that everything that happens to you is part of a prearranged plan.

The opposite tendency to those who find meaningful patterns everywhere is to find them hardly anywhere. There are people who make efforts to guard against thinking there is some kind of deeper meaning when there might be only coincidence. They point out, for example, that while it might seem that meeting someone you eventually marry was planned or even fated, it could be just a random event that had a happy ending. Similarly, it might seem that a stranger who is at the right place at the right time to provide lifesaving help was somehow sent there, but fortunate coincidences are likely to occur occasionally.

Psychic phenomena complicate the issue of when we should attribute what happens to coincidence. There are undoubtedly occasions where we have little reason to think that anything more than chance is involved, but if psychic powers are real, some things that might be ascribed to luck or coincidence may come about because of extrasensory knowledge or psychokinetic influence. You pick up the phone to call someone who is already on the line because she is calling you. It might be coincidence, or it might be a telepathic connection between minds. You become uneasy about taking a particular flight and cancel your reservations on a flight that subsequently crashes. Was it a coincidence, or might you have had some precognitive awareness of a danger? You are trying to stop someone from driving while intoxicated, and just as this person is driving off, the car's fuel pump stops working. Was it a chance occurrence, or might it have been an unconscious psychokinetic influence on your part?

The Hand of God?

Some cases where psychic phenomena may be involved are also cases where we might suspect that God is involved. However, the urge to see God's involvement can be excessive. Rachel Held Evans describes her experience of going to a wedding in Ohio the weekend Hurricane Katrina hit.[4] A number of guests were coming from out of town, and there were multiple delays at airports in the region from which many of the guests would depart. Despite the obstacles, the entire family made it to the event. Someone at the wedding referred to the fact that everyone had made it as "a God thing." Presumably this guest meant that God had somehow arranged events so that the wedding would go well. Evans felt a disconnect. She had been watching news reports of desperate families trapped on rooftops during the hurricane as they waited for rescue, and of death and injury from storm surges that had breached the levees. She found it disconcerting to imagine that God was concerned enough to make sure the wedding went well, but not concerned enough to help those in more desperate circumstances. Evans adds that she later heard the phrase "God thing" applied to a range of benefits, including scholarships, job offers, new cars, and remodeled kitchens.

There is, of course, a sense in which all good things can be thought of as divine blessings. But the picture of God taking action to arrange it so that Christians are shielded from inconveniences most people face or given extra material benefits because of their piety makes us wonder about God's priorities. Why would God act to secure relatively unimportant benefits, but fail to act to prevent or ameliorate suffering from real disasters? Are we to imagine that God has special favorites who get blessings, but cares less about those who aren't given such help?

The point is that assessments of God's involvement are tied to particular ideas of God. If we have defective ideas about God, those defects are likely to be reflected in how we assess what God does in relation to particular events. We might, as the Evans example shows, have extravagant views about God micromanaging the world to benefit favored individuals. Or we might project our ideas of a vengeful God onto cases in which people experience tragedy. Biophysicist Joyce Hawkes reports that she was in graduate school when her mother died suddenly. The pastor of her fundamentalist church told her over the phone that her mother's death occurred because she was being punished for choosing to study science. She says that this encounter pushed her into atheism.[5]

Recognizing that defective theology can lead to misguided interpretations of how God is involved doesn't show that we should refrain

---

4. Evans, *Faith Unraveled*, 151.
5. Hawkes, "Following the Thread," 186.

from any claims about God's involvement in the world. If we understand the nature of God to be revealed in Christ, we can often find particular outcomes that resonate with our understanding of what God seeks to do. Some of these cases may also be instances in which we can suspect that something paranormal was the means by which God's purposes were achieved.

A young man who had decided to kill himself was sitting in his car at an isolated lake, ready to end his life. Another car pulls up, and his brother steps out of that car. The man asks his brother why he is there. The brother says he doesn't know. He got in the car not knowing where he was going, but he knew that he needed to get in the car and drive.[6] If you accept telepathic influence, you might suspect that a connection between minds was the means through which the beneficial result occurred. If you also believe in God, you might think that God did something to activate this kind of telepathic influence, or you might think of this event as a fortunate result of the kinds of powers of mind that are a part of the created order.

It is understandable why Christians toward the progressive end of the theological spectrum might shy away from tales of remarkable events that are sometimes used to affirm questionable views of God. But thinking that paranormal processes are sometimes a means through which God acts can be combined with a critical judgment that informs our assessments of when and how to speak of God. Furthermore, our understanding of psychic phenomena may help in deciding when to give particular claims about extraordinary events serious consideration.

Adjusting Our Pictures

One reaction to claiming that God works through powers that we might think of as human potentials is to say that it explains away the miraculous. I think that it is more accurate to say that alters a common way that Christians have conceived the miraculous. We sometimes imagine God doing something that is analogous to Harry Potter casting a magical spell. God says the proper words, so to speak, and some result occurs in the world. In this picture whether something remarkable happens is entirely due to what God does.

---

6. Netburn, "Strange Coincidences" paras. 16–17.

But how should we think about the involvement of human beings in extraordinary events? In many biblical stories of miraculous events a human being does something, and then there are results that go beyond what we ordinarily think of humans as capable of producing. For example, Moses stretches out his hand, and the sea parts (Exod 14:21). Someone might claim that the human acts in these stories have nothing to do with bringing about the results. Stretching your hand over waters, for example, won't make the sea part. God has to do it. But would that make what Moses does just extraneous? One answer might be that God could part the sea without Moses stretching his hand over it, but having Moses stretch out his hand is the equivalent of saying "abracadabra." It is done for the sake of dramatic effect.

But how sure are we that the human acts described in these stories have nothing to do with causing the remarkable results? We might feel confident that they don't if we had never heard of human beings producing results that are inexplicable in terms of what we know of physical causality. But as this book makes clear, stories of people doing things that have extraordinary results are abundant. People can doubt such stories, but those of us who are convinced that psychic powers sometimes enable people to do extraordinary things may suspect that such powers play a role in biblical accounts of extraordinary events. Such a view does not conflict with the possibility of God's involvement, since we can conceive of God as working through latent potentials of human agents.

Some may worry that if there are potentials for extraordinary powers of human agents that can be used for good, those powers could also be used for evil purposes. Admittedly so, but finding the prospect deplorable or frightening is not a reason for denying it. There are biblical texts that describe people who are not aligned with God's purposes as having extraordinary powers (e.g., Exod 7:11; Matt 24:24). Both ordinary and extraordinary powers can be used for evil. But as I pointed out in a previous chapter, we can recognize the dangers without exaggerating them or despairing over them.

Signs of the New Creation

The standard New Testament terms for acts of power described in Gospel accounts are translated as signs and wonders. The healings and exorcisms are signs of a kind of liberation God seeks for human life. John the Baptist was apparently bothered that Jesus's achievements seemed limited in relation to his expectations of what would happen when the Messiah came (Matt 11:2–6; Luke 7:19–23). But what occurs on a limited scale in Jesus's ministry becomes for Christians a kind of template for projecting a more far-reaching transformation that God is seeking for our world.

The pivotal event that shapes this expectation is, of course, the resurrection of Jesus. Christians thought of his resurrection as the definitive sign of a new order God was bringing about. New Testament scholar N. T. Wright calls the resurrection a signal that God has begun to complete what Hebrew Scriptures had promised. It was understood to be "an initial and representative act of new creation."[7]

Physicist and theologian John Polkinghorne says, "The new creation represents the transformation of the universe when it enters into a new and close relationship with its Creator so that it becomes... suffused with the divine presence."[8] The "old creation" might be thought of as bringing into existence something that can have a degree of independence from God. But this independence carries with it the likelihood of resistance to what God seeks for the world. Thinking of creation as being "suffused with the divine presence" suggests a new kind of harmony between God's purposes and creaturely freedom.

Such a harmony would make possible an expansion of human control. The signs and wonders we see in the life of Jesus can be thought of as previews of the kind of control over nature that God seeks for us. Healing miracles, for example, are a foretaste of what it would be like to have a control over our bodies that allows us to alter the conditions that lead to disease and physical defects. Nature miracles point toward an adjustment between human life and the natural environment that allows both to flourish. The expansion of human powers should be thought of in relation to God's intention that we become co-creators who are involved in bringing God-given potentials of the created order to fulfillment.

However, giving us greater powers of knowledge or influence over material things makes sense only if our concerns can be brought closer to God's concerns. For early Christians, joining a Christian community meant accepting an understanding of God's purposes that was shaped by particular communal ideals deriving from the teaching of Jesus, such as concern for the weak and vulnerable and rejection of coercive

---

7. Wright, *Resurrection of the Son of God*, 729–30.
8. Polkinghorne, *Faith of a Physicist*, 167.

power. So, we might think of this community as intended to be a kind of training ground for sensitizing people to the divine presence in a way that allows proper use of powers that will eventually be more fully available. Obviously, the Christian community hasn't always functioned in this way. Too often Christian teachings have been distorted by cultural assumptions alien to the community's central ideals. But we can also see ways in which Christianity has transformed fundamental societal assumptions in a desirable direction.[9]

Many of the powers displayed in early Christianity appear to be connected to shifts away from ordinary consciousness to states in which influences from the subconscious mind can be received. In practices such as speaking in tongues (*glossolalia*), ordinary consciousness gives way to utterance that comes from an unconscious level. There is a similar diversion from conscious control in visions, which are mentioned as a sign of the Spirit's coming (Acts 2:17), as well as in prophetic utterances, and likely in acts of healing. In the early church, practices and rituals conducive to letting go of the kind of rational control that our culture prizes were a means to entering into states in which extraordinary powers could become available.

Philosopher Jules Evans remarks, "Secular modernity shaped us into walled-off rational selves disconnected from our subliminal mind, our bodies, each other, the natural world, and (perhaps) from God."[10] Christians have not escaped this shaping. But even in the modern world, there are experiences that seem to connect us to the subliminal mind in a way that opens access to a level of reality from which we are ordinarily blocked. Of course, experiences of giving up control are not all benign. There are dangers. New Testament passages call for discernment (e.g., 1 John 4:1). But we might think of Christian practices as helping to open us to beneficial potentials of the spiritual realm.

If we think that the world God has created is more mysterious than our culture leads us to expect, we can be alert for events or experiences that reveal a spiritual dimension of reality. If we have reason to think that extrasensory perception occurs, we can sometimes expect dreams, visions, and intuitions that convey an awareness of God and God's purposes that motivates and directs us. If our minds have powers to influence other minds or physical states, we may sometimes in

---

9. Hart, *Atheist Delusions*, 166–82.
10. Evans, *Art of Losing Control*, xxiii.

prayerful states utilize these powers in harmony with what God seeks for the world. If we can break free of the constraints of a view of reality in which physical causes account for everything, we may find events or experiences that call our attention to God's presence in the world.

Bibliography

Alexander, Eben. *Proof of Heaven: A Neurosurgeon's Journey into the Afterlife*. New York: Simon and Schuster, 2012.
Allison, Dale C., Jr. *Encountering Mystery: Religious Experience in a Secular Age*. Grand Rapids: Eerdmans, 2022.
———. *Resurrecting Jesus: The Earliest Christian Tradition and Its Interpreters*. London: T&T Clark, 2005.
———. *The Resurrection of Jesus: Apologetics, Polemics, History*. London: T&T Clark, 2021.
Almeder, Robert. *Death and Personal Survival: The Evidence for Life after Death*. Lanham, MD: Rowman and Littlefield, 1992.
Arcangel, Dianne. *Afterlife Encounters: Ordinary People, Extraordinary Experiences*. Charlottesville, VA: Hampton Roads, 2005.
Augustine. *The Literal Meaning of Genesis*. Vol. 1. Translated by John Hammond Taylor. Ancient Christian Writers 41. New York: Paulist, 1982.
Barrett, Justin. *Why Would Anyone Believe in God?* Walnut Creek, CA: Rowman and Littlefield, 2004.
Barrett, William. *Death Bed Visions*. London: Methuen, 1926.
Beauregard, Mario, and Denyse O'Leary. *The Spiritual Brain: A Neuroscientist's Case for the Existence of the Soul*. New York: HarperCollins, 2008.
Braude, Stephen E. *Immortal Remains: The Evidence for Life After Death*. Lanham, MD: Rowman and Littlefield, 2003.
———. *The Limits of Influence: Psychokinesis and the Philosophy of Science*. London: Routledge and Kegan Paul, 1986.
Broad, C. D. *Lectures on Psychical Research*. London: Routledge and Kegan Paul, 1962.
Callanan, Maggie, and Patricia Kelley. *Final Gifts*. New York: Simon and Schuster, 1992.
Carter, Chris. *Science and Psychic Phenomena: The Fall of the House of Skeptics*. Rochester, VT: Inner Traditions, 2012.
Chalmers, David. "Facing Up to the Problem of Consciousness." *Journal of Consciousness Studies* 2 (1995) 200–219.
Cheung, Theresa, and Julia Mossbridge. *The Premonition Code: The Science of Precognition: How Sensing the Future Can Change Your Life*. London: Watkins, 2018.

Clark, Nancy. *Divine Moments: Ordinary People Having Spiritually Transformative Experiences*. Fairfield, IA: 1stWorld, 2012.
Devers, Edie. *Goodbye Again*. Kansas City, MO: Andrews and McMeel, 1997.
Dossey, Larry. *Healing Words: The Power of Prayer and the Practice of Medicine*. New York: HarperCollins, 1993.
———. *One Mind: How Our Individual Mind Is Part of a Greater Consciousness and Why It Matters*. New York: Hay House, 2013.
Ducasse, C. J. *Paranormal Phenomena: Science and Life After Death*. New York: Parapsychology Foundation, 1969.
Dugan, Maxie. *The Workbook of Intercessory Prayer*. Nashville, TN: Upper Room, 1979.
Dyson, Freeman. "Foreword." In *Extraordinary Knowing: Science, Skepticism and the Inexplicable Powers of the Human Mind*, by Elizabeth Lloyd Mayer, ix–xi. New York: Bantam, 2007.
———. "One in a Million." *New York Review of Books*, March 25, 2004. https://www.nybooks.com/articles/2004/03/25/one-in-a-million/?srsltid=AfmBOooEjmMoDc51N7MSJOfoVjnXFq-OSQGYVDrp5dB3k3JMsAWqVYiE.
Eire, Carlos. *The Good, the Bad, and the Airborne: Levitation and the History of the Impossible in Early Modern Europe*. Burlington VT: Ashgate, 2009.
Ellens, J. Harold. *Light from the Other Side: The Paranormal as Friend and Familiar*. Eugene, OR: Resource, 2011.
Elliott, T. S. "The Waste Land." Owl Eyes. https://www.owleyes.org/text/waste-land/read/poem-text#root-56120-5.
Emmons, Charles F., and Penelope Emmons. *Science and Spirit: Exploring the Limits of Consciousness*. Bloomington IN: iUniverse, 2012.
Epperly, Bruce G. *Angels, Mysteries, and Miracles: A Progressive View*. Gonzalez, FL: Energion, 2017.
Evans, Jules. *The Art of Losing Control: A Philosopher's Search for Ecstatic Experiences*. Edinburgh: Canongate, 2018.
Evans, Nancy Bush. *Dancing Past the Dark: Distressing Near-Death Experiences*. Cleveland, TN: Parson's Porch, 2012.
Evans, Rachel Held. *Faith Unraveled: How a Girl Who Knew All the Answers Learned to Ask Questions*. Grand Rapids: Zondervan, 2014.
Feather, Sally Rhine, and Michael Schmicker. *The Gift: ESP, the Extraordinary Experiences of Ordinary People*. New York: St. Martins, 2005.
Finney, Jack. *Invasion of the Body Snatchers*. New York: Scribner, 1998.
Flood, Derek. *Healing the Gospel: A Radical Vision for Grace, Justice, and the Cross*. Eugene OR: Cascade, 2012.
Fontana, David. *Is There An Afterlife?* Winchester, UK: O Books, 2005.
Fox, Mark. *The Fifth Love: Exploring Accounts of the Extraordinary*. Kidderminster, UK: Spirit and Sage, 2014.
———. *Lightforms: Spiritual Encounters with Unusual Light Phenomena*. 2nd ed. Kidderminster, UK: Spirit and Sage, 2016.
———. *Spirituality, and the Near-Death Experience*. London: Routledge, 2003.
Gaub, Ken. *God's Got Your Number*. Green Forest, AR: New Leaf, 1998.
Gauld, Alan. *Mediumship and Survival: A Century of Investigations*. London: Heinemann, 1982.
Geiger, John. *The Third Man Factor: Surviving the Impossible*. New York: Weinstein, 2009.

Greyson, Bruce. *After: A Doctor Explores What Near-Death Experiences Reveal About Life and Beyond.* New York: St. Martins, 2021.

———. "Near Death Experiences." In *Mind Beyond Brain: Buddhism, Science, and the Paranormal,* edited by David E. Presti, 22–44. New York: Columbia University Press, 2018.

Griffin, David Ray. *Parapsychology, Philosophy, and Spirituality: A Postmodern Exploration.* New York: State University of New York Press, 1997.

Gross, Terry. "Two Nights Before the Attack, Salman Rushdie Dreamed He Was Stabbed Onstage." *NPR*, April 16, 2024. https://www.npr.org/2024/04/16/1244847366/salman-rushdie-knife.

Grosso, Michael. "Evidence for St. Joseph of Copertino's Levitations." 2015. https://assets.website-files.com/602d8561ae2fe611c947c905/602d8561ae2fe6f4dc47ca05_01-Ch-1-Supp-Joseph.pdf.

———. *The Man Who Could Fly: St. Joseph of Copertino and the Mystery of Levitation.* Lanham, MD: Rowman and Littlefield, 2016.

———. *Smile of the Universe: Miracles in an Age of Disbelief.* San Antonio, TX: Anomalist, 2020.

Gurney, Frederic, et al. *Phantasms of the Living.* 1886. Edited by Eleanor Sidgwick. Abridged ed. London: Kegan Paul, Trench, Trubner, 1918.

Haig, Scott. "The Brain: The Power of Hope." *Time* 169 (2007) 118–19. https://time.com/archive/6596785/the-brain-the-power-of-hope.

Haraldsson, Erlendur. *The Departed Among the Living: An Investigative Study of Afterlife Encounters.* Guilford, UK: White Crow, 2012.

Hardy, Alister. *The Spiritual Nature of Man.* Oxford: Clarendon, 1979.

Hart, David Bentley. *Atheist Delusions: The Christian Revolution and Its Fashionable Enemies.* New Haven, CT: Yale University Press, 2009.

Hart, Hornell, et al. "Six Theories About Apparitions." *Proceedings of the Society for Philosophical Research* 50 (1956) 153–239.

Hawkes, Joyce. "Following the Thread from a Crack on the Head." In *Spiritual Awakenings: Scientists and Academics Describe Their Experiences,* edited by Marjorie Woollacott and David Lorimer, 185–88. Tucson, AZ: AAPS, 2022.

Heaney, John J. *The Sacred & The Psychic: Parapsychology and Christian Theology.* New York: Paulist, 1984.

Hick, John. *The Fifth Dimension.* Oxford: Oneworld, 1999.

Horgan, John. "The Complexologist Tragedy and Telepathy." *Johnhorgan.org* (blog), n.d. https://johnhorgan.org/books/mind-body-problems/chapter-four.

Horn, Stacy. *Unbelievable: Investigations into Ghosts, Poltergeists, Telepathy, and Other Unseen Phenomena from the Duke Parapsychology Laboratory.* New York: HarperCollins, 2009.

Hufford, David. "The Healing Power of Extraordinary Spiritual Experiences." *Journal of Near-Death Studies* 32 (2014) 137–56.

———. *The Terror That Comes in the Night: An Experience-Centered Study of Spiritual Assault Traditions.* Philadelphia: University of Pennsylvania Press, 1982.

———. "Visionary Spiritual Experiences in an Enchanted World." *Anthropology and Humanism* 35 (2010) 142–58.

Hume, David. *An Enquiry Concerning Human Understanding.* 1777. Project Gutenberg, 2006. Edited by L. A. Selby-Bigg. https://www.gutenberg.org/files/9662/9662-h/9662-h.htm.

Hunter, Jack. *Spirits, Gods and Magic: An Introduction to the Anthropology of the Supernatural*. London: August Night, 2020.
James, William. "Certain Phenomena of Trance." In *William James on Psychical Research*, edited by Gardner Murphy and Robert O. Ballou, 102–11. New York: Viking, 1960.
———. "The Final Impressions of a Psychical Researcher." In *William James on Psychical Research*, edited by Gardner Murphy and Robert O. Ballou, 309–25. New York: Viking, 1960.
———. "On Mediumship." In *William James on Psychical Research*, edited by Gardner Murphy and Robert O. Ballou, 47–55. New York: Viking, 1960.
———. *The Varieties of Religious Experience*. 1902. Reprint, New York: New American Library, 1958.
———. "The Will to Believe." In *The Writings of William James*, edited by John J. McDermott, 717–35. Chicago: University of Chicago Press, 1977.
Kastrup, Bernardo. "Analytic Idealism and PSI." In *Consciousness Unbound: Liberating Mind from the Tyranny of Materialism*, edited by Edward Kelly et al., 257–82. Lanham, MD: Rowman and Littlefield, 2021
———. "Apparitions, Ghosts, and Mediumistic Communications." *Meditations on Life, the Universe, and Everything* (blog), September 2012. https://www.bernardokastrup.com/2012/09/apparitions-ghosts-and-mediumistic.html.
———. *Why Materialism Is Baloney: How True Skeptics Know There Is No Death and Fathom Answers of Life, the Universe, and Everything*. Winchester, UK: IFF, 2014.
Keener, Craig. *Miracles: The Credibility of New Testament Accounts*. 2 vols. Grand Rapids: Baker Academic, 2011.
———. *Miracles Today: The Supernatural Work of God in the Modern World*. Grand Rapids: Baker Academic, 2021.
Kelly, Edward. "Introduction." In *Irreducible Mind: Toward a Psychology for the 21st Century*, edited by Edward Kelly et al., xvii–xxxi. Lanham, MD: Rowman and Littlefield, 2007.
———. "Introduction: Science and Spirituality at the Crossroads." In *Beyond Physicalism: Toward Reconciliation of Science and Spirituality*, edited by Edward Kelly et al., xi–xxix. Lanham, MD: Rowman and Littlefield, 2015.
———. "A View from the Mainstream." In *Irreducible Mind: Toward a Psychology for the 21st Century*, edited by Edward Kelly et al., 1–46. Lanham, MD: Rowman and Littlefield, 2015.
Kelly, Edward, and Michael Grosso. "Mystical Experience." In *Irreducible Mind: Toward a Psychology for the 21st Century*, edited by Edward Kelly et al., 495–575. Lanham, MD: Rowman and Littlefield, 2015.
Kelly, Emily Williams. "Mediums, Apparitions, and Deathbed Experiences." In *Mind Beyond Brain: Buddhism, Science, and the Paranormal*, edited by David E. Presti, 69–90. New York: Columbia University Press, 2018.
———. "Psychophysiological Influence." In *Irreducible Mind: Toward a Psychology for the 21st Century*, edited by Edward Kelly et al., 117–239. Lanham MD: Rowman and Littlefield, 2007.
Kelsey, Morton T. *The Christian & The Supernatural*. Minneapolis, MN: Augsburg, 1976.
———. *God, Dreams, and Revelation: A Christian Interpretation of Dreams*. Rev. ed. Minneapolis, MN: Augsburg, 1991.

Klopfer, Bruno. "Psychological Variables in Human Cancer." *Journal of Projective Techniques* 21 (1957) 331–40.
Kripal, Jeffrey. *The Flip: Epiphanies of Mind and the Future of Knowledge*. New York: Bellevue Literary, 2019.
Krohn, Elizabeth G., and Jeffrey Kripal. *Changed in a Flash: One Woman's Near-Death Experience and Why a Scholar Thinks It Empowers Us All*. Berkeley, CA: North Atlantic, 2018.
Lamont, Peter. *The First Psychic: The Peculiar Mystery of a Notorious Victorian Wizard*. New York: Little Brown, 2005
Laubach, Frank. *Prayer: The Mightiest Force in the World*. New York: Revell, 1946.
Lerma, John. *Into the Light: Real Life Stories About Angelic Visits, Visions of the Afterlife, and Other Pre-Death Experiences*. Pompton Plains, NJ: New Page, 2007.
Lewis, C. S. "The Efficacy of Prayer." In *The World's Last Night and Other Essays*, 3–11. New York: Harcourt Brace Jovanovich, 1952.
Long, Jeffrey, and Paul Perry. *God and the Afterlife*. New York: HarperCollins, 2016.
Mayer, Elizabeth Lloyd. *Extraordinary Knowing: Science, Skepticism, and the Inexplicable Powers of the Human Mind*. New York: Random, 2007.
McClenon, James. *Wondrous Events: Foundations of Religious Belief*. Philadelphia: University of Pennsylvania Press, 1994.
McTaggart, Lynne. *The Field: The Quest for the Secret Force of the Universe*. New York: HarperCollins, 2008.
Montefiore, Hugh. *The Paranormal: A Bishop Investigates*. Leicester, UK: Upfront, 2002.
Moody, Raymond. *Glimpses of Eternity: Sharing a Loved One's Passage from This Life to the Next*. New York: Guideposts, 2010.
———. *Life After Life*. New York: Bantam, 1975.
Morris, Thomas. "Suspicions of Something More." In *God and the Philosophers: The Reconciliation of Faith and Reason*, edited by Thomas Morris, 8–18. New York: Oxford University Press, 1994.
Morse, Melvin, and Paul Perry. *Parting Visions: Uses and Meanings of Pre-Death, Psychic and Spiritual Experiences*. New York: Villard, 1994.
———. *Where God Lives: The Science of the Paranormal and How Our Brains Are Linked to the Universe*. New York: HarperCollins, 2000.
Morton, R. C. "Record of a Haunted House." *Proceedings of the Society for Psychical Research* 3 (1892) 311–32.
Mossbridge, Julia, and Dean Radin. "Precognition as a Form of Prospection: A Review of the Evidence." *Psychology of Consciousness: Theory, Research, and Practice* 5 (2018) 78–97.
Mossbridge, Julia, et al. "Predicting the Unpredictable: Critical Analysis and Practical Applications of Anticipatory Activity." *Frontiers in Human Neuroscience* 8 (2014) 1–10.
Murphy, Michael. *The Future of the Body: Explorations into the Further Evolution of Human Nature*. New York: Tarcher/Perigee, 1992.
Murray, Craig, ed. *Mental Health and Anomalous Experience*. New York: Nova Science, 2012.
Myers, Frederic W. H. *Human Personality and Its Survival of Bodily Death*. 1907. Reprint, Scotts Valley, CA: CreateSpace, 2016.

Nagel, Thomas. "Is Consciousness an Illusion?" *New York Review of Books*, March 9, 2017. https://www.nybooks.com/articles/2017/03/09/is-consciousness-an-illusion-dennett-evolution.

Nahm, Michael, and Bruce Greyson. "Terminal Lucidity in Patients with Chronic Schizophrenia and Dementia: A Survey of the Literature." *The Journal of Nervous and Mental Diseases* 197 (2009) 942–44.

Nahm, Michael, et al. "Terminal Lucidity: A Review and a Case Collection." *Archives of Gerontology and Geriatrics* 55 (2012) 138–42.

Netburn, Deborah. "Strange Coincidences: Are They Fluke Events or Acts of God?" *Los Angeles Times*, December 1, 2022. https://www.latimes.com/california/story/2022-12-01/how-coincidences-help-us-make-sense-of-the-world.

Origen. *Against Celsus*. In vol. 4 of *Ante-Nicene Fathers*, edited by Alexander Roberts et al. Translated by Frederick Crombie. Buffalo, NY: Christian Literature, 1885. Revised and edited by Kevin Knight. http://www.newadvent.org/fathers/04161.htm.

Osis, Karlis, and Elendur Haraldsson. *At the Hour of Death*. Rev. ed. Guilford, UK: White Crow, 2012.

———. "OOBEs in Indian Swamis: Sathya Sai Baba and Dadaji." In *Research in Parapsychology*, edited by J. D. Morris et al., 147–50. Metuchen, NJ: Scarecrow, 1976.

Pannenberg, Wolfhart. *Jesus—God and Man*. Philadelphia, PA: Westminster, 1968.

———. *Systematic Theology*. Vol. 2. Grand Rapids: Eerdmans, 1994.

Patanjali. *The Yoga Sutras of Patanjali*. Translated by Sri Swami Satchidananda. Rev. ed. Yogaville, VA: Integral Yoga, 2012.

Penberthy, J. Kim, et al. "Impact of Meditation versus Exercise on Psychological Characteristics, Paranormal Experiences, and Beliefs: Randomized Trial." Journal of Scientific Exploration 38.1 (2024) 28–40. https://doi.org/10.31275/20242849.

Phillips, J. B. *Ring of Truth: A Translator's Testimony*. New York: Macmillan, 1967.

Pinnock, Clark, et al. *The Openness of God: A Biblical Challenge to the Traditional Idea of God*. Downers Grove, IL: InterVarsity, 1994.

Plato. *Apology*. In *The Trial and Death of Socrates*, edited by Shane Weller, 19–41. New York: Dover, 1992.

———. *Crito*. In *The Trial and Death of Socrates*, edited by Shane Weller, 43–54. New York: Dover, 1992.

Polanyi, Michael. *Personal Knowledge: Towards a Post-Critical Philosophy*. New York: Harper & Row, 1958.

Polkinghorne, John. *Belief in God in an Age of Science*. New Haven, CT: Yale University Press, 1998.

———. *The Faith of a Physicist*. Princeton, NJ: Princeton University Press, 1994.

———. "Kenotic Creation and Divine Action." In *The Work of Love: Creation and Kenosis*, edited by John Polkinghorne, 90–106. Grand Rapids: Eerdmans, 2001.

Post, Stephen G. *God and Love on Route 80*. Coral Gables, FL: Mango, 2019.

Powell, Diane Hennacy. *The ESP Enigma: The Scientific Case for Psychic Phenomena*. New York: Walker, 2009.

Radin, Dean. *The Conscious Universe: The Scientific Truth of Psychic Phenomena*. New York: HarperCollins, 1997.

———. *Entangled Minds: Extrasensory Experiences in a Quantum Reality*. New York: Simon and Schuster, 2006.

———. *Real Magic: Ancient Wisdom, Modern Science, and a Guide to the Secret Power of The Universe*. New York: Random, 2018.

———. *Supernormal: Science, Yoga, and the Evidence for Extraordinary Psychic Abilities*. New York: Crown, 2013.

Rees, Dewi. *Pointers to Eternity*. Talybont, UK: Y. Lolfa, 2010.

Reichenbach, Bruce. *Divine Providence: God's Love and Human Freedom*. Eugene, OR: Cascade, 2016.

Rowling, J. K. *Harry Potter and the Deathly Hallows*. New York: Scholastic, 2007.

Sabom, Michael. *Light and Death*. Grand Rapids: Zondervan, 1998.

———. *Recollections of Death: A Medical Investigation*. New York: Wallaby, 1982.

Sanders, John. *The God Who Risks: A Theology of Providence*. Downers Grove, IL: InterVarsity, 1998.

Sanford, John. *Dreams: God's Forgotten Language*. New York: Harper Collins, 1989.

Schmicker, Michael. *Best Evidence*. 2nd ed. New York: Writers Club, 2002.

Schroll, Mark A. "Personal Encounter with Paranormal Dreaming." *Academy for the Advancement of Postmaterialist Sciences*, January 1, 2001. https://www.aapsglobal.com/tag/mark-a-schroll.

Sheldrake, Rupert. *Science and Spiritual Practices: Transformative Experiences and Their Effects on Our Bodies, Brains, and Health*. Berkeley, CA: Counterpoint, 2017.

———. *Science Set Free: 10 Paths to New Discovery*. New York: Random, 2012.

Sidgwick, Eleanor. "On the Evidence for Clairvoyance." *Proceedings of the Society for Psychical Research* 7 (1891) 41–46.

Simonsen, Terje G. *A Short History of (Nearly) Everything Paranormal*. London: Watkins, 2020.

Smith, Huston. "Intimations of Mortality: Three Case Studies." *Harvard Divinity Bulletin* 30 (2001) 12–15.

Society for Psychical Research. "Cheltenham Ghost." *Psi Encyclopedia*, October 5, 2015. https://psi-encyclopedia.spr.ac.uk/articles/cheltenham-ghost.

Stevenson, Ian. *Twenty Cases Suggestive of Reincarnation*. Charlottesville, VA: University of Virginia Press, 1974.

Streett, R. Alan. *Exploring the Paranormal: Miracles, Magic, and the Mysterious*. Grand Rapids: Eerdmans, 2024.

Sweeney, Marvin A. *Jewish Mysticism: From Ancient Times to Today*. Grand Rapids: Eerdmans, 2020.

Targ, Russell, and Jane Katra. *Miracles of Mind: Exploring Nonlocal Consciousness and Spiritual Healing*. Novato, CA: New World, 1998.

Tarrant, Jeff. *Becoming Psychic: Lessons from the Minds of Mediums, Healers, and Psychics*. Boca Raton, FL: Health Communications, 2023.

Taylor, Charles. "Disenchantment-Reenchantment." In *Dilemmas and Connections: Selected Essays*, 287–302. Cambridge: Harvard University Press, 2011.

Teresa of Avilla. "Christ Has No Body." Journey with Jesus, n.d. https://www.journeywithjesus.net/poemsandprayers/3637-Teresa_Of_Avila_Christ_Has_No_Body.

Tucker, Jim. *Life Before Life: A Scientific Investigation of Children's Memories of Previous Lives*. New York: St. Martins, 2005.

Twain, Mark. *Autobiography of Mark Twain*. Vol. 1. Edited by Harriet Elinor Smith. Berkeley, CA: University of California Press, 2010.

———. "Mental Telegraphy." 1891. *Robert A. Heinlein: The Home Page for Science Fiction's Grand Master.* https://www.nitrosyncretic.com/rah/telepath.html.

Ullman, Montague, et al. *Dream Telepathy: Experiments in Nocturnal Extrasensory Perception.* 1973. Reprint, Charlottesville, VA: Hampton Roads, 2001.

Walton, John H., and J. Harvey Walton. *Demons and Spirits in Biblical Theology.* Eugene, OR: Cascade, 2019.

Ward, Keith. *Pascal's Fire: Scientific Faith and Religious Understanding.* Oxford: Oneworld, 2006.

Wargo, Eric. *Precognitive Dreamwork and the Long Self: Interpreting Messages from Your Future.* Rochester, VT: Inner Traditions, 2021.

———. *Time Loops: Precognition, Retrocausation, and the Unconscious.* San Antonio, TX: Anomalist, 2018.

Weber, Max. "Science as a Vocation." 1918. In *Max Weber: Essays in Sociology,* edited by H. H. Gerth and C. W. Mills, 129–58. New York: Oxford University Press, 1946.

Webster's New World College Dictionary. 4th ed. Foster City, CA: IDG, 2000.

Weddle, David L. *Miracles: Wonder and Meaning in World Religions.* New York: New York University Press, 2010.

Weil, Andrew, "Foreword." In Tolly Burkan, *Extreme Spirituality*, xviii–xxi. New York: Atria, 2011.

White, Ernest. *Christian Life and the Unconscious.* New York: Harper & Row, 1955.

White, Rhea. "An Analysis of ESP Phenomena in the Saints." *Parapsychology Review* 13 (1982) 15–18.

Wiebe Phillip. *God and Other Spirits: Intimations of Transcendence in Christian Experience.* Oxford: Oxford University Press, 2004.

———. *Visions of Jesus: Direct Encounters from the New Testament to Today.* New York: Oxford University Press, 1997.

Wilson, C. Roderick. "Seeing They See Not." In *Being Changed By Cross-Cultural Encounters*, edited by David E. Young and Jean-Guy Goulet, 197–208. Orchard Park, NY: Broadview, 1994.

Wink, Walter. *The Powers That Be: Theology for a New Millennium.* New York: Doubleday, 1998.

Winner, Lauren. *Girl Meets God: On the Path to a Spiritual Life.* Chapel Hill, NC: Algonquin, 2002.

Wright, N. T. *The Resurrection of the Son of God.* London: SPCK, 2003.

Name Index

Abraham, 67, 81, 82
Alexander, Eben, 183, 184, 186
Allison, Dale, xii, xv, 15, 129n11, 134n3, 166n14, 193, 195, 200, 203
Arcangel, Dianne, 177, 178
Augustine, 12

Barrett, Justin, 123
Barrett, William, 208
Bohm, David, 53
Braude, Stephen, 102, 105, 106
Broad, C. D., 39, 40, 61

Callanan, Maggie, 208, 209
Chalmers, David, 14

Damer, Bruce, 98
Devers, Edie, 194, 200
Ducasse, C. J., 39
Dugan, Maxie, 136
Dyson, Freeman, 59, 60

Eire, Carlos, 119
Elisha, 111–13
Emmons, Charles, 160
Evans, Jules, 223
Evans, Rachel Held, 218–19

Finney, Jack, 32
Fontana, David, 196, 197
Fox, Mark, 63

Garrett, Eileen, 175, 176
Gaub, Ken, 131–32, 143
Gauld, Alan, 160
Gilligan, Carol, 46
Greyson, Bruce, 179–80, 181
Griffin, David Ray, 52, 94, 98
Grosso, Michael, 119

Haig, Scott, 206–7
Haraldsson, Erlendur, 159, 194, 199
Hardy, Allister, 57, 137
Hawkes, Joyce, 219
Hick, John, 136, 137, 138
Home, Daniel Dunglas, 104–5, 106, 107
Hufford, David, 78, 85, 129n11
Hume, David, 22–25

Isaiah, 78–80, 82, 83, 85

James, William, 38, 50, 128, 174, 178, 191
Jesus, 5, 19, 24, 72, 74, 75, 76, 80, 82, 83, 116, 144, 149, 186, 200–204, 222
Joseph (O. T.), 88
Joseph (N. T.), 67
Joseph of Copertino, 118–19
Jung, Carl, 72, 73, 103

Kastrup, Bernardo, 51, 199
Katra, Jane, 147–48, 149, 150, 152, 154
Kauffman, Stuart, 93

233

Keener, Craig, 18, 19, 144, 148, 153
Kelley, Patricia, 208, 209
Kelly, Edward, 40
Kelly, Emily Williams, x
Kelsey, Morton, ix, x, xv, 15, 78, 83
Kripal, Jeffrey, 53
Krohn, Elizabeth, 90

Lamont, Peter, 105
Laubach, Frank, 136, 141
Lewis, C. S., 61, 62, 192–93
Loewen, Jacob, 1–2, 3, 4, 5, 6, 7, 8, 10, 11

Mayer, Elizabeth, 43–49, 51, 53
McCoy, Harold, 44–46, 49, 53, 112, 150
Merton, Thomas, 140
Montefiore, Hugh, 76–78, 81, 83, 86
Moody, Raymond, 180, 210–12
Morris, Thomas, 7–8, 98
Morse, Melvin, 145–46, 160
Mueller, George, 138, 139n14
Myers, F. W. H., 69, 73

Nagel, Thomas, 14

Origen, 82

Padro Pio, 116, 118
Pannenberg, Wolfhart, 81, 203
Patanjali, 114, 117, 119
Paul, 67, 80, 166n14, 202, 203, 213

Pauli, Wolfgang, 103
Peter, 72, 105, 144, 149
Phillips, J. B., 192–93, 195
Piper, Leonora, 38, 174
Polkinghorne, John, 108, 222
Puthoff, Harold, 136

Radin, Dean, 10, 53, 107
Reichenbach, Bruce, 122
Rhine, J. B., 175
Rhine, Louisa, 70, 96, 199
Rushdie, Salmon, 89

Sabom, Michael, 181, 184
Sanford, John, 72–73
Saul, 112, 170–71
Schroll, Mark, 65–66
Stevenson, Ian, 163–65
Sullenberger, "Sully," 90

Teresa of Avila, 215
Twain, Mark, 87–88

Weber, Max, 40–41
White, Rhea, 118
Wilkinson, Ed, 5–6
Wilson, C. Roderick, 3
Winner, Lauren, 74–75, 75n13
Worrall, Ambrose, 149
Worrall, Olga, 149
Wright, N. T., 202, 203, 222

Subject Index

after-death visitations, 192–204
    experiences, 192–96
    explanations, 198–200
    resurrection of Jesus, 200–204
altered states of consciousness, 12, 13, 41, 59, 60, 107, 113, 117, 128, 192
angels, 40, 83, 124, 166, 210
anomalous presence, 128–29
anomalous voice x, 15, 72, 81, 82, 85, 124, 125, 127, 132, 145–48, 192

belief in extraordinary, 6–8, 25–28, 35–36, 37–40,
    opposing motivations, 35–36
benevolent helpers, 125–30
body, control over, 115–17

Cheltenham House, 158
clairvoyance, 9, 94, 118, 198
coincidence, 39, 121, 122, 218
crisis apparitions, x, xi, 9, 21, 79, 157, 199

debunking explanation, 33, 39, 42
demon, demonic, 21, 24, 40, 73, 83, 104, 129n11, 166n14, 175n7
divine guidance, 61–62, 68, 171, 216, 217
divine-human encounters, 81–84, 215–17,
dowsers, 44, 45, 150

dreams, 12, 15, 20, 21, 50, 55, 56, 58, 60, 65–75, 79, 80, 81, 88, 89, 90, 91, 94, 95, 96, 146, 194, 196, 209, 216, 223
    biblical, 67–68, 69, 70. 72, 81–84, 215–16
    experiments, 70, 91–92
    precognitive, 89–90, 91, 94

enchantment, disenchantment, 40–42, 41n16
entanglement, xiv, 52
evidence
    anecdotal, 46, 59, 61, 91–92, 93, 107
    experimental, 7, 46n4, 52, 60, 91–92, 106, 136, 151
    observational, 46
evil, 16–17, 19, 129n11, 142–43, 160, 166n14, 175n7, 221
evil spirit, 19, 129n11, 166n14
extrasensory (perception, awareness), ESP
    definition, 9
    emotions, 59, 63, 89, 132,
    pervasiveness of, 216–17
    spontaneous, 55, 56, 59, 61, 63, 70, 92, 101, 118
    unconscious mind, 50, 61, 64, 68, 69, 71, 117, 122, 123, 128, 130, 136, 138, 140, 147, 151, 152, 160, 162, 163, 167, 216, 217

ghost stories, 101, 157
God's action
   excessive attribution of, 218–20
   powers other than God, 16–20
   through natural order, xv, 18–20, 27, 28, 29, 42, 121–23, 153, 214–15, 220–21
   using psychic powers, 28, 29, 30, 122, 141, 154, 221

hallucinations, 12, 39, 57, 77, 78, 80, 124, 128, 129, 194, 198, 199, 200, 201, 206, 212
   veridical, 57, 85, 86, 199
hauntings, 101, 157–61
healing
   hearing a voice, 145–48
   placebo effect, 150–52
   power, 149–50
   prayer for, 2, 4, 5, 10, 133, 136, 138, 140, 141, 143
   self-healing, 150–53
   unsuccessful, 139–40
hypnosis, 69, 116, 138

levitation, 104, 119

magic, ix, 4, 15, 17, 24, 27, 40, 41n16, 105, 135, 142, 220
materialism, 14, 51
mediums
   biblical, 170–71
   contact with spirits, 170, 175–77, 178
   deceptive techniques, 169–70, 172–73
   extrasensory powers, 172–73, 177–78
   investigation of, 172–73
mind
   powers of, 11, 14, 15, 21, 103, 113, 135, 220
   relation to brain, 9, 14, 15, 51, 182–84, 200, 207, 208
   subliminal, 69–74, 75, 77, 162, 176, 223

miracles
   and natural law, 24–25, 122
   biblical, 108–9
   Christian concerns, 28–31
   Hume's argument, 22–25
   in other religions, 22–23
   signs and wonders, 24–25
mystery, definition of, 12

naturalism, scientific naturalism, 26
near-death experiences
   extrasensory information, 179–82
   life-review, 184–86
   negative, 187–88
   subsequent effects of, 186, 190–91
new creation, 221–24

organ transplants, 161–63
out-of-body experience, OBE, 180–84, 197, 210–12

paranormal, 27, 29, 30, 31, 40, 50, 53, 64, 65, 76, 77, 88, 103, 111, 119, 152, 174, 194, 195, 215, 220
panpsychism, 52
panexperientialism, 52
petitionary prayer
   magic, 142–43
   revised model, 134–37, 141–43
   standard model, 133–34
   unsuccessful, 139–40
Princeton Engineering Anomalies Research Project, 106
physical causality, x, xi, xiv, 9, 13, 14, 15, 27, 41, 51, 56, 77, 78, 97, 100, 107, 129, 135, 142, 158, 192, 199, 200, 221, 224
poltergeist phenomena, 100–103, 157
possession, 165–66, 166n14, 175n7, 176
premonitions, 8, 89–90, 91, 92, 94, 95, 96, 97, 98
   possible or actual future, 95–97
   preventative action, 94, 95–97
presentiment, 91–92

psychic superpowers, 110, 111, 117–20, 143
  in Bible, 111–13
  religious contexts, 113–15, 117–20
psychokinesis, PK, 9, 10, 15, 94, 101, 102, 106, 107, 108
  and biblical miracles, 108–9
  recurrent spontaneous, 101

quantum phenomena, xiv, 52, 53, 103, 107
  zero-point field, 107

reality, theories of, 40–53
reincarnation, 163–67
Religious Experience Research Centre, 57, 63, 84, 137
resurrection of Jesus, 200–204, 222
retrocognition, 160
Rhine Research Center, 54, 70

saints, 114, 116, 117, 118, 188
science
  and extraordinary events, xiv, xv, 6, 7, 11, 15, 26–27
  attitude toward mystery, 13
  future development, 10, 16, 38

séances, 60, 102, 103, 104, 172, 173
shaman, 59, 114, 115
siddhis, 114
skepticism, xiii, 6, 7, 18, 26, 30, 35, 37, 38–40, 65, 68, 92, 155
Society for Psychical Research, 59, 103, 158, 172, 174, 197
stigmata, 116
Superman, 110

telepathy, 9, 38, 49, 94, 118, 136
terminal lucidity, 206–8
third-man factor, 125, 126, 127, 128

visions
  biblical, 78–84
  deathbed, 208–13
  of Paul, 67, 80, 202, 213
  revelatory, 69, 80, 76–86
  shared, 210–13

worldviews, 25–28

Yoga Sutras, 114, 117

www.ingramcontent.com/pod-product-compliance
Lightning Source LLC
Chambersburg PA
CBHW031731230426
43669CB00007B/317